Conversations in Cultural Rhetoric

and Composition Studies

Critical Studies in the Humanities
Victor E. Taylor, Series Editor

This open-ended series provides a unique publishing venue by combining single volumes issuing from landmark scholarship with pedagogy-related interdisciplinary collections of readings. This principle of cross-publishing, placing scholarship and pedagogy side by side within a single series, creates a wider horizon for specialized research and more general intellectual discovery. In the broad field of the humanities, the Critical Studies in the Humanities Series is committed to preserving key monographs, encouraging new perspectives, and developing important connections to pedagogical issues.

Proposals for submission should be directed to the Series Editor, Victor E. Taylor, Department of English and Humanities, York College of Pennsylvania, York, PA 17405-7199.

Conversations in Cultural Rhetoric
and Composition Studies

Keith Gilyard and Victor E. Taylor, editors

The Davies Group, Publishers
Aurora, Colorado

Library of Congress Cataloging-in-Publication Data

Conversations in cultural rhetoric and composition studies / Keith Gilyard and Victor E. Taylor, ed.
  p. cm. -- (Critical studies in the humanities)
 ISBN-13: 978-1-934542-17-0 (alk. paper)
 ISBN-10: 1-934542-17-2
 1. Rhetoric--Social aspects. 2. Culture--Study and teaching. 3. Language and culture. I. Gilyard, Keith, 1952- II. Taylor, Victor E.
 P301.5.S63C66 2009
 808--dc22
                                        2009030323

Cover photo: © budda | dreamstime.com

Printed in the United States of America

0123456789

Contents

Preface

Conversations in Cultural Rhetoric and Composition Studies is not a traditional collection of commonly focused or rigidly formatted interviews, although the interview is the obvious form of presentation. The volume strives for something beyond this very familiar model of one-to-one exchange or fact-finding "Q&A." As the titles states, it offers conversations, which we view as critical and complex arrangements of people, concepts, and contexts; that is to say, it "presents" conversations that are understood to be open *networks,*[1] extending and multiplying as they proceed from and through speakers into an infinitely textured and changing world.

Why do we privilege conversations over interviews? Interviews are no doubt a useful genre, but they tend to delimit communication. For instance, interviews track information, creating a series of openings and closings—question asked, question answered, with an occasional follow-up query. Conversations tend to pursue a different, more circuitous communicative path, with questions opening spaces for discussion and, then, leading to elaborations of the same topic or explorations of related ones. Conversations, as we have been defining them, are not finite communicative acts and do not, then, necessarily move in the direction of stasis or closure. Conversations, especially the ones contained in this volume, continuously open new and related discursive and rhetorical possibilities.

Conversations, as we present them in this volume, thus belong to a speaking and thinking that form multiple points of contact in a complex, shared, *expanding* world of rhetorical exigencies, concepts, references, events, actions, and actors. It is this possibility of unlimited expansion that we have tried to capture in this work. *Conversations in Cultural Rhetoric and Composition Studies,* through the form of the *conversation,* begins in the middle of a communicative process in which scholars in CRCS are joined in a wide and volatile *networked* world of ideas.

While it may not be an approach to human communication that is prevalent in composition and rhetoric, actor-network-theory (ANT) has a strong and revealing connection to studies in the field. ANT contends that all communication is, in effect, dynamic, multiple, plural, "thick,"[2] and interwoven by design; ANT is conversation theory.[3] In *Reassembling the Social: An Introduction to Actor-Network-Theory*, the theorist and sociologist Bruno Latour describes a *network* as a field in which actors "*make* other actors *do* unexpected things" (129), which is rhetorically different from but related to the more common notion of actors making other actors do *expected* things.

Compositionists and rhetoricians certainly will see a family resemblance between this central idea in actor-network theory and other theoretical frameworks for describing the linguistic, social, and rhetorical effects (expected and unexpected) speakers and writers have on audiences. Presented in this way, actor-network theory resembles Kenneth Burke's dramatistic pentad, with its emphasis on action, motive, and the relational dynamic across act, scene, agent, agency, and purpose.[4] While one is able to identify shared themes between the two theoretical frames, the Burkean pentad and actor-network theory are not completely symmetrical or equivalent; there are fundamental differences. Actor-network theory, for instance, strongly emphasizes institutional, technological, and historical systems, with "actors" understood as both human and non-human points of action within an open system.[5] In other words, actor-network theory is postmodern in its emphasis on the global context for motive, action, and effect. While Burke's concept of nonsymbolic motion may, in fact, correspond well with Latour's understanding of "network," the pentad, however, which some may argue pre-figures postmodernism, focuses on a notion of individually varied perspectives and motives in dialogue with changing dramatistic conditions—the "scene-behind-the-scene." Nevertheless, the two approaches are in "conversation," and this may help to provide a useful, transdisciplinary framework for our volume.

There is not an opportunity in the space of this preface to fully analyze the similarities and differences between Latour and Burke. However, it is worth noting that actor-network theory and Burkean rhetoric allow for a strong consideration of the significance of conversation as a mode of intellectual inquiry, and this is the point of bringing the two figures together. Differences aside, in the work of both Latour and Burke an important, persistent similarity exists—a focus on the ratio of *relation, context, actor,* and *action* … rhetorical occasions, exigencies, and effects. By emphasizing the *relational, contextual,* and *active* over the *monadic, autonomous,* and *static,* as both Latour and Burke advocate, we invite the reader to see the "interviews" in this volume as spiraling *conversations* within *systems,* sprawling networks of engagement in which scholars speak with other scholars, with critical works in the field, concepts of identities, histories, and, finally, with disciplines and institutions.

How do these conversations take shape? What is it that we need to know from these scholars? What do we need to discuss with them? The conversations, as a practical matter, begin with an invitation to explore an uncertainty; they begin with a question that seeks to open a discussion. The first interrogative draws attention to a moment of uncertainty or unknowing—something to be filled in, elaborated, or explained—not necessarily something that needs to be directly answered. In these instances uncertainty simply could be about an historical fact or perspective on an issue or topic, but that uncertainty always is presumed to be in a context or have a "thickness" to it. The first answer, then, demands a second question: How is the "clarified" uncertainty connected to other areas? It is when the conversations begin to explore these contexts or networked areas that the volume shows that it is more than a compilation of interviews. In all the conversations, we were careful to begin with each figure's scholarship and work our way to key issues in his or her thinking and scholarship. In this respect, one is able to see an "internal network" of ideas and issues in the conversations. "This is what I think and this is how I arrived at it" runs across the conversations.

How are connections connected? Just as one finds an internal network of ideas and issues in the conversations assembled here, one also finds that the internal dynamic references other external networks. These are the points in the conversations when autobiography or self-description begins to relate to wider cultural, historical, institutional, and intellectual contexts. These also are the points of multiplication in the conversations, moments when uncertainty of content becomes an uncertainty of connection. To highlight this notion of connecting connections, which can seem complicated, we turn again to one of the principle figures in actor-network-theory, Bruno Latour, who in *Reassembling the Social* discusses the various "design" difficulties that he and his colleagues encounter in defining and connecting (in)congruous multiplicities of contexts and networks:

> An actor-network is traced whenever, in the course of a study, the decision is made to replace actors of whatever size by local *and* connected sites instead of ranking them into micro and macro. The two parts are essential, hence the hyphen. The first part (the actor) reveals the narrow space in which all the grandiose ingredients of the world begin to be hatched; the second part (the network) may explain through which vehicles, which trace, which trails, which types of information, the world is being brought *inside* those places and then after having been transformed there are being pumped back *out* of its narrow walls (179–80).

Latour's description of the actor-network problem leads away from a focus on "ranked" hierarchies or causal linearities. Every so-called "point of origin" has a "thick" history and complex relation to a wider contextualizing system; in other words, nothing exists in strict isolation and nothing is created *ex nihilo* within the social space. If we accept this description of the actor-network, then our inquiry necessarily will take into account actors and the connections between actors, as Latour suggests. It also is important to consider that the complete network within which everything exists is never made visible in actor-network theory. The network is, for Latour, never finished, which means that new connections and emerging actor-network relationships are perpetual and never totalized.

In this context, Latour's actor-network theory (supplemented by the Burkean dramatistic pentad, or hexad, given Burke's late addition of *attitude* as a category) provides an interesting backdrop for *Conversations in Cultural Rhetoric and Composition Studies*. If this were a book of interviews on a specific topic, then one simply could view it as a collection of differing and agreeing points of view on the same issue. This isn't that kind of book. Cultural rhetoric and composition studies is a vast field, and a volume that compresses it into a precise set of topics would have missed the opportunity to show its unruly, rich complexity. In order to approach this complexity of the field properly it is important to ask, how do the different "actors" connect to each other? To their contexts? Beyond their immediate contexts? At some level, like Latour, we must embrace or, at least, accept a certain degree of uncertainty if it allows the dynamic nature of the wider field of study to emerge. For Latour, it is important to underscore the circuit connecting the actor to his or her direct and indirect context. It is this emphasis on connecting or tracing the circuits of actor-networks that is reflected in the conversations assembled in this volume. In this regard and in the absence of a shared controlling, discursive hub, Latour's theory is helpful in understanding the ways these conversations could be read.

How does one read for connections? Initially, the conversations begin with a reflection on scholarship and the critical issues shaping a figure's thinking. From this point, the conversations travel in a variety of directions. For instance, Louise Wetherbee Phelps, in her conversation, autobiographically charts her early search to find a meaningful intellectual environment for her work in writing and linguistics. Steven Mailloux, on the other hand, begins with an analysis of *cultural rhetoric* and the importance of the term in defining his scholarship as it appears between literary studies and rhetoric more broadly defined. Jack Selzer, too, addresses his earlier scholarship and its relationship to archival research and technical writing. The wider context or extended network for Phelps, Mailloux, and Selzer is, then, the significance of disciplinarity on thinking. Phelps, Mailloux, and Selzer discuss how their thinking was/is shaped by a relation to a highly specific linking of the disciplines literary studies, rhetoric, linguistics, and composition. C. Jan Swearingen "joins" this conversation by discussing her earlier work in classical rhetoric, and Jaime Armin Mejía brings together his early experience as a teacher and the emerging field of composition pedagogy—a topic Phelps develops in the context of curricular design in her conversation. The features of the network, however, do not end simply on the coincidence of topic. Thinking and disciplinarity are highly contextual and, in these instances, theoretical. Mejía, for instance, discusses in his conversation the teaching of writing in a situation informed not only by disciplinarity but ethnicity as well. In each conversation, there are layers of discourse that simultaneously speak to the specificity of a topic or issue; these discursive specificities, however, exist in larger contexts and this is where the conversations begin to form wider networks.

In addition to the network of Phelps, Mailloux, and Selzer, the participants Swearingen, Kirkland, Hoang, Mao, Wardle, Pough, and Mejía all network issues of identity and writing, but from differing vantage points. This plurality of perspectives is further evidenced when Michael Bérubé's conversation turns to rhetoric and disabilities studies and their connection to issues of identity. Bronwyn Williams, Haivan Hoang, LuMing Mao, Ernest Stromberg, David Kirkland, James Zebroski, and Gwendolyn Pough add to the identity and writing conversation by including the important interconnecting elements of race, class, and gender. Again, these issues create a network of threads or circuits about thinking and disciplinarity in the academy.

The concept of *network,* as Latour describes it, takes on an added significance when conversations about disciplinarity, identity, pedagogy, and culture "spiral" toward the problem of institutions. Again, we see a network of perspectives forming in a conversation "with" all the participants. In these conversations, we are given a "history" of composition and rhetoric in the context of disciplinary-institutional upheavals. Jaime Mejía, James Zebroski, and Elizabeth Wardle re-join this network as they discuss the specific triangulation of student-teacher-institution. The point to keep in mind is that all of the conversations in the volume connect across multiple topics and multiple levels. One could place each conversation under a single heading, but that would prove to be misleading since the conversations always are moving toward and through a variety of themes, contexts, and issues.

Reading the conversations collected in this volume as network-forming events creates the sense of a simultaneously widening and contracting world. Each figure has a precise focus, but that focus assumes extra meaning when it is placed into a wider or sharper context or, simply, paired with a related set of concerns from another perspective. With each new opening or introduction of a topic or issue, the conversations assembled here re-connect to a network of discourses in a multitude of ways—even beyond this assemblage. This is the strong, defining feature of the volume and one that we hope will invite others into these conversations.

We would like to express our thanks to our "conversation partners" for their insight, thoughtfulness, and patience. We also thank The Davies Group, Publishers for their interest in the project and their work bringing it forward. Research assistants Ersula Ore and Kevin A. Browne, Penn State University, were magnificent in helping to put the final manuscript together. Finally, we are grateful for the love and support of our families.

Works Cited:

Kenneth Burke. "Questions and Answers about the Pentad." *College Composition and Communication* 29 (1978): 330-35.

Bruno Latour. *Reassembling the Social: Actor-Network-Theory.* New York: Oxford University Press, 2007.

John Law and John Hassard, eds. *Actor Network Theory and After.* London: Wiley-Blackwell, 1999.

Notes:

1. *Network* is used in the context of the social sciences; more specifically, it relates to actor-network theory and the work of Bruno Latour. Latour describes his use of the term in "On recalling ANT" in *Actor Network Theory and After* by John Law and John Hassard: "Now that the World Wide Web exists, everyone believes they understand what a network is. While twenty years ago there was still some freshness in the term as a critical tool against notions as diverse as institution, society, nation-state and, more generally, any flat surface, it has lost any cutting edge and is now the pet notion of all those who want to modernize modernization.... What is the difference between the older and the new usage? At the time, the word network, like Deleuze's and Guattari's term rhizome, clearly meant a series of transformations—translations, transductions—which could not be captured by any of the traditional terms of social theory. With the new popularization of the word network, it now means transport *without* deformation, an instantaneous, unmediated access to every piece of information. That is exactly the opposite of what we meant"(14).

2. See Clifford Geertz's *The Interpretation of Cultures*. New York: Basic Books, 1977.

3. This is an "equivalence" based on the importance "relation" or "ratio" in ANT and narrative theory, which is described as "conversation" theory.

4. In "Questions and Answers about the Pentad," Kenneth Burke refers to an example of "circumference" in his concept of "dramatism." Given a situation in which people are involved in a crisis, in this instance a shipwreck, their actions are interpreted through the headings of "scene-act ratio" and "agent-act ratio," with each showing some aspect of the crisis in the context of relationship. In other words, scenes, agents, and acts are meaningful only in respect to "ratio" or the dynamic between the terms.

5. This inclusion of non-human "actors" has been a controversial aspect of ANT. Many have critiqued this extension of the "actor" category as "apolitical" or "ahistorical." Latour, et al, however, see it differently, with the expanded concept of actor as a further development of the relationships that make "human actors" part of a network.

Louise Wetherbee Phelps is a Visiting Scholar at Old Dominion University and Professor Emerita of Writing and Rhetoric at Syracuse University, where she was founding director of the Writing Program, establishing it as an independent department with a doctoral program. A former Fellow of the American Council on Education, she is a consultant on post-secondary writing instruction, writing program administration, and doctoral education in rhetoric and composition, specializing in program design and review, professional development, and processes of transformational change in higher education. She currently coordinates efforts to include rhetoric and composition/writing studies in classification systems used for disciplines and instructional programs in scholarly and governmental data bases. A pioneering scholar in the field, Professor Phelps is author of *Composition as a Human Science* and two co-edited volumes, *Feminine Principles and Women's Experience in American Composition* and *Rhetoric and Composition in Four Keys* as well as numerous essays on topics in composition, rhetoric, doctoral education, and writing program administration. She is currently completing *Poetics of Composition: Footprints of an Intellectual Journey*, the first of a two-volume autobiographical collection of her published and unpublished writings, entitled *Madisonian Research*.

The Conversation

Victor Taylor: Could you describe what drew you to the field?

Louise Wetherbee Phelps: My first formal encounter with composition as a field occurred in 1971, when I attended a 4Cs conference in Cincinnati, traveling on the bus and attending as a complete outsider (I remember being the only person with no institution on my badge). I wasn't teaching then and didn't plan ever to make it a career. With young twins and a baby, I had my hands full just managing from day to day, with only nebulous plans for the future. I aspired to be an editor when they were old enough for me to work, but hadn't figured out how (since there were no major publishing houses where I lived). For the moment, I was trying to write a book, living by the family dictum to "proceed as way opens."

My path to composition began long before that conference, although I only understood that in retrospect. It is more a quest story than the conversion narrative that so many tell about their entry into the field, and the differences profoundly shaped my identity as a scholar.

Taylor: How did this early "quest" eventually shape your career?

Phelps: I was interested in writing as soon as I learned to read, identifying with characters like Jo in *Little Women* and Betty in the Little Colonel series, who kept a diary while growing up and became a writer. I learned to write from my parents and talked with them about writing from grade school on. As writers, they offered very different models. My father, a former journalist-editor and author of occasional medical case studies, wrote limericks, collected malapropisms, composed crossword puzzles, and wrote wittily about his medical practice and about language. My mother wrote humorous accounts of family life and personal essays with strands of memoir and cultural criticism. Her writing is steeped in deep reading across a remarkable range of topics and sources. (I think the passionate, eclectic, and appropriative model of reading she embodies, and her abiding influence on the works and authors I read, are even more important to my writing than her example as a writer.) My father admired Hemingway and Dashiell Hammett; my mother's all-time literary hero was Dr. Samuel Johnson. Both parents composed book-length memoirs that embodied their strikingly disparate writing processes, purposes, and prose styles. Although I wrote short stories and poems, my most vivid early memories of feeling creative and esthetically satisfied with my writing are in nonfiction genres.

Taylor: You are describing a rather complex interdisciplinary or cross-disciplinary world view. Were you able to sustain it formally in academic settings?

Phelps: In college, I tried to "major" in writing, even though there was no such major. In practice that meant taking all the courses I was allowed to in creative writing (in an English major) and writing a novella as my senior thesis. (Enough to determine that I had no gift for fiction or poetry.) Meanwhile I fell in love with philosophy, where I wrote a prescient essay on Austin's performative utterances, and took courses on language wherever I could find them. I never connected to English as a department, a discipline, or an academic career. I was only a sophomore when I realized that literary analysis (New Criticism then) was a game I could play, but didn't want to—it just didn't seem serious enough to spend your life on. I stayed in the English major only because I was told there was no such thing as an interdisciplinary major and I couldn't write a creative thesis in philosophy.

Looking back, I suspect my dreams about the future then, with virtually no advising, were based more on intellectual attraction—what I hoped to learn—than on any knowledge or informed consideration of job prospects. (Yet I never doubted I would eventually have a career!) I'm not sure I even made the direct connection between getting a doctorate and becoming a college teacher. So I didn't take up scattered hints that I might apply to a Ph.D. program, though I might have gone to graduate school in linguistics if I had known it was undergoing a cognitive revolution. Without a clear-cut path, I temporized. Since I believed in the concept of universal national service, in lieu of military service I decided to teach for a few years in the public schools. I accompanied my new husband to graduate school at Johns Hopkins and got one of the first Master of Arts in Teaching degrees to make me eligible to teach. After an initial assignment in a junior high, I taught tenth through twelfth grade, 5 classes of 40 plus students each.

Taylor: It is almost a universal pre-condition for educators. We struggle to find a space for our own intellectual interests and then find ourselves creating these spaces for others. Did you see "teaching writing" as your future?

Phelps: Although I grew better at it from sheer stubborn persistence, I was not a natural teacher. I struggled with the constant deficit of time and sleep, a feckless bureaucracy, an overstuffed and incoherent curriculum, and the high standards I had for myself, which were in tension with the low expectations (for teachers *and* students) entrenched in the whole system. I came away resolved not to teach again, but this experience did plant the seeds for my entry into composition years later. I became deeply engrossed in the intellectual challenges presented by the models of writing implicit in the prescriptions, assignments, and sequences we were mandated to follow in the course of study. Everything I knew about writing—from my own processes and strategies of writing, my observations of peers and now my students, my critical training to analyze texts, and the teaching and example of my parents—told me that what was being taught was totally misconceived. It had nothing to do with real writers, their diverse and idiosyncratic composing processes, the development of writing abilities, or the structures of real-world texts.

I also understood immediately that the underlying theory of learning didn't work: telling people about writing (the rules, descriptions, generalizations, and prescriptions of the textbooks) did not engender the ability to do it. I knew the complexity of building up over time a set of skills, techniques, rhetorical moves, conscious knowledge, and tacit, non-analytical abilities (intuition, judgment, improvisation) that would allow one to keep writing and learning more about writing. Already I was deeply interested in development and sequence. The curriculum called for tenth graders to memorize and practice an artificial typology of self-contained paragraphs (which none of us could find real-life examples of). The next year, eleventh graders were suddenly writing multi-paragraph literary criticism. I wondered how they were supposed to make this leap.

On one level, I tried to come up with practical moves that would actually help students. For the literary analysis, I offered students a "simple model" of the structure of a critical essay and asked them to imitate the pattern. The results were so successful (unexpectedly transferring to their history class) that I was assigned the next year to the writing class for seniors, where I continued trying to design assignments and respond to students' writing in ways that would help them develop sustained writing skills as well as produce "good writing." But on a deeper level, this challenge rekindled my intellectual curiosity about the underlying questions that writing had always stirred in me, about language, meaning, thought, mind, communication, interpretation, symbolic action, and more. Meanwhile, I was picking up information that would later prove relevant, since the array of topics I was required to cover included not only writing but also logic, rhetoric, literature, history of the English language, grammar and style, linguistics (structural grammar), and speech.

What I was experiencing was the classic beginning of inquiry, described by so many scientists and artists (and, later, compositionists) as a sense of discrepancy or anomaly—a "felt tension"—that prompts them to search, experiment, or engage in sustained contemplation. Rather than solving a known problem, this is how you discover a new one: perceiving a situation in fresh terms that reorient your thinking to new questions, objects, purposes, and relationships. In my experience, the most characteristic quality of a generative problem is not its sheer fecundity, but its capacity for surprise … the serendipitous connections and unforeseen consequences that follow from pursuing its implications. The structural model that I constructed for my students was the first idea I formulated in composition that proved generative in this sense.

Taylor: Fortunately, the story doesn't end there. You, in a sense, turned back to philosophy, a philosophy of education.

Phelps: It was some years afterwards, at home with three young boys and no car, that I began to work on a book that would capture for other teachers what I had learned in these experiments. But this goal, especially as it involved making models of discourse, seemed to lead me ever deeper into the fundamental study of language and its relationships to meaning, mind, and activity—the same questions that had engaged me in college. I pursued an eccentric project of reading, determined in part by what I found in the local library, which uncovered everything from Barrett Wendell's *English Composition* (1891) to Martin Steinmann's *New Rhetorics* and W. Ross Winterowd's *Rhetoric: A Synthesis*. When I introduced myself to Ed Corbett at that 1971 4Cs conference, I was searching for ways to learn rhetoric and linguistics as sources for my book, which was becoming a much broader theoretical investigation. He asked to see some chapters and, encouraging me to continue, recommended I approach Louis Milic, a rhetorical scholar specializing in eighteenth-century stylistics, at Cleveland State University. It turned out that Milic (along with a newly hired Chomskyan linguist) was starting a new M.A. degree focused on practical linguistics and practical criticism and suggested that I enroll to get the background I wanted for my project, including independent study with him. So I reentered the academy (part-time) self-identified as a writer, not as a prospective teacher or academic scholar. I fell into a teaching post by accident when offered a chance to earn tuition as a teaching assistant. I ended up working in the writing center and then becoming its director. But the more I learned in my studies and teaching, the more I perceived the complexity and scope of writing as a subject; and the book receded into the distance as I measured my aspirations against my knowledge. Ultimately, I decided the only way to understand writing from the full range of disciplinary perspectives was to get a Ph.D.

Taylor: It is a challenge to find interdisciplinary programs or, less ambitiously, interdisciplinary-sensitive faculty. Did you build your own program of study?

Phelps: Originally, I intended to do my degree through a University without Walls program, but before taking that route I decided to find out whether Case Western Reserve University (where my husband's faculty position gave me free tuition) would agree to host an interdisciplinary doctorate. Since I naively equated "interdisciplinary" with an interdepartmental, cross-institutional program, I was surprised to learn that such a degree would need a department to host it, where I would be required to take half my courses. The English department looked like the best bet because it had recently acquired a linguist and also offered stylistics, while the linguistics department was defunct and the speech department had given up rhetoric for communication sciences. Lacking any precedents or models, I simply decided what I wanted to learn and canvassed the city for possible mentors and courses. Then I went to the department with a complete design for a program in hand, including courses and independent study in about 14 research areas (including both composition and rhetoric), reading lists, instructors at three universities who had agreed to work with me, and a plan for supervision by an interdisciplinary committee. Fortunately, one of the members of the proposed oversight committee was the sympathetic English graduate director, and I got word that I could go ahead (although there were some bumps along the way).

By then I knew there was a nascent discipline in composition. When I encountered it as such in my readings, my study of writing already had a long history and a firm shape as an interdisciplinary inquiry. What I needed was an intellectual community and an imaginable place to situate my project. So my move into composition and rhetoric was not a matter of conversion but of convergence—finding scholars whose inquiries intersected with mine and making the joyful discovery that our joint interests defined a possible intellectual home and profession.

As best I can recall, academic composition was most salient to me originally as a potential audience for my writing, rather than a primary source of knowledge or even an institutional location for a potential career. In writing my master's thesis (after starting Ph.D. courses part-time), I reconstructed the history of composition and its roots in rhetoric (and elsewhere), studied contemporary work, and began to identify with the scholars working to develop it as a research discipline. I had extended person-to-person contact with this community only after I finished my doctoral course work, at a two-week, in—residence graduate and postdoctoral seminar offered by Janice Lauer and W. Ross Winterowd (which became the Purdue Seminar offered by Janice for many years). The seminar was a heady experience because I was so perfectly primed to absorb and integrate the new information and sources it offered, while for the first time I had an audience excited by, and able to understand, my original ideas. It was a revelation to discover both the overlap of my work with other composition scholars and also its distinctiveness. For example, Ross and I had an uncanny number of extradisciplinary sources in common, which we had independently discovered and appropriated for our own writing studies. Janice became a remarkably generous mentor and helpful critic for my dissertation, while, of course, Ross hired me to teach in the University of Southern California's "RLL" doctoral program when I graduated (after warning me I would never get a job with a self-designed Ph.D.).

Taylor: I find this ironic and interesting given the fact that much of your career has involved developing curricula for undergraduate and graduate composition and rhetoric programs.

Phelps: I can't emphasize enough how profoundly this long path to composition shaped the entire intellectual trajectory of my career. I can trace virtually every major thread and motive of my work back to this antecedent, not simply in the studies I undertook and the intellectual experiences they created, but in the entire process of curiosity, questioning, discovery, and invention beginning in childhood that led up to and through my doctoral program. I can point to just a few of the enduring patterns these experiences set.

The first legacy is the two primary modes in which I approach scholarship: phenomenological and philosophical. As a writer and a beginning teacher, I found my own experience and that of others to be complex, diverse, and quite incongruent with the descriptions and prescriptions that constituted school knowledge of writing. I became interested in developing my own descriptions and understandings of these events and activities *as experienced.* The desire to observe lived experience closely led me to phenomenology; the effort to express it led me to experiment with metaphors, multiple voices, and other literary techniques. I didn't dismiss objectivist studies like empirical research and critical analyses of systems and structures; in fact, I thought them an essential complement to subjective inquiries like dramatism or hermeneutical interpretation, which foreground the perceptions and self-understandings of subjects or agents. But this starting point made me question theory and scientific models of writing that falsified or contradicted human experience, or seemed inadequate to its complexity and variety. My work later on teachers' appropriation of theory was an extension of this instinctive respect for what practitioners and social actors themselves know about what they do and what they need from formal knowledge.

The anomalies I discovered by comparing conventional wisdom about writing with my own direct knowledge as a writer and teacher motivated me to build my own theories, which I ultimately defined—and came to practice deliberately—as philosophical work. Susanne Langer called this "the systematic construction of meanings" (52). My philosophical bent was innate, not learned from books, but Langer taught me to recognize, name, and practice it systematically—theory as method. Coming to theory by this route explains why my intellectual work has never just presented finished theories, but has always included, as equally important, accounts of theorizing as process, experience, reflection, and self-understanding. It's the same impulse that determines the fundamentally esthetic structure of my academic writing: I'm trying to dramatize for readers to experience what it feels like to discover and think through particular problems and ideas, experiencing states of confusion or flashes of insight, in movement that has rhythms of tension and resolution. This dramatistic dimension of theory appeared first in my master's thesis ("the autobiography of an idea") as the master narrative and runs through all my work, representing theorizing as a practice that "presumes a historical person with passions, values, responsibilities, interests, and a degree of involvement in the object of study" (CNK 107–08).

Taylor: I recall, long ago, as a new graduate student at Syracuse University in the late 1980s, this emphasis on discovery and problem-solving. When I was introduced to the "spiral curriculum," I remember thinking, "Hegel!" Describe how composition, for you, became a practice of "concept-formation."

Phelps: Puzzles in writing and teaching practice became conceptual analyses, which in turn led me to propose in my dissertation a philosophical framework to integrate and generalize them. The staying power of these early inquiries is striking, taking many forms and directions over time. My questions about discourse structure, for example, produced a critique of process theory and prompted an attention to time and temporality that appears recurrently in my work as themes of history, process, and change. My studies of coherence and of interpreting student writing had equally rich and unexpected histories, and those three veins of scholarship are not exhausted.

The second legacy of my long route into composition lies in the patterns set by the process itself, which indelibly shaped my identity and my relationship to the academy. Well into adulthood, including my Ph.D. work, I studied writing essentially as an independent scholar. Having envisioned a multidisciplinary graduate education, I carried it out without the benefit of teachers who were scholars in composition, or had even read the literature. As a result, my background and way of thinking were never "disciplined" by an establishment with privileged methods, canons, conventions of writing, and so on; and my scholarly identity was not formed in this crucible, even as heretic or rebel. Composition itself came too late in this process for me, and didn't yet have the institutional solidity and presence, to serve the usual function of a discipline to acculturate me in its norms. All this left me with a much looser sense of belonging, even to composition and rhetoric itself, than most academics have (or, at least, want). I am most comfortable in an ambiguous or hybrid identity, for myself and the field. Even though (ironically) I've spent much of my career thinking about and working for the symbolic construction of rhetoric and composition as a disciplinary identity, I understand disciplinarity as pluralistic, mutable, and pragmatic. The multiple intellectual paradigms that are laminated and blurred in the "discipline" enable it to join or identify strategically with a variety of interdisciplinary alliances, coalitions, and intellectual formations.

Taylor: All of this belongs to a specific time and place. Could you discuss that aspect of it?

Phelps: I haven't said much about the intellectual climate of the times, much less the broader societal context—which was turbulent during the 1970s when composition really began to coalesce as a discipline. Composition is indelibly marked by its birth during this period of social conflict and change, but it would take a historian (and a lot more space!) to do it justice. Because of my isolation, these broader developments had less direct influence on me than on composition scholars who were more fully immersed then in the public world and the academy as a political institution. But I grew to be a scholar during a period of intellectual instability and change in the understandings of language, symbols, meaning, and knowledge, and I was absorbed in the conflicts going on in this world of ideas. Disciplines concerned with language and communication were evolving, however grudgingly, toward a more rhetorical view recognizing the context-dependency of meaning. Simultaneously, a postmodern consciousness was emerging in the human sciences, undermining the Cartesian-Newtonian worldview and challenging the values of the Enlightenment that had long dominated the modern sciences, humanities, and public life. For me, this called for a new positive framework, which I found broadly in an affirmative notion of context. The process theme of early composition studies appeared to me a limited expression of a broader philosophical transformation toward a contextualist worldview that takes event as the master metaphor, often turning to the sphere of discourse for its vocabulary.

Taylor: How willing was the academy, particularly through English departments, to accept C/R as more than a sub-field of a traditional discipline, namely literary studies? Could you situate your work in this dynamic? To what extent were you attempting to write for a new or different intellectual community?

Phelps: When I began to involve myself formally in higher education in the early 1970s, I don't think the academy at large was so much unwilling to accept composition as completely oblivious to it as an aspiring discipline. It had an institutional presence mainly inside English departments (because of their responsibilities for writing instruction), and a precarious foothold at that. Within English, there was no widespread acceptance of it as a scholarly focus: attitudes ranged from sheer ignorance of its existence to dismissiveness or active hostility. But attitudes were softening slightly as pioneering scholars vigorously pushed for space to do their work and, especially, train graduate students. By the end of my graduate studies, composition and rhetoric had established a few outposts where these scholars had founded programs (Carnegie Mellon, Purdue, the University of Southern California), or were mentoring would-be scholars of composition; and other places where by hook and by crook students found ways to prepare for a career in writing studies. For a brief but crucial period (around the time I graduated), the National Endowment for the Humanities lent some credence to writing studies by sponsoring year-long seminars where many went to "retool" in composition and rhetoric.

My own travails and triumphs in getting a Ph.D. are a wonderful synecdoche for both the latent potential of composition and also the barriers and resistance to its full development and acceptance as a distinct discipline. On the positive side, I did succeed, through the support of a few individuals, in setting up my graduate program as a special interdisciplinary study located (by default) within the department of English. During my coursework, working directly with the supervising committee I had set up, I had little contact with the department as a whole, and was blissfully ignorant of the bureaucracies, rules, and procedures that govern academic life. It was a shock, therefore, to suddenly receive a call telling me that the English department had rejected my exam proposals (approved by my committee), one outraged faculty member accusing me of deceiving the department about my program. After some sleepless nights, I demanded a meeting with the Graduate Committee to defend myself. It was a close call. It turned out that the charge of deception rested on an ambiguity in the requirement that I take fifty per cent of my courses in "English." Although I had taken half my courses in the department, the Graduate Committee members said they were not in "English"—i.e., literature. The committee seemed amazed and skeptical about the idea that studying writing could be a scholarly goal. Most said I should complete a Ph.D. in literature, and then could be allowed to write a dissertation in composition. I told them I would give up the degree rather than destroy its integrity. I won this argument, and the chance to continue, by one vote. The person who cast that vote said it was only because she figured I would have to study literature in one of my proposed exam areas, the history of style.

The faculty quickly tightened the rules to prevent other students from reproducing my heresy (although my example did open the door for students to write composition/rhetoric dissertations after completing requirements for a literature degree). It was two decades before the department established a Ph.D. in "Writing History and Theory." I didn't realize how old this battle was until my mother told me at the time about her own experiences in college in the late 1930s. She majored in writing in a department of "English Composition," where she studied what we would now call creative writing, criticism, theory, and history of the English language. She remembers a lot of friction and ill feeling between this department and the department of "English"— i.e., literature, which regarded composition as an illegitimate upstart. Sometime after she graduated, the literature faculty succeeded in eliminating the composition department.

Taylor: That, unfortunately, seems to be a story that could still be told today. Could you describe the dual struggle for intellectual and institutional identity?

Phelps: History repeated itself again when I was at the University of Southern California, whose English faculty managed to destroy one of the most successful and long-lived Ph.D. programs in the country, in Rhetoric, Linguistics, and Literature (RLL). It's my impression that departments of English (or Humanities) began to hire scholars into composition/rhetoric positions in rising numbers around the time I graduated, but there was a backlash when those candidates came up for tenure about 6–7 years later. Many, including me, were denied tenure. When those candidates were rehired elsewhere, often as program directors, I think that was the tipping point when composition gained a critical mass of tenured faculty and began to expand the graduate programs that allowed it to reproduce the discipline as a social formation in the academy, rather than simply an intellectual movement. This, along with evolving responsibilities for writing instruction, gave composition a greater measure of security and made possible its growth, activity, even a degree of power. But none of that has brought full acceptance as a discipline, or even simple recognition of its existence by the higher education establishment. That remains a work in progress.

Taylor: How did this further shape your identity as a writer and scholar?

Phelps: Situating my work as a writer during the formative years of composition was a delicate and difficult problem, especially when writing my dissertation and in the next few years. The channels for publication were not only severely limited but almost entirely practice-oriented. I was advised to stop writing about concepts and write about "the real thing"; to drop critiques, eschew theory, and focus on practical applications; to use plain English and avoid complex syntax. I was told that my work was unpublishable because it was too philosophical; or that it was unacceptable because it didn't privilege the literary theory familiar to most readers. If the intellectual community I wanted to write for existed, as I hoped and believed it did, it wasn't accessible. The best I could do was to invent a fiction of the ideal reader in my writing and try to persuade readers to become this audience. Although enough readers accepted this invitation eventually for me to find a place in the field, I don't think I was broadly successful in this rhetorical task. If there is a "mainstream" intellectual community in composition, I am an outlier; and, as an inveterate generalist, I don't fit any better into the specialized communities that have developed.

Taylor: As a "generalist," could you give an assessment of the major issues in composition and rhetoric today? To what extent are these related to or beholden to the issues that dominated the early period of the field?

Phelps: For me, making such an assessment is an integral, recurrent part of my intellectual work as a generalist and student of the discipline—and it really is *work*. Probably the major exigence for my doing this work, other than certain professional occasions or invitations, is the need to introduce new scholars to the discipline and teach them strategies for making sense of a chaotic flow of input about a complex, confusing domain. Rather than make an assessment and present it to students, I structure courses to model and practice the process of speculative thinking that I use myself. It's a more systematic version of what members of the field do all the time as they try to keep up with a fire-hose of information: paying attention selectively, deciding what's significant, situating their work in this scene, scouting the territory for a problem or opportunity, and so on. It's best done in a group whose members can compare findings, develop interpretations of them, and mutually test their judgments. I think of it as forming a hologram by skimming and scanning a range of materials with an alertness to what is meaningful and relevant, through a faculty I call "resonance." I first used this method with graduate students in a mapping project at USC, which led to the anthology *Composition in Four Keys* (and our identification of a social turn across all positions in the mid-eighties). I most recently did it in 2006, in a course called "Mapping the Future: Theory and Practice of 'Writing' the Discipline," an exercise in informed speculation on how observed phenomena in current materials from the field can be extrapolated as "turns" or trends of major significance.

Taylor: And the future?

Phelps: In trying to anticipate the future, I tend to look beyond the hot topics or issues of the day and focus on events or trends with the potential to reshape what issues we take up, or how we think about them. Here are a couple I've observed recently, one pedagogical and political and the other scholarly: (1) the meteoric rise of undergraduate majors in writing and rhetoric; and (2) the recent convergence of international writing studies with American rhetoric and composition, specifically in its disciplinary identity as "writing studies," with a socio-cultural focus and orientation to "research" (social sciences). I'll sketch these briefly, with some speculative comments on their implications.

As leader of a CCCC task force attempting to get codes for instructional programs in rhetoric and composition/writing studies (used in making reports of educational data to the federal government), I discovered that we have skimpy and unreliable data about both graduate (especially M.A.) and undergraduate programs. This is precisely because, without proper codes, they have been undercounted or miscounted in federal databases, largely because they have been conflated with other programs and hidden in generic "English" degrees. However, a CCCC committee has developed preliminary documentation on the striking growth of undergraduate majors in writing and rhetoric, with new ones continuing to form rapidly. This data correlates with informal scans and experts' sense of trends. These majors appear to be responding to student interest and workplace needs, attracting many students—including double-majors and minors—as they are established as tracks or separate degree programs.

Majors, most obviously, diversify the pedagogical imperative of composition, with potential implications for scholarly agendas and allocation of faculty time. Their curricula, often emphasizing professional and technical communication, tend to connect the discipline more fully with external sites and genres of writing (workplace, community) while also enabling greater attention to theory and history. Although most majors will not become faculty scholars, students entering graduate school with undergraduate background and intellectual interest in the field (rather than a conversion experience based on teaching in a literature or creative writing MA program) would cause a sea change in the content and approach of these programs. On the national scene, undergraduate majors make writing studies more visible to the higher education establishment and a wider public, including prospective students, as a distinct field of study and research.

Taylor: The question seems to be, "How can we imagine and then shape the future of a writing major or even writing in a turbulent academic space?"

Phelps: The establishment of majors could create a cascade of more far-reaching effects through its conjunction with other trends. First, a long-predicted generational change is now underway, in which a huge cohort of senior faculty is retiring and being replaced by young hires, simultaneous with accelerating changes in student demographics. Second, as a consultant I've noticed a conceptual shift in understandings of general education across U.S. institutions. Many top administrators and state policy makers are no longer viewing it as simply "basic skills" instruction, but as the continual acquisition of increasingly advanced skills, requiring a comprehensive program stretched out over the college years and distributed throughout the curriculum. Most of the advanced abilities targeted in such programs are associated with writing and rhetorical education, especially as our field expands "writing" to multimedia and multimodal communication: they include, for example, critical thinking, digital literacy, research, communication, and collaborative skills. Inevitably, writing programs and writing faculty are being called on to participate in, lead, and/or support this new, expanded general education agenda, which also recontextualizes and alters the purpose and nature of first-year writing.

The convergence of these developments adds up to an increasing demand, and potential for hiring, larger numbers of writing faculty to administer complex responsibilities for multiple programs, combining redesigned general education requirements for the majority of students (in writing courses and WAC/WID programs, supported by writing centers) with a popular, growing departmental major. If writing faculty are hired to meet such needs, they could change the whole power dynamic of English departments by replacing many literature slots with positions in rhetoric, professional and technical communication, and program administration. Those who *are* hired in literature and other areas in these departments are likely to have more familiarity and respect for writing studies than the retiring generation. All this might make moot the question of whether composition should leave English and form new departments, although there are other reasons that may continue. At the same time, the establishment of undergraduate majors fills in the last gap to complete what I call the "departmentalization" or disciplining of rhetoric and composition into something more like a conventional academic field, whether that is in English departments where the balance of power has shifted, in writing departments, or in new multidisciplinary colleges organized around problems or themes. If I am right about this, composition could find itself in a radically transfigured field of problems: some of those that have obsessed us for decades—like the "abolition" movement or the "composition-literature split"—may quietly disappear or look very different, while entirely new ones will suddenly emerge.

Taylor: You are suggesting a "university model" beyond the traditional American context. Is this the next step for composition?

Phelps: The second development is a recent event that promises to redefine the boundaries and constitution of our intellectual community. In a rather stunning breakthrough, signaled by a series of research volumes and conferences (with important leadership from Charles Bazerman), multi-national research on writing studies and literacy development has coalesced as a global, interdisciplinary field and connected up with U.S. composition and literacy studies. Scholars from a wide range of disciplines and research areas are beginning to explore the possibilities for collaboration and interchange in a world-wide intellectual community. I see this encounter as potentially reconfiguring the internal structure of our own field, like a new tectonic plate, by revitalizing certain elements of the original conception of writing studies as "composition" that have been lost, altered, or devalued over the years. There is a cluster of features I am thinking of. For a certain period in its formative years, the humanities and social sciences, as influences (from other disciplines) and modes of intellectual work, were relatively balanced, as suggested by the preference for a title combining "rhetoric" with "composition." Philosophically, this produced a creative tension between objectivist-realist modes of thought and subjectivist-idealist ones. This balance was upset by the critique of science in composition and the influence of cultural studies and postmodern theory (facilitated, ironically, by a degree of acceptance and success within English departments). Relatedly, many of us conceived the study of writing as a multidisciplinary enterprise, not located exclusively or even necessarily at all in "English." Some founding scholars came from ESL, linguistics, education, cognitive science, or communication; and many more had studied these and other fields. Third, our focus was on writing, not pedagogy, as the primary object of study, even though the motive was understood as (teaching) practice. The largely science-based spectrum of research on writing across national and cultural borders could strengthen the core group that has retained this original conception (under the rubrics of "writing studies" or composition or literacy studies, rather than rhetoric), giving new vigor and prestige to social science approaches and broadening the range of disciplinary sources. In turn, this international community could benefit from integrating into these studies the humanities-based scholarship, including the entire legacy of rhetorical studies, and the pedagogical expertise and theoretical sophistication of contemporary composition and rhetoric.

Finally, connecting its scholarship to global writing studies may restore to "composition" the broadened scope of subject matter it was originally intended to have, which drew strength from its integration and identification with rhetoric but had its own motive and integrity. In recent years, the field at large has drifted toward perceiving and even promoting divergences between "rhetoric and "composition," "theory" and "practice," or "scholarship" (humanities) and "research" (sciences), stressing and fracturing integrations that were important to the consolidation of the field as a scholarly discipline. The net effect has been to resurrect in many minds a retrograde, reductive notion of composition as concerned solely with academic (student) writing—more precisely, required lower division writing, and as exclusively pedagogical, having neither knowledge nor theory. In contrast, many founding scholars, including myself, specifically called for expanding the scope of composition to include writing, literacy development and education, and rhetorical practices at all ages, among all social groups, in all possible sites and contexts of activity. In incorporating rhetoric in the subject matter, we implicitly broadened "writing" from even the most generous concept of inscribed or composed language (covering reading and speech) to all sign systems and media in their rhetorical function, even though we had not yet experienced the digital revolution. Classrooms, or more broadly educational settings and functions of all kinds, were a somewhat privileged context because of the field's responsibilities in higher education, but we by no means intended to limit the field to this compass—quite the contrary. Because the interpretation of writing in the new "writing" studies is so inclusive and expansive in every dimension (media, mode, setting, culture, age), they may help to liberate composition studies from its narrow identification with college writing and pedagogy, restoring the central role of both scientific research and theory to its intellectual work.

Taylor: Looking back, could you discuss the trajectory of your writing? What are the intellectual patterns?

Phelps: This is relatively easy to answer, because I am in the process of finishing (hopefully soon!) the first volume of a collection of my writings from 1973 to the present. Grouping the pieces thematically and chronologically has become an unexpected journey of self-discovery, and I see the work now as a kind of hermeneutical autobiography. The patterns within each volume, and the relationship between them, express the harmonies and rhythms, themes and movements of my career. The first volume is called *Poetics of Composition: Footprints of an Intellectual Journey.* The second is called *Prosaics of Composition*, tentatively subtitled "The Rhetorical Portfolio of a Scholar in Action." Together, the set is called *Madisonian Research*, referring to James Madison's work on the

Constitution as my ideal model for integrating intellectual work and constructive action. The contrast between the two books is between "poetics" as the more essentialist or ideal form of intellectual work (the equivalent of basic research in science) and "prosaics" as rhetorical action, in which intellectual work is fully integrated into practice (paralleling applied research). However, all my activities and characteristic approaches in both arenas are "poetic" in a different sense: that composing and rhetorical action are both metaphor and means for the way I accomplish my work. As I've suggested, my career expresses, enacts, and examines many patterns of oppositions that are both truly in conflict and also necessary complements, entwined and interdependent.

In the first volume, I've collected published and unpublished work that represent "poetics" in two senses, which may be roughly equated with the "philosophical" and "phenomenological" modes described earlier. The philosophical work there includes characterizations of the discipline, studies in disciplinarity/interdisciplinarity and disciplinary issues, and the development of fundamental concepts and integrative theories of "composing" (both writing and reading). Some of the later work takes a historical turn. The phenomenological dimension appears both in the experiential foundations for philosophical work and also in some works of phenomenological description. Within these broad categories, there are clusters of work on professional identity, criticism, literacy development, graduate education, and feminism, including some experiments with alternate style and mixed genres.

The second volume will include writings in the context of teaching, administration, and institutional or professional leadership, illustrating and analyzing the perspectives of design and rhetorical action. That means it will include some rhetorically active documents like curriculum proposals, memos, policy documents, strategic plans, and so on.

The interdisciplinary reading I did prior to my appointment at the University of Southern California gave me a knowledge base to ground my philosophical project. During my years in the RLL program I worked to exploit, advance, refine, and revise the conceptual framework of my dissertation. Situating the discipline as a human science, I formulated a transactional theory of discourse and a developmental perspective on literacy, and developed specific concepts like coherence, discourse structure, process and product, literacy development, and the psychology of composition. By the mid-eighties I was moving into a new phase, poised to continue a trajectory that was moving toward something like today's socio-cultural theory of writing or cultural-historical activity theory. I knew this project was methodologically challenging, and ideally I would have joined a research group in order to learn from and collaborate with more objectivist researchers whose methods and expertise I needed to complement mine. I'm thinking of social scientists, developmental psychologists, linguists, cognitive scientists, and philosophers working on issues of discourse and language. At the same time, I would have loved to work with artists, media and technology scholars, and practitioners across disciplines who could enrich my own interests in craft, technique, tools, and design.

Taylor: What led to the change in course?

Phelps: This was the moment I left USC to become founding director of the Syracuse Writing Program, an abrupt transformation of my own context that precipitated major changes in the focus of my scholarship. In this phase of my career, my thinking and writing took a radical turn toward a form of intellectual and rhetorical work more deeply integrated with action. Taking a leadership role opened up broad new areas of inquiry, a significant gain, but at a heavy cost in scholarship along certain paths that became impossible, at least at the pace and in the ways I had originally planned. Materially and intellectually, the conditions of my job as an administrator designing and implementing a major writing program (and department) precluded the intensive reading program (eclectic, multidisciplinary, wide-ranging) and sustained, deep writing projects that I had been able to pursue at USC. There, my passionate engagement with these projects had been facilitated by the department's exclusion of me from its business (an unintentionally benign neglect) and the catalyst of graduate teaching. It was not simply time that the new job consumed; it demanded intellectual energy and attention at the highest level. The consequences were that the issues and opportunities facing me—curricular, professional, administrative—became the subject matter of my new intellectual work and the motive for new lines of scholarship.

One way to put the difference is in the acquisition of a new material reality, and therefore a new definition, of practice as an experiential grounding for my work. At the Syracuse Writing Program, for the first time I participated in (and helped conceive and support) a full-scale teaching community, enabling a form of distributed invention and reflective practice that transformed and recontextualized my prior, largely solitary experience as an individual practitioner. (I had only had hints of this possibility in the writing center at Cleveland State and in the RLL community at USC). This community had a sufficient size and integrity to constitute a human activity system with important characteristics for study *and* action. It was complex enough to be rich and rewarding, yet sufficiently intelligible to be open to study as a system, embedded in other systems, both hierarchically and horizontally. In making it possible for me to observe and conceptualize social dimensions of writing in a natural context, the Writing Program played a role in my work comparable to that of workplace sites for other researchers of that period, exemplifying features of social systems like distributed cognition and leadership, the dynamic of change and tradition, and the role of texts, genres, and genre systems in activity.

Among the consequences were to resituate my interest in things like invention or artistry of practice into systems of human activity and interaction, and to understand and practice rhetorical action as a collective, deeply contextualized activity, in very much more practical, prosaic, and political terms. Living the difficult role of a woman administrator in a feminized discipline (and program) brought to the surface a tacit feminism in my own experience of composition, prompting me to explore feminism as a "subterranean" feature of the field and contribute to its explicit development. My interest in human development shifted toward professional development for teachers and advocacy for non-tenure track instructors. In this new phase, I didn't abandon earlier concerns and concepts—they just took new forms and directions. In fact, just as I framed writing development in the Writing

Program as a "spiral" curriculum, my own work spirals back constantly to its earliest themes.

There's an overlap between the period when I took major leadership responsibilities and, recurrently, administrative roles in the Writing Program, and the most recent, fourth phase of my career, where I turned back toward graduate education (requiring more intensive engagement with the conceptual content and evolution of the discipline) and simultaneously outward, into broader arenas of action. An important catalyst for this reorientation was a transitional year as an American Council on Education (ACE) Fellow, where I studied higher education administration in a national program that trains people for potential presidencies and helps them explore their talents and interests in leadership and administration.

This marvelous experience of studying higher education from the highest levels and most diverse perspectives of leadership helped me to discover and affirm that my primary talents and interests as a teacher and administrator lay in graduate education, professional development for faculty throughout a career (in the framework of my long-standing interest in life-span development), and innovative program design and development, in the context of higher education reform. When I returned to Syracuse, I resolved to pursue these interests wherever I found myself, shaping roles for myself to do this kind of work there or elsewhere as the opportunity arose.

Taylor: After this training, why didn't you go into upper level administration?

Phelps: Although at times between then and now I have looked seriously at possible positions in higher education administration, nothing was a perfect match, and this potential career path never materialized. In part, I realized, the problem was my unwillingness to give up either side of myself—the scholar and writer or the action-oriented administrator—or, especially, to sacrifice the integration of the two that marked my work in each sphere. As a scholar, I was always drawn to practice, both as an object of study and as a context for my own reflective action. As an administrator, I approached leadership through the same modes of intellectual work (conceptual and phenomenological), more broadly addressed to institutional practices and contexts; in the same design attitude; and with the same primary tools—writing, rhetoric, symbolic action, inquiry, and collaboration. I was really interested only in jobs that would allow me to innovate and build new programs in a context of constructive change and educational reform, on the action side, and, as a scholar and writer, to continue my intellectual work to ground and interpret that activity. Those were few and far between and not usually accessible, for reasons ranging from geography (family considerations) to background (an unorthodox degree, discipline, and career were often a handicap), but especially because both scholars and administrators tend to be deeply suspicious of this combination.

As it turned out, then, this time was spent at Syracuse, where, as I became increasingly free of leadership responsibilities to the undergraduate program, I split my time and primary focus between graduate education in my department and action projects of two types: institutional reform and service to the profession, both becoming new sites of my intellectual work and writing.

Following my ACE Fellowship, after serving again in an interim administrative role in the Syracuse Writing Program, I led the development of a doctoral program in Composition and Cultural Rhetoric and turned my attention to graduate course design and pedagogy. Besides drawing on my work in human development, I came to see graduate education as a critical factor in understanding and constructing disciplinarity. Once they reached critical mass, doctoral programs became not only the means for populating the field with new scholars, but also the centers where its definition and directions are constantly renegotiated—and, it turned out, the political route to disciplinary acceptance. Responsibility for graduate courses and students motivated me to return to earlier theoretical problems, develop new topics of inquiry (like method), and, especially, turn my work in composition increasingly in a historical direction. At the same time, inspired by the Fellowship (and continuing to follow the literature on higher education reform), I devoted an enormous amount of time and intellectual energy to leadership of two action projects. As chair of the Senate Academic Affairs Committee, I led several multi-year change projects at Syracuse, two of them accomplishing reforms in the areas of tenure and promotion policies and the status of non-tenure track faculty. In a third project I coordinated the committee's inquiry into community engagement in its local and cosmopolitan aspects, written up in a monograph-length white paper triangulating the perspectives of higher education reformers, university administrators, and faculty ("Learning about Scholarship in Action"). During the same period (and still ongoing), I initiated the Visibility Project for the profession, working to gain full recognition for the field as a research discipline by focusing on the information structure of the academy and higher education bureaucracies. We have had two major breakthroughs in making rhetoric and composition/writing studies more visible to the academy and higher education policy makers (including federal agencies) by assigning its programs and products codes and descriptions in important educational data bases.

Taylor: What about the wider field? Where do you see it leading you in the future?

Phelps: I am retiring from Syracuse University in May, 2009 and moving to the Hampton Roads area of Virginia, but I intend to remain active as a scholar, writer, and consultant. I will maintain a connection with doctoral education through an appointment as a Visiting Scholar at Old Dominion University as well as completing commitments to graduate students at Syracuse, from a distance. This will certainly inaugurate a new phase of my intellectual work, though it is hard to predict all the possible directions it will take. I am a multi-tasker and, as I described in "Rhythm and Pattern in a Composing Life," I lead a composing life, with writing ideas constantly dancing through my head and an accumulating stock of speculative writing in files and notebooks, from which texts will eventually crystallize in ways I can't quite predict. Periodically, I organize these thoughts and materials into plans and projects and try to prioritize them. But this is not one of those fallow periods when I pause to reflect, so there is a certain randomness in selecting here from this spectrum of possibilities, especially since I know that what determines which I act on is synergy.

A lot of my current preoccupations come from my graduate teaching. I must conduct research in order to develop constantly new content for courses, and since I design them as inquiries to which I don't know the answers, I am learning and, therefore, writing. A number of my current interests center on time and temporality. I foresee, for example, undertaking more historical work on the modern development of composition, since I am very dissatisfied with current historical representations of the mid-to-late twentieth-century development of American rhetoric and composition. References to this period, in what you might call the "public memory" of the discipline, rely too much on commonplaces and conventional wisdom rather than inquiry and the study of primary sources.

Just as I work on teaching students how to navigate the field contemporaneously as a domain of problems and activities, including how to notice things, judge importance, and extrapolate future directions, I am concerned with the converse problem of cultivating historical consciousness in new scholars. Recently I wrote a response piece on the temporal dimensions of graduate education ("Traveling Time's Arrow") and am contemplating another on this topic. I would also like to go back to give more attention to an argument I made in the 1980s, that composing process models were wrongly built on short-term composing episodes and should have taken "composing over time" as the paradigm case. Janet Emig and I planned to edit a research volume on this subject, but life events derailed these plans.

One issue I'm thinking of revisiting, in response to several recent discussions I've read, is the theory/practice binary, which seems to be returning as a perceived problem in graduate programs (often conflated with an opposition between rhetoric and composition). I've already indicated a critique of this position that is grounded in history. I have some thoughts about reformulating my own earliest work on both sides of this binary and on their relationship. In the case of theory, I have long been interested in developing a concept of theory as a language that would "afford" the work of writers as composers and rhetorical actors, instead of making teachers the primary audience for theory—and therefore to an extent subjugated by it. The other side of this coin is to contest the assumption that "practice" refers exclusively to teaching practice, and specifically to an individualist concept of practice as what a single teacher does in "the classroom." I see it as encompassing a spectrum of historical and contemporary "practices," referring to both individual and collective agency and activity in writing, rhetoric, and literacy education.

I have too many other projects and interests to name, from an interest in international writing education to quirky projects like reading a shelf of writings on architecture and design that I expect to inspire a book someday. A high priority will be to complete my two-volume collection. Generally, though, a great deal of my work is opportunistic and responds to exigence and opportunity. Intellectual work should, I think, surprise the person who does it—that is what qualifies it as growth and learning. I expect mine to be unexpected at the same time as it will be "me"—reflecting my characteristic modes of inquiry, themes and problems, styles, principles and commitments. In retirement, I will continue to "proceed as way opens."

Steven Mailloux is President's Professor of Rhetoric at Loyola Marymount University. Previously, he taught rhetoric, critical theory, and U.S. cultural studies as Professor of English and Comparative Literature and Chancellor's Professor of Rhetoric at the University of California, Irvine. He also served in several administrative positions during his years at UCI including Associate Dean of Humanities for Graduate Study, Acting Director of the UC Humanities Research Institute, Director of the Critical Theory Emphasis, and Interim Chair of English and Comparative Literature. For the latter position, he received on-the-job training as Chair of English at Syracuse University when that department initiated a comprehensive reform of its literature curriculum in the direction of critical theory and cultural studies. He is the co-editor of *Interpreting Law and Literature* (1988) and editor of *Rhetoric, Sophistry, Pragmatism* (1995) as well as the author of *Interpretive Conventions: The Reader in the Study of American Fiction* (1982), *Rhetorical Power* (1989), and *Reception Histories: Rhetoric, Pragmatism, and American Cultural Politics* (1998). His most recent book is entitled *Disciplinary Identities: Rhetorical Paths of English, Speech, and Composition* (2006).

The Conversation

Keith Gilyard: Thanks for doing this, obviously. As you know, I have followed your work for some time with much appreciation, especially as you have laboriously developed the concept of rhetorical hermeneutics, which is a method for studying the production and reception of texts. Moreover, you are closely associated with the idea of *cultural rhetoric*, which you have defined on various occasions as the political effectivity of trope and argument in culture, and have made a case that English departments should be organized along lines of cultural rhetoric studies. I bring up all of this because sometimes folks in Rhetoric and Composition, many of whom see you as one of them, become nervous when cultural studies faculty try to become too involved in Rhet-Comp searches and hires. Yet, you provide strong intellectual support for the idea of cultural studies expanding into what some consider the realm of Rhetoric and Composition. In *Reception Histories*, for example, you use additional terms like *rhetorically oriented cultural studies*. In *Disciplinary Identities*, you term cultural rhetoric study a "specific rhetorical form of that heterogeneous movement known as cultural studies." Could you play with these ideas a bit more, speak some about the rhetorical paths that you have traveled on the way to your present advocacy and how you might address the concern I have noted? Any more magic triangles? Like culture, theory, textuality?

Steven Mailloux: Well, thanks a lot for the opportunity to talk with you. The issues that you note in your question are still important to me, and you raise some of the challenges relative to where I'm going. I continue to be interested in thinking and rethinking the institutional context for our work in humanities and the social sciences through cultural rhetoric studies. Cultural rhetoric studies continues for me to be a way of rethinking various relationships among disciplines in the human sciences. There are some very specific reasons why I have adopted the term *cultural rhetoric*, and I hope we can have a chance to talk about these.

Gilyard: What are the specific reasons? Let's go into it.

Mailloux: One of those has to be the particular configuration of the discipline that I was trained in—English Studies—and the particular way that discipline has developed over the last hundred and twenty years as a study of language that ends up privileging a particular part of language, a particular kind of language: the literary. What that has meant over time is that other aspects of language, other fields within English Studies, have not been given the intellectual respect or the economic recognition of their importance for the discipline. One of those fields is the teaching of writing, what has come to be called Rhetoric and Composition.

Gilyard: It's a cash cow for a lot of departments.

Mailloux: That's right. A cash cow in different ways at different institutions. Each of the research institutions where I trained and have worked depended on English departments controlling the teaching of composition in order to fund the graduate program. So, as I sometimes say, I am able to teach my course Rhetoric and Political Theology with twelve students at the graduate level because the graduate students are being funded through the teaching of composition. That's just one aspect of the way that composition is the economic base.

Gilyard: That doesn't make you the bad guy, though, does it?

Mailloux: That doesn't make me the bad guy. But what it does, given my institutional conscience, is make me feel responsible for the way that the field of composition has developed and the way people are treated within that field. One of the reasons that I hold on to the term *rhetoric* is that it has been traditionally associated with Rhetoric and Composition within English studies. I prefer the term to *discourse* or *literacy* or even *writing.* Rhetoric, conceived in a particular way as the use of language in contexts, the use of language that has effects in those contexts, bridges the activities of literature professors, students of literacy, teachers of composition, etc. Someone might say, "Well, you're doing Foucauldian discourse analysis. Why don't you just call it that? This will play better, be more persuasive within the way that the humanities are currently configured."

Gilyard: But it wouldn't play better in a lot of places I know, though. I mean, that would just take you further out of the game.

Mailloux: That's my point. It would take you further out of the game if the game is that you're trying to reconceptualize English Studies in such a way that Rhetoric and Composition as an intellectual field is not just supplemental or subsidiary but actually central. It seems to me to be very hard for somebody who embraces a notion of cultural *rhetoric* to simply privilege literary history, critical theory, or cultural studies.

Gilyard: Then why do you get this trepidation that I notice? Some people really fear that cultural rhetoric or cultural studies is an imposition on English Studies. But you say it belongs.

Mailloux: That's correct.

Gilyard: And they're saying that it's an interloper.

Mailloux: Here's where you have to have, not necessarily a double consciousness, but a double conscience. That is, for me the overall project is to reconceptualize not only literary and English Studies but, in my more grandiose moments, the human sciences more generally as Cultural Rhetoric Studies. Not just that, my project also is to provide a basis for Rhetoric and Composition to gain more institutional power. Now, the double conscience that I'm talking about is that I have responsibilities as an academic intellectual to the larger university project, but I also have a responsibility to the particular field of Rhetoric and Composition. That field may, in fact, not go along with my particular vision because of reasons internal to the field. And it certainly has been the case that for some compositionists cultural studies just takes the place of literary studies directing composition. So, in that view, rather than being an empowering institutional strategy, advocating rhetorical studies becomes a way that cultural studies can interfere in composition. But following a double conscience means that you have to play at least a double game, which means that you not only say that Rhetoric and Composition should be at the table in discussions of the future of English Studies, but that one of the reasons that it should be at the table is that it is one of those disciplines or fields that has a disciplinary identity and a professional legitimacy, just as nineteenth-century American literature or creative writing or whatever.

Gilyard: But that's kind of what I wanted to ask about because you couple *rhetoric* and *composition*. I know there's a historical association, but it seems that in some places, especially since the 1960s, composition has become an area of practice and study not tied so consciously to rhetoric. I remember being at conferences where people announced, "*I'm a rhetorician.*" In other words, "I don't do that composition stuff *you* do." So composition and rhetoric have been linked strategically but not in all places. I'm wondering how you see this playing out, this kind of negotiation that you're talking about.

Mailloux: I am a rhetorician and thus have to be very sensitive to the particularities of the context in which the term *rhetoric* is used. It certainly is the case that there would be some places where an argument about linking rhetoric and composition would first have to be argued within the composition faculty.
Gilyard: Exactly.

Mailloux: And that's part of my point. You can't simply impose any kind of structure or terminology. I can't all of a sudden, for example, start calling creative writing rhetoric. But I could, as I tried to do at Syracuse University, unsuccessfully....

Gilyard: That was the magic triangle reference....

Mailloux: To get creative writers to think of rhetoric as a possible way of rethinking the relationship of creative writing to literary studies and composition. I understand that some people who identify themselves not as rhetoricians but as writing experts or literacy scholars might not want to use the term *rhetoric*. And my job in a particular situation is to try to give them reasons why the term will empower them and at the same time support them in developing their own identity. So that's basically the trick in the positive sense. What that ends up meaning, though, is that you have to convince not only the composition specialists but also your other colleagues in the English department that composition is itself a field and thus you can't just declare expertise simply because you have expertise in cultural studies. No. It's the same way that a creative writer doesn't claim to have expertise in critical theory, necessarily.

Gilyard: So in your searches, you still have to vet applications with respect to this dialogue that has to take place.

Mailloux: That's right. And then you get into some really interesting situations. For example, UC Irvine once did not recognize composition as a scholarly field and thus thought of composition only as a service. As it has moved from thinking of it as a pedagogical service to a scholarly field that has a pedagogical component—just like critical theory or cultural studies or literary history—the kinds of people the department wants to hire in composition lines has changed. But it is also different, I would argue, than in departments where composition is already fully established, a place like Penn State, or in an entirely separate department like at Texas at Austin. So that's where you get into the micro strategies. You might say that you don't want to get somebody, for example, who was trained in literary studies and does writing on the side, who doesn't recognize composition as a discipline, maybe only had to teach it in order to get through graduate school. On the other hand, in the particular situation at Irvine, where you only have a small number of lines in composition, and you're thinking about wanting to empower yet simultaneously integrate composition into the larger arena, you don't want to get somebody that is, let's call it, a separatist writing scholar.

Gilyard: That won't give you traction on that campus.

Mailloux: What that means is that there is a narrow range of composition specialists who self-identify also as rhetoricians that you want to hire. So this means recruiting somebody who knows the history of the field of composition, who knows the theoretical debates that are going on in writing pedagogy, who has a specific research project within composition that might relate to fields outside of it but at the same time is self-identified as a compositionist, is recognized at CCCC professionally, publishes in the composition journals but also can build bridges to those outside of composition. It's that kind of person whom you would end up hiring that fulfills what I'm calling a double institutional conscience.

Gilyard: That's based on particular contexts and readings of those contexts, which links to my next question because behind your whole project is philosophical pragmatism. Moreover, you are keenly concerned about politics. Do you still feel that pragmatism is a forceful political statement on its own? I think you've said something tantamount to that; at least I read it that way. But do you think pragmatism needs an adjective with some punch?

Mailloux: The answer to the first part of the question is, yes, I still think, both inside and outside the academy, that various forms of pragmatism are useful for supporting various kinds of political interventions. Having said that, though, the second part of your question is the more interesting for me, and that is, "Do you need an adjective in front of pragmatism to give it more rhetorical punch?" And I think that it's more important within the academy than outside for it to have that adjective. I think of pragmatism as having not an inherent but a historical politics associated with it. I'll come back to that notion of inherency. I think that it's been associated with progressive movements since its beginning—with James and Dewey, and, in some of its more interesting formulations, with certain public intellectuals like one that you work on, Cornel West, and also, in a more problematic way, Richard Rorty. Outside of the academy, pragmatism has a good record up to a point given the way that pragmatists have entered the public sphere on questions of democratic deliberation, on questions of protection of human rights, on questions of examining and reconfiguring the unequal distribution of justice and the unequal distribution of wealth. Academically, though, we have a different case.

Gilyard: Let me hold on to the outside piece first because you mention West, and this is part of what was driving my question. It's that he put *prophetic* up in front of his pragmatism because he wanted to dissociate it from what he called some rather benign politics of Dewey and some of the other people that you mentioned. He said they didn't go far enough in certain areas, particularly in terms of race. So I'm thinking about this association of pragmatism with progressivism, but I'm also thinking about the far-left criticism of pragmatism. They say, "Is it any coincidence"—I think Howard Selsam, a student of Dewey at Columbia University, raised the question—"that the nation that developed pragmatism is the nation that developed the hydrogen bomb and stuff like that?" What I'm saying is that if you judge things just in pragmatist terms, meaning you're looking at the outcomes, the effects of things, you can use it to justify nearly anything.

Mailloux: That's right.

Gilyard: So then…

Mailloux: Now here's where I think pragmatism is like rhetoric: you could end up using it to undertake just about any political program. That is to say that I could train somebody in rhetoric—and even put it within a critical literacy or critical pedagogy context—and I might be training somebody to go out, enter into the public sphere, and argue for the oppressed. Or I might be training somebody to go out to oppress more effectively. It's always a risk.

Gilyard: And that's exactly my point. And that's why I was asking about the term to which you might link pragmatism. If you could come up with a notion we agree on, something about, let's say, democracy or genuine democracy, you could tie that to pragmatism and take the philosophy off neutral.

Mailloux: I have used the term pragmatism with an adjective—rhetorical pragmatism. But that doesn't solve the problem that you're talking about. But let me just try to elaborate why I think that that's useful still. First of all, I wish I had come up with the term prophetic pragmatism. I do think that prophetic pragmatism, as West describes it, with its commitment to critical temper and democratic faith, is consistent with what I'm calling rhetorical pragmatism.

Gilyard: I think so.

Mailloux: I would see rhetorical pragmatism being the broader category and one version of rhetorical pragmatism being prophetic pragmatism. The two are not inconsistent. I do think that West's particular brand of prophetic pragmatism is an intersection of three traditions: Marxism, Protestant Christianity, and pragmatism. I only identify with one of them. He then, in a mix, is able to stir them up and come out with prophetic pragmatism that is theoretically antifoundationalist and politically committed to the analysis of inequalities, including those of race, gender, and economics. It would be a contradiction in terms if this prophetic pragmatism were then used by a reactionary force.

Gilyard: That's what I'm saying.

Mailloux: But I'm as committed to pragmatism as West. That's kind of a silly way to put it, but I think I'm fully committed and think that has been reflected in my institutional work, scholarship, and, to a certain extent, in any work that I've done as a public intellectual.

Gilyard: Well, one could see that in the work.

Mailloux: However, I view things a bit differently. For example, part of what drives prophetic pragmatism is an economic analysis that

I'm not completely committed to, a certain Marxist class analysis. Then there is my own struggling relationship with Christianity. I still consider myself self-identified as a Roman Catholic, but it's an ongoing struggle. Pragmatism is perfect for me in the sense that it reflects a kind of uncertainty and critical self-consciousness. But that isn't always the best attitude to have for a political project. So I've struggled with this idea and decided that rhetorical pragmatism is consistent with other left pragmatisms but doesn't have built into it certain kinds of certainties that those pragmatisms do.

Gilyard: Those pragmatisms really shouldn't be all that certain if they are indeed pragmatist, right?

Mailloux: That's the issue. And then you get into my particular formation as a pragmatist that owes so much to Stanley Fish and Richard Rorty. And they would make the argument—and I've been convinced by it—that theory has no necessary theoretical consequence. Now I think Fish goes too far because I think theory has rhetorical consequences, which are political. And he doesn't give enough acknowledgment to that. But Rorty makes the argument that a political commitment, or a political agenda of radical democracy, for example, or liberal democracy does not need to be undergirded foundationally by a philosophy. So this is another way of saying that, given the right historical circumstances, any theory can be used for any political agenda. Among those so-called circumstances are social and economic conditions. I might even say that there are certain ways of using prophetic pragmatism that could be, from a particular perspective, seen as reactionary. Just as you can use certain forms of Marxism—state Marxism—for certain kinds of totalitarianism. But, still, also as a pragmatist, I'm not only interested in the possibilities, I'm interested in the probabilities. And the probabilities are that it's pretty hard to use prophetic pragmatism for that sort of thing. So I can't go too far in that direction. But the point is that some academic versions of pragmatism restrict the necessary linkages between pragmatism as a theory and pragmatism as a politics. Then I end up having to make arguments that there are associative reasons, that there are shared tropes, arguments, and narratives that relate what I call rhetorical pragmatism to a commitment to radical democracy. Both rhetorical pragmatism and radical democracy, for example, share tropes of conversation and dialogue; they share arguments about the primacy of empowerment and the protection of minority rights; and they share narratives about the way that you come up with knowledge of truth: through deliberation. For those reasons, I would argue that there's no necessary connection between rhetorical pragmatism and a commitment to radical democratic politics, but there are associative reasons. And at this particular time and place, within the academy and outside, rhetorical pragmatism, then, still seems to me to be a valid theoretical and political position.

Gilyard: I want to ask you a little bit more about pragmatism in relation to terminology, shifting back to the cultural rhetoric term because you prefer it to critical literacy, though the latter term may have more currency in the academy and seems to do significant work. At the same time, your notion of rhetorical hermeneutics is sometimes criticized, though you dismiss much of the criticism handily, often to my amusement. I love the way you take on and debunk the folks who are messing with you. You're such a careful writer. One of my students was upset. He said, "You know, Mailloux should just let it go." But I told him that you had to turn over everything carefully because you didn't know where the attack would come from. That's just the way he writes, I tell people. You have to leave it alone. Appreciate it.

Mailloux: That's a good observation.

Gilyard: Don't hate; congratulate, you know. But I'm wondering if a strong pragmatist impulse might kick in and cause you to abandon some of your patented terminology if you find yourself spending too much time defending yourself—effects and results, right?—in the discursive spaces in which you operate. Some of the people are sympathetic, like my department colleague Rosa Eberly, for example, whom you mention in your work. She's not hostile to the project of rhetorical hermeneutics, but she's going to question the linking of production and reception. She sees rhetorical hermeneutics as a critical method whereas her focus is on rhetoric as a productive art. Of course, you counter that rhetorical hermeneutics contains tools and advice for both production and interpretation. In fact, you spend a lot of time arguing that we shouldn't separate production from reception. And I agree with that, but it seems that if we spend all that time debating terminology, it might be time to use other terms.

Mailloux: Let me give you even more ammunition. Even using the term rhetoric in a more nonacademic public sphere is problematic. The term gets associated with something specious and with mere talk as opposed to action. People outside of the academy question why I continue to use the term, especially, as you indicate, because I have to spend considerable time defending it. Or the best example would be proposing cultural rhetoric at Syracuse and spending two years trying to argue for a curriculum. I couldn't even get my friends to agree with this. Why keep doing it? Should I give it up just on the basis of my own premises about probabilities and effects and about pragmatism looking at outcomes to judge the truth about something? The short answer is "yeah, probably." So why don't I? The trivial reason is probably that it's just too late in the day. But the less trivial reason is historical and theoretical. The fact is there are different ways to win debates that are internal to the academy and outside. Losing a particular battle doesn't mean you necessarily lose the war. I do think that there are more people interested in rhetoric now within the humanities than there were twenty years ago. So within the academy, I do think that holding on to the term can have positive effects. Wayne Booth, someone with whom I disagreed somewhat but also praised in many ways, is an example of a person who held on to the term rhetoric. He did coin other terms, *rhetorology* and things like that. But rhetoric was something that he remained committed to, and that commitment had effects throughout literary studies and composition. That represents the sort of the political-institutional reason for holding on to it. That is, I gave you a rhetorical answer in response to the rhetorical critique. But the theoretical answer, which is situated within this historical moment, is that I don't know of another term that does as much effective intellectual and political work as rhetoric. I mean, rhetoric can allow you to speak to those that are interested in ancient classical traditions, but, at the same time, there's nothing more postmodern than rhetoric. Rhetoric gives you the classical and the postmodern. For those in English departments that are arguing between cultural studies and literary studies, between attention to the historical context of culture and close reading of texts, rhetoric is on both sides. I can do really close readings of texts and say I'm doing rhetorical work, but I also then do historical contextualizations of reception. So, again, rhetoric does both kinds of work. In addition, I think one reason theorists of various types have adopted rhetoric is because of certain Sophistic traditions that allow you to avoid certain essentialist, foundationalist, and other kinds of traps. Rhetoric does all that work.

Gilyard: Yeah, but it's funny because when we were trying to bring the doctoral program in cultural rhetoric on board at Syracuse—you had left by then—rhetoric was considered the new thing. You know, some of the colleagues in the College of Arts and Sciences who were against our proposal wanted to know why we were pushing this new discipline and felt that we should get in line and wait. I was sitting there, Louise Wetherbee Phelps also, thinking that rhetoric was older than any other discipline represented in the room. We also ran into trouble because of the term *cultural*. The anthropology department felt some ownership there, wanted to flex a little territorial muscle. As a result of all this, we were voted down the first time around. We came back, however, with a successful strategy, rhetoricians that we were.

Mailloux: These kinds of issues—and I wrote on this in my last book— have to do with disciplinary identities. Because of the work that I've done in administrative positions, as well as in my teaching and in scholarship, I've seen how disciplinary identities can get in the way of productive intellectual work. I found many times it wasn't generation or gender or race or ethnicity or region or any of those kinds of identity markers that got in the way of really interesting conversations among scholars. It was disciplinary blinders that did. Rhetoric brings you so much that helps to break down certain kinds of divides, including the divide between the social sciences and the humanities. Rhetorically, it's about acknowledging certain kinds of vested interests and knowing that you have to get into conversation with them, yet having a vocabulary that's going to bridge different gaps.

Gilyard: That's what I think is the strength of *Disciplinary Identities*. You set up, as you usually do, rhetorical hermeneutics as the use of rhetoric to practice theory by doing history. Then the book moves into these contemporary problems, problems we have to deal with. I'm thinking about the 9/11 stuff, the comments about the panel you were on at Cardozo Law School with *New York Times* columnist Edward Rothstein. This is a bit different from some of your earlier work in which you set up the same theoretical move and then take us immediately back to the nineteenth century and to close reads. You don't want to give up that type of thing; it's part of your project also. But I think it is powerful, maybe an advance, to talk about contemporary issues and about how we might envision the academy. Unfortunately, you were not successful in convincing Mr. Rothstein of the value of your perspective. He saw you as just another academic postmodernist.

Mailloux: Because rhetorical hermeneutics is the use of rhetoric to practice theory by doing history, that leads me to do historical work, to do reception studies that are often in need of an archive. My training is in nineteenth-century American literature, so you get the reception study of Margaret Fuller reading Frederick Douglass's slave narrative or of the Concord Public Library banning *Huckleberry Finn*. And then as I try to do that also in theory, that is, use rhetoric to practice theory by doing history, I end up doing a reception study of Heidegger's statement that phronesis is conscience. It becomes harder as you try to relate that to contemporary issues. I do think that what I try to do with respect to the 9/11 issue is do a sort of reception history of my own argument.

Gilyard: I thought that was very effective. Very powerful.

Mailloux: Really, in the case of Syracuse or the 9/11 panel story, the work is partly a rhetorical history of my own failure and then an attempt to analyze why the failure occurred. Then I consider other ways of proceeding.

Gilyard: You talked about some identity markers earlier, and I want to go to this identity question because I find useful your notion of identity as interpreted being. And I know, of course, that you also argue that any such interpretation is historically and socially situated among other interpretations, including interpretations by the original being in question. But this formulation won't be quite as satisfying to some folks unless a system of weighing, some sort of semiotic analysis is involved. For example, my sense of identity as a slow-walking, peaceful African American cannot simply be canceled by the negative construction of me by a hard-charging, club-wielding, noose-carrying white bigot. I can be canceled, but I can think of more useful contributions to discussions about identity. In other words, it seems that identity cannot equal the sum total of interpretations. Consider, for example, if I were an African American who did not identify with the ethnic group at all but claimed to identify primarily with my profession. I could still get attacked by the same club-wielding, noose-carrying bigot. So it seems that no useful definition of identity can be that it does not matter. I lean more toward performance explanations than essence explanations, but it seems a strong performance thesis has to be qualified, no?

Mailloux: This is a really good question, which means it's really hard to answer! Let me try to think aloud here.

Gilyard: I say this in reference to some of what you've written about William Scarborough and then Booker T. Washington to some extent. I have that in mind.

Mailloux: Scarborough's a good example of somebody who at certain moments and in certain contexts identified more as a professional classicist, one might argue, than as an African American. But that identification did not keep him from being discriminated against and not being able to get a hotel room at a professional conference or even, in the example that I give in *Disciplinary Identities*, in one of the activities of the conference itself. But he did say repeatedly, at least early in his career, he self-identified as a professional classicist and in those contexts of the professional conferences felt that he was treated as an equal. And he himself felt an equal. But that doesn't provide a counter to your question. It actually just further elaborates it. So my initial response is to say you're right; yes, performance theories of identity need to be qualified. On the other hand, let's look again at the example that you talk about here: the idea of somebody who self-identifies as an African American and a human rights holder, a civil rights holder, as part of his or her identity, and in various ways performs that. And when I'm talking about performance here, I mean the performance of rhetoric and interpretation, that is, the way that you interpret yourself and the language you use in thinking and expressing that interpretation. So we have the situation of this African American that you've given me, and then some club-wielding, noose-carrying white supremacist has a very different interpretation of this person, one aspect of which would be that this person maybe isn't even a person or is an innately inferior person. So that is an interpretation that then leads to actions.

Gilyard: Then the actions cancel out my identity, no matter what I interpreted that identity to be. It cancels out either way. That's why I suggest we need a fuller definition of identity.

Mailloux: Okay. It cancels out, and your question said it very well that the *I*, the very being of the person, could be canceled out; he could be killed. Now, the interpreted being, the identity of the white supremacist leads him not only to identify himself in a particular way but to identify his object of violence. And the identity of the African American does not prevent him from that.

Gilyard: That's why I relate it back to when you were talking about your pragmatism. That's part of what my point is. It's that if I assume a particular identity, it should have particular consequences. But if I get canceled from without irrespective of the interpreted being I assume, then it means that my identity makes no difference. I'm saying that can't be your argument for identity, can it?

Mailloux: Well, I originally was going to say "no it can't"; but now I'm going to say "yes it can" because, if you look at identity's relationship to action, what would actually happen would be the following. Obviously, if the guy is coming at me wielding a club, you know, I'm not going to say, "Hey! My interpreted being is different than what…" That isn't what I would do. I would put my arm out or respond in kind. Then I'm identifying not as a passive but as an active person; so my identity, my interpreted being, mobilizes me.

Gilyard: This is what I'm talking about in terms of the weighing. That's why I was asking you about weighing. Isn't there a way to talk about layered identity or some things being more salient than others? It's like when we go abroad. We know how American we feel when we're in Africa or Europe, and we don't necessarily feel so American here.

Mailloux: In a very unoriginal way in *Disciplinary Identities*, I would call that hybrid identity. And so layered identity, multiple identity—we in different times and different places function with a different interpreted being.

Gilyard: You see, I go with layered over hybrid because what I'm saying is that hybridity assumes a sort of stasis, like I'm two fixed and more or less equal things at once. Let's say, for example, I can't get my arms up in time. Let's say I'm captured and being lynched or something. Then I say, "Well, I don't really identify as an African American. I'm hybrid, so just lynch the left half of me. At least I can get out of this halfway okay." That wouldn't work, would it? Or let's say if somebody's accused of a hate crime against me and I say, "No, you can't charge them with a hate crime. You can charge them with assault but not a hate crime because I don't identify as African American." You get to absurd points, right?

Mailloux: But just a kind of metacomment. What we're doing here—this is what seems to me to be so useful about rhetoric—is that we can go metarhetorical and analyze the way that the metaphor of hybridity and the metaphor of layeredness work in particular contexts. And so rhetoric is always able to do that kind of move. We're using rhetoric to talk about rhetoric, and I just really think that's a useful kind of tool. Okay, end of metacomment.

Gilyard: A good metacomment.

Mailloux: Right after 9/11, when some of the responses by American citizens of European descent were to go and beat up Arabs, there was an incident in which a Sikh was beaten up. That Sikh doesn't identify as an Arab, let alone as an Arab terrorist. His identity doesn't change when he's beaten up. What he might try to do actually is use rhetoric to convince them, "Look, I'm not an Arab! Here are my credentials! I'm a Sikh!" There are ways that you can actually answer violence through interpretation and rhetoric.

Gilyard: Again, that's if you get a chance. It's like that scene toward the end of Spike Lee's movie *Do the Right Thing*. After the rioters seize the pizzeria, they approach the Korean deli, and the shopkeeper is swinging a broom to ward them off while exclaiming, "I'm black, I'm black!" One African American responds indignantly, "What do you mean you black?" and proceeds to explain that the Korean is not black like him. But another African American man intercedes, "Leave the Korean alone. He's all right."

Mailloux: It seems to me that if we ask what kind of identity that privileges, then we need something even different from hybrid or layered. We have to use something like strategic. But that it ends up being from a rhetorical perspective strategic all the way down. And then you get into interesting kinds of theoretical…

Gilyard: And then that crosses with the politics because some people would criticize the notion of strategic without obligation.

Mailloux: That's right.

Gilyard: It doesn't mean identity is not strategic. It doesn't mean it's not rhetorical. It's just that it's more than that in some minds and people are definitely going to chime in politically.

Mailloux: This gets to the theoretical debates, which I certainly wouldn't want to have if somebody were about to beat me but can have in a context like this. I could make the antiessentialist argument about identity. I do acknowledge, though, that sometimes that argument is just irrelevant. For example, early on in my career, there was a law and literature conference at which two women were giving papers. One gave a very sophisticated feminist analysis that used poststructuralist strategies to rethink the notion of *woman* and argued what relationship that had to contemporary domestic politics. Another woman got up and said, "Women make the best leaders." Period. And then she gave some historical examples of women and said that women are inherently better leaders of countries. A couple of us who were sympathetic to feminism—but were more sympathetic to a poststructuralist version of it—began to respond. The first person raised his hand and challenged the second presenter and also asked the first presenter what she thought of her co-panelist's argument. She wouldn't answer the question directly. Then other people in the audience—males—raised their hands to say, "But you didn't really answer the question, you know. What do you think about..." She still refused. It took another questioner or two before we realized that she was not going to turn on the other woman. The theoretical issue of essentialist versus antiessentialist was much less relevant at that particular moment politically than their showing some solidarity. So there are some times when theoretical issues just seem to be beside the point. On the other hand, antiessentialist, antifoundationalist critiques of identity politics have been very effective in broadening inclusiveness.

Gilyard: You mentioned Richard Rorty earlier. Rorty and Edward Said saw no role for religion in the public sphere. I don't think you quite take the same stance. Now that I'm hearing comments about your conflicted Roman Catholicism, I'm interested in hearing you elaborate on that issue.

Mailloux: In the places that I talk about Said and Rorty, for example, in *Disciplinary Identities*, I do group them as public intellectuals...

Gilyard: Secularists, right?

Mailloux: Secularists and, at least in Rorty's case, an atheist. But now I would differentiate them further. Said had a particular political reason for pushing religion off the table —in the Middle East situation, for example: as a Palestinian, as somebody who both in his scholarship and in his public intellectual activism saw that the religious claims that were made, especially by fundamentalists on both sides of the Israeli-Palestinian conflict, made the situation worse rather than better. So he had a very good rhetorical reason not to bring religion into that kind of context. Said at one point talks about public intellectuals in terms of the rhetorical tradition. He says what we need is what the rhetoricians call *inventio*. And I've quoted that a couple of times. I just think it's wonderful and really true about Said. He would go into a situation, and he would then say that the best intellectuals are those who are trying to move the conversation by inventing new ways to conceptualize the situation for the better. That's what he tried to do with *Orientalism*. That's what he tried to do with all of his work. For him, religion was not part of that, which was for me very understandable. Rorty is a different case. He felt for most of his career that the separation of church and state should really be absolute. He was traditionally liberal on that point. This goes back to that connection between theory and politics. He would say that there's no connection, but those two presuppositions led him to doing very odd rhetorical performances. For example, he is invited to go down to South America to a conference to talk to liberation theology intellectuals. He goes down there and says to this group, who have based their politics on Catholicism and tried to change the status quo at great personal risk to themselves, "There's no relationship between politics and philosophy.

There's no relationship between politics and theory." And that seemed so oblivious to that particular rhetorical-political context.

Gilyard: In other words, he didn't see religion as a language of negotiation and therefore part of the public sphere.

Mailloux: That's right.

Gilyard: So if your public sphere constitutes itself as religious, then you're not making good rhetorical moves if you take Rorty's stance.

Mailloux: I sometimes tell my students that rhetoricians are supposed to (though there are no rules for this) use *phronesis*, meaning practical wisdom, go into a situation and be able to tell what the most effective means of persuasion are. To go into a church and claim, "There is no God. Now listen to me and what I'm going to talk to you about" is not very effective. Now, it's very interesting that Rorty, at the end of his career, when he started working with Vattimo, actually said, "Well, you know, I really shouldn't have been arguing for antireligion but anticlericalism."

Gilyard: Right.

Mailloux: When he made that switch, he was fine-tuning the liberal critique of bringing religion into the public sphere, and I think he was more accurate in terms of what he really opposed, the various kinds of fundamentalisms that Sharon Crowley talks about in *Toward a Civil Discourse*. For various reasons—it's not just 9/11—there's been a return of religion to public culture and the academy.

Gilyard: Well, you know, Fish said it would be the next big thing.

Mailloux: It makes so much sense in terms of the public, nonacademic side, globally and domestically. If we don't as rhetoricians pay more attention to how religious rhetoric works, then we're just throwing up our hands at really being public intellectuals. So that has to be on the agenda in a way that it wasn't years ago. That means, though, that there are going to be many different kinds of discussions, some of which aren't going to be that useful. But I think Sharon's book is just a really good example of trying to analyze things. And that book, by the way, is so interesting because of her own struggles with representation. She doesn't tolerate the fundamentalist political position that she's analyzing but yet tries to analyze the rhetoric of that position fairly. Rhetoric again becomes a useful tool. I'm teaching this course next quarter called Cultural Rhetoric and Critical Theory: Subjects, Events, Theologies, and we're starting…

Gilyard: There is another triangle!

Mailloux: Yeah, well, I've got the triangles there—using rhetoric, practicing theory, and doing history. That is another triangle. In this course, we'll start with Paul and Augustine, and then we'll jump to twentieth-century receptions of Paul and Augustine. This we would start with Heidegger's Paul and Augustine 1920s seminars, go to Arendt's dissertation on love in Augustine, and then Kenneth Burke's *Rhetoric of Religion*, and then come up to some of the recent turns of later theorists like Derrida. Lyotard's last book is on Augustine's *Confessions*. There is Alain Badiou's book *Saint Paul*.

Gilyard: That kind of answers the last question because I was going to ask you what you were up to. This course is one of the latest things you're up to.

Mailloux: I would say there are two things that might be further developments. I will continue to look at identity in its various performances within and outside the academy, to think about disciplines, interdisciplines, and transdisciplines, and the relationship of academic intellectuals to public intellectuals. And there rhetorical studies has a great deal to contribute. I think of public intellectuals as being translators, commentators, inventors, and metacritics. To be a metacritic means that you can analyze how expert discourses are translated or new ones are invented in the way Said talked about or are simply applied in commentary in the mass media. Rhetoricians not only can participate actively as what I call hybrid intellectuals who are public and academic; but can also analyze such events and processes as metacritics. And so that's one project. The other project really has to do with the rhetoric of political theologies. This is a historical and theoretical project that is probably way too ambitious and unrealistic. What I'd like to do is to look at the way Pauline Christianity over the last two hundred years has been appropriated by various interpreters and activists: for example, appropriated by both sides on the slavery question in the nineteenth century, and the ways, after the Civil War, it was used on both sides of the immigration debate. Also how Frederick Douglass identified with Paul throughout his career to the point of visiting Athens, standing on the Areopagus and hearing Paul's speech to the Athenians. Next I'd like to take up how Pauline Christianity gets used in twentieth-century critical theory, in rhetorical hermeneutics from Heidegger through Badiou (exemplified in the course I just described). Then, and this is the stretch, I'd like to read back in a kind of feedback loop the twentieth-century theoretical perspectives into and out of the nineteenth-century receptions.

Gilyard: Ambitious. As you say. But you'll get to some of it, though.

Mailloux: Some of it. Maybe.

C. Jan Swearingen is Professor of English at Texas A&M University, and a Past President of the Rhetoric Society of America. Her books include *Rhetoric and Irony: Western Literacy and Western Lies* (Oxford 1991), and *Rhetoric, the Polis, and the Global Village* (Lawrence Erlbaum 1999). She has written numerous chapters and articles on the history and theory of rhetoric, African American rhetorical cultures, comparative rhetorical studies, feminist approaches to rhetoric, and rhetoric and religion. An NEH Fellowship in 2008-2009 funded her study of rhetoric and religion in colonial Virginia, *From Church to State: Rhetoric, Religion, and the Transformation of Liberty in Colonial Virgina 1740–1776.*

The Conversation

Keith Gilyard: I know you have much to say about the contemporary scene relative to rhetoric and culture. But first I want to go back to some of your relatively early work that is summed up in *Rhetoric and Irony*. You expressed a wide range of concerns in that book, but central purposes seemed to be the recovery of the dialogic, the expression of tolerance for various epistemologies, the view of literacy as multivariable, some of the ideas that one can recover, at least in part, from Plato, Aristotle, Cicero, and Augustine. In retrospect, I find such a project interesting in that the Western classical tradition is often posited as a norm against which folks invested in cultural diversity have to push. Would you speak about your work in this regard and how your earlier thinking is reflected, if it is, in your current thoughts about education and discourse studies?

C. Jan Swearingen: We need to learn from the diversity of the classical world. It was and is all too common to think of the classical world as uniform, as elite, as made up of patrician men who all spoke the same and talked the same. Quite the reverse was true. It was a very multiracial, multicultural world in which there were slaves of a very different kind than we think of in our own history, slaves who were educators and tutors of families. The cross-fertilization with the ancient Near East, Persia, and Egypt was very strong. So it was a bubbling cauldron of different cultures, traditions, and histories all talking to one another. The thing about Plato that most interested me was the discovery that his dialogues are intended to not conclude on any particular point. They're not intended to teach doctrines. They're intended to bring voices together to create an improved understanding of a topic or subject. And that can only happen through interactions. One person can't do that. That's something that we need to keep revisiting like we are right now through this discussion, that truth doesn't come from single people, it comes from exchange.

Gilyard: That implies a critique of writing, at least Plato's critique of writing as a final, delivered product. It implies a critique of rhetoric, too.

Swearingen: If it's a monologue.

Gilyard: When most students think about classical rhetoric, they don't think of it in terms of cultural diversity the way you pose it.

Swearingen: The need to standardize a curriculum removed a lot of that diversity. Once it became a classroom tradition, it became more uniform, and then classrooms themselves became the domain of an elite. Missing was the kind of living exchange between people outside of classrooms, which is where Plato was, although I think we don't remember that. And he was having conversations outside of any classroom setting. Aristotle, on the other hand, set up a school with outlines for how to compose things.

Gilyard: Speaking of standards, the series of symposia that you and your colleagues have begun here at Texas A&M on vernacular rhetorics—this year's theme being Africana and African American identities and voices—recalls your long-standing interest in language policy concerning African Americans. Over a quarter century ago you were commenting on the King case, which many refer to as the Black English trial or the Ann Arbor decision. Since then we have had a sort of King II, the Ebonics controversy. I'm sure another sequel is on the way.

Swearingen: In Ann Arbor, a misunderstanding came about on the part of the teachers who were required to go through what we would call today sensitivity training, which would focus on awareness of Black English as the students' native language. Then, as with the Oakland Ebonics case, the public misunderstanding and the teachers' misunderstanding were that teachers were being forced to teach Black English. That was never the issue at all. It was about improving the responses of teachers to what they faced in classrooms. But the conversation got stuck on this issue of teaching Black English, and that resulted in much of the negative response to the trial in Ann Arbor and to the Ebonics situation later. I'm frustrated and amazed at this stubbornness, this willful misunderstanding of what the issue is and the continued negative use of that phrase "teach Black English." It makes me sad for the future that people so willfully misunderstand what the issue is.

Gilyard: We can look right here in Texas. Wasn't an anti-Ebonics resolution introduced in the state legislature?

Swearingen: It was part of the English Only movement.

Gilyard: What's the state of the conversation out here now?

Swearingen: Actually, Texas has a complicated history. Texas is the only state with a large number of Hispanics that has not passed English Only legislation. I think that's part of our regional history, our border history with Mexico. You may have noticed that the airport in Houston has announcements being broadcast in both English and Spanish. Both Bush the father and Bush the son have always been proponents of bilingualism, partly for political reasons. They wanted the Hispanic vote. So it's interesting to me that California and Florida have both gone totally English Only while Texas has not. Now, on Ebonics, it's not quite the same history. But I think there's at least lip service given to the teaching of what Black English is in our linguistics program in our education college. So there's not just this blind refusal to look at it. And I'm curious about that, too, because Oakland just blew up and I don't know whether it's ever recovered or whether anything finally happened to resolve it. But we're going through the motions here; I wouldn't say there's great enthusiam for it but on campus some people are honoring the discussion of Black English and language variation. We've got four linguists in our department doing that work.

Gilyard: Is that connected to public schools in any way as a project?

Swearingen: I don't know the form that it takes in the public schools.

Gilyard: It seems to me the whole thing blew up in Oakland because of the language that was used by the school board, in particular the phrase *genetically based*. Talking about genetics is a legitimate conversation in linguistics. I have a book in my office right now called *Language Contact, Creolization, and Genetic Linguistics* (by Sarah Grey Thomason and Terrence Kaufman). Ironically, it was published by the University of California Press. *Genetic* can be used as a specific linguistic term that has nothing to do with biology as we generally think of biology. However, it was taken up as a biological term by the public, and the school board didn't do a good job of clarifying its position.

Swearingen: Of course, there's another wrinkle. Many middle-class African Americans, in line with comments made by the likes of Bill Cosby and Whoopi Goldberg, don't want to hear about Ebonics. In Texas we've had variations on the same theme happening within both the black community and the Hispanic community over Ebonics-oriented African American education and over bilingual education. Some of the upwardly mobile African Americans don't want to hear about Ebonics. Some of the upwardly mobile Hispanics don't want bilingual education. They want assimilation.

Gilyard: There's always a class-language dynamic. You can map language and pedagogical attitudes on to class positions to a significant degree. You know, Cosby made some pretty good money off of Ebonics, with Fat Albert and those Ebonics-speaking characters. So things are rarely simple. I'm thinking of this town near the border where they outlawed English. Where was that?

Swearingen: You got me on that one. I don't know.

Gilyard: I saw it on Robert MacNeil's documentary *Do You Speak American?* He talked about it. There was this controversy where they banned English from this town. I think it's down near the Rio Grande.

Swearingen: When I was in junior high here in the late 1950s and early 1960s, everybody was required to take Spanish from the first grade through the eighth grade. It was mandatory bilingual education for English speakers. That has since changed. But there's been more tolerance for that or acceptance of it.

Gilyard: You think it had to do with sort of a frontier sense? Trade was an issue.

Swearingen: A fluid border, a very open border at that point.

Gilyard: Still open—kind of open. I think some of the English Only stuff has to do with people not being certain about the stability of borders, not just in a physical sense but in a rhetorical sense. You figure you can't influence people the way you want to if their primary allegiance lies elsewhere.

Swearingen: Another thing that's happened has been a reaction against the terms *diversity, multiculturalism,* and *tolerance* because of new mandatory curricula that uses that language in a lot of public schools. I find that my college students here are just fed up with it. They're tired of Black History Month. They don't want to hear about Women's History Month. They've experienced a cafeteria-style menu of obligatory multiculturalism, and I'm sorry to see that it's had that effect because it's made people resist the front door of all those issues. They don't want to hear about African American writers and Hispanic history because in their perception it's been shoved down their throats. There was a joke on Garrison Keillor's *Praire Home Companion* that there was going to be an Anglo-Saxon march in New York City. It's a backlash.

Gilyard: Well, I remember being a kid in school in New York City talking about, even writing about, white backlash. You know, the black revolution and the white backlash. That was the era. Langston Hughes wrote about backlashes. When I thought at length about the matter, I realized that people in backlash operations have power. That fact was often hidden in conversation and hidden in discourse. Anybody that can lash back and win the day by lashing back wields a certain measure of power and enjoys a certain degree of dominance. This undercuts the argument about not wanting to be bothered. I'm not saying all students are powerful, but even a perceived relationship to power and privilege enables some to feel they have the luxury of not being bothered.

Swearingen: There's also a split in the faculty. There's an argument whether or not we should even have programs like Africana Studies. Some ask whether we should have programs in African American literature. Why not just study that as part of American literature?

Gilyard: Well, we would have if folks hadn't segregated the stuff in the first place.

Swearingen: Exactly.

Gilyard: That's an issue that's been in the national press for the past few years, the question of the continued justification of ethnic studies programs. It's a serious issue. Ethnic studies programs arose in response to exclusion. That has to be remembered, and I think the original rationale is still relevant in some places. But one of the things that these disciplines do have to come to grips with is the question of intellectual distinctiveness. If you do, for example, offer a psychology or sociology course in an African American studies program, there should be something about the course that represents a difference beyond the fact that it is housed in an African American studies program, maybe has an African American professor, or uses material about African Americans. It has to have a perspective that represents a different intellectual contribution than would be made in more established departments. That's a thing to grapple with as the future of ethnic studies is discussed.

Swearingen: You know, one thing that interests me about the liveliness of African American literature or Hispanic literature or Latino literature, Latino Studies, is that these works are wonderfully impervious to deconstruction and the theory crowd because they are living vernaculars. It's fresh, new, vernacular literature that's doing the work of identity construction. It's doing the work of history. Toni Morrison's talking about her own work as a case of fiction doing the work of history is really rich and exciting and deep. This links to another question, a conversation I would like to have with you. We've been hiring recently here in Africana Studies, and we've been trying to educate our department and the Africana Studies department about the intersection of African American and Africana Studies with rhetoric. I've had a hell of a time trying to convince some of my colleagues who are in American Literature and African American Literature that's its really hard to study African American literature without knowing something about African American oral traditions and rhetoric.

Gilyard: Oh, without a doubt.

Swearingen: They go blank and don't know what I'm talking about, so I'm looking for ways to make that argument more accessible. That's one of the purposes of this topic that we're addressing in the symposium later today: Africana and African American Voices and Vernaculars. Even the idea of vernacular rhetoric is not entirely clear to some of my colleagues. When I speak of idiomatic oral traditions, it's like "What? What? What?"

Gilyard: Africana Studies is a broad rubric both ethnically, ideologically, and in terms of discipline, so different discourse communities are operative. If you look at African American Studies departments traditionally, you can see that there's frequently been a split between humanities and social sciences faculties. In some places, the social sciences advocates dominate. I have colleagues who argue African American Studies should be political science and nothing else. When humanities scholars have been prominent, that has tended to mean literary scholars. Certainly, some of them have had an appreciation for the rhetorical. They build theories on it. Skip Gates' *Signifying Monkey* is a theory of rhetoric that he applies to literature. They also understand African American oratory and African American music to be two strong and persuasive cultural forms. What

I think you may be encountering is that people don't have the language to talk with you when you declare rhetoric as your interest. They may discern, say, the importance of Martin Luther King Jr. as an orator, but they are unlikely to be familiar with systematic rhetorical projects about King, say Keith Miller's work over the years. I don't think a lot of people in Africana Studies, or even African American literature, have read that work. That's why in our textbook *African American Literature*, Anissa Wardi and I reserved two chapters expressly for rhetoric. We don't call it rhetoric because we don't want to scare anybody away. But there's a chapter on the African American Jeremiad as a major rhetorical form and a chapter on black-nationalist discourse that is really about the tropes that comprise what we would call Black Nationalism or Black Nationalist Rhetoric. So I'm trying to bridge the literature and rhetoric gap, focusing on folktales for that purpose also.

Swearingen: As I'm trying to work my way through these discussions and disagreements, I'm trying to figure out exactly how Africana Studies is different from African American Studies. I know that there's something about Africa in there, but there's something about Africa in African American, too. There's a spin thing that I need to understand.

Gilyard: This is part of what I'm talking about, discourse communities and fissures. African American Studies often has implied a sort of ethnic studies model. You build programs around the distinctive sociopolitical and sociocultural situation of African Americans viewed within an American context. But alongside this type of thinking has existed a strand of Pan-Africanist thought. Folks have viewed Africa to be the center of their theoretical and curricular models. Africa is at the center and the diaspora revolves around it. We can look at the Caribbean, North America, and South America from an African-centered perspective. If that's the case, if Africa is at the center and the orbiting is diasporic, then African American Studies is an inappropriate label. It's not encompassing enough. So just as we have had the humanities-social sciences split, we have had the ethnic model-diasporic model split. This has been exacerbated at times by the fact that faculty have hailed from Africa and other parts of the African diaspora and joined departments—whether called Africana or African American—that have been founded largely by African American scholars who operated under an ethnic studies model. In some cases, faculty members from abroad have not only joined departments but have been hired to head them. So you can imagine some of the ideological, cultural, and ethnic tensions that continue to unfold. I have worked in an African American Studies department and noticed that some of my colleagues addressed their external correspondence "Department of Africana Studies." As individual faculty members, they rejected the institutional nomenclature. Those folks, who were not natives of the United States, felt they fit into the Africana box but not the African American box. But then me, when I get up in the morning, don't feel like I'm revolving around Africa, you know. I'm from right here. One way to look at this tension—though I don't necessarily argue that it's the best way and this is no declaration of right or wrong—is that Africana Studies tries to be truer to the evolution of world history whereas African American Studies tries to be truer to American history and the history of American higher education.

Let me shift gears somewhat. I want you to talk a little bit about the time you spent in Cape Town. I know it wasn't long but you commented on it in your writing. I'm interested in what you saw.

Swearingen: It was fascinating. I'm still downloading it in my mind. There were so many issues. The relationship between Europeans/whites and Blacks in South Africa, going back to the 1600s, is eerily similar to the history of Sparta in the seventh through fourth centuries B.C. when a minority, the Spartans, enslaved a majority, the Messenians, who became state slaves, serfs known as helots. They nonetheless served in war under their masters, and if they fought well, could win their freedom. Helots had no political rights. The minority Spartans developed and sustained universal military training of everyone, men, women, and children, to be constantly ready to defend themselves against external invasions and slave uprisings, much like the fears of slave uprisings in pre-Civil-War and colonial southern states. The majority of Athenian Greeks were non-citizens as well, including most of the sophists, and Aristotle, who was from Stagyria. In addition to the slave population in Athens were the metics, or resident aliens, without political rights but with the right to work: Aspasia, Gorgias, and Aristotle among them. These examples further illustrate the diversity of Greek culture(s), and the variety of non-citizen and slave populations they included. The Cape Town Centre for Rhetoric Studies has been doing a lot of work with the new South African legislature, especially in formulating education policy. For a time the parliament was discussing whether to cease using English as the language of education and revert back to fourteen different tribal, regional languages—and so have different schools in all those different languages—or to use a bilingual system like India uses where English is the default common language and yet you do have schools that use the native languages in the various regions.

Gilyard: India, the country with the most native speakers of English, right?

Swearingen: Right, and it's a different native English than ours. But back to South Africa. They were debating education policy, but what was also happening within the legislature, the more immediate issue, was that each of the representatives from the regions was using his or her native tongue to speak, and so the Centre for Rhetoric Studies was creating a handbook for parliament to use that annotated gestures in each of these fourteen languages because they mean different things. If somebody points, or uses a smile, or moves his or her head in a certain way, the meaning is different in the different languages.

Gilyard: In other words, it's a concern with what linguists call suprasegmentals.

Swearingen: There was this picture book that annotated each of the gestures. It was like the UN. It was like a translator in your ear but also a translator so you can see what the gestures mean. That was very interesting. Moreover, there are some very interesting bodies of research coming out of that center at Cape Town. One of them, for example, was on Zulu epideictic oratory. There are traditions that are still in evidence today. When the chief speaks to the people, he uses certain time-honored forms of speaking. The praise singers are still active in a lot of traditions. Nelson Mandela's political oratory draws on his tribal background. His father was a leader in a tribe. All of these nuances are now being analyzed and recorded that were previously not studied because it was forbidden. But people knew about it; it wasn't being formally studied. I think those rhetorical studies are really exciting and will eventually cross the Atlantic, I'm sure, into Africana Studies. I think we're going to learn a lot about genres of rhetoric and linguistic forms from just hearing the languages and seeing the gestures that have been transmitted and preserved in cultures.

Gilyard: You have addressed in similar fashion over the years the multi-rhetorical nature of the American Southwest. We have talked a little bit about that, especially the influence of Chicano/Chicana culture. Do you see strides over the decade since you addressed these concerns in your introduction to *Rhetoric, Polis, and the Global Village* in terms of improved scholarship, instruction, and policy?

Swearingen: I'm very interested in how the Latino, Hispanic, Chicano community is being rhetorically constructed nationally and regionally. Within Texas, there's been a pretty heated debate about whether to use the term *Hispanic* or *Latino* or *Chicano* or *Mexicano*. Latino is generally thought of as not acceptable because it's more about Puerto Ricans in New York City or Chicago or Los Angeles. But if you use Chicano, that's too political for some because it connotes the farm workers' union and grassroots political movements. Many middle-class, upwardly mobile Hispanics don't want to use that. *Tejano* is sometimes used. Hispanic is a problem because it denotes Spanish rather than Mexican. So there's a lot of identity politics going on. There are also debates about whether writers like Sandra Cisneros and others who write in English but are Latino/Latina are abandoning their culture to write in English. Do you write in English or do you write in Spanish? Then in San Antonio, in particular, there are very funny debates about whether Sandra Cisneros even belongs here because she's really from Chicago. Some amusing loyalty, identity, origin issues are going on.

Gilyard: I'll have to speak with Jaime Mejía about these matters. He explained some of this at CCCC a couple of weeks ago up in New York. If I'm not mistaken, Jaime has embraced Chicano for exactly the reasons you articulate. He wants to make that political statement, but he also understands why other people don't embrace the term. What do you think about this rhetorical construction that we have been handed since the last census about Hispanics now making up the largest ethnic minority group in the United States? To me, if you think about ethnic groups having significant cohesion around history, interests, and culture on a number of fronts, it doesn't appear that Hispanics constitute an ethnic group.

Swearingen: I think I can go with you on that because I have seen people identify much more with being Puerto Rican in Chicago or Dominican in New York City. They're not identifying with Hispanic as a uniform category. But I've seen the same disputes go on within African American communities.

Gilyard: Sure. Of course.

Swearingen: There's a guy name David Bradley who used to teach at Temple.

Gilyard: The guy who wrote *The Chaneysville Incident*. Sure.

Swearingen: Well, he spoke a couple of times at The University of Texas at Arlington while I was on the faculty there, and he started out one of his lectures by saying, "I'm not going be your African American experience." He was deconstructing the whole notion that there was this coherent, cohesive African American identity that he represents or that anybody else represents.

Gilyard: There's no cohesion in that everyone's the same, but there is a sense of a community or commonality. Every member of any family can deconstruct the family photo. Ralph Citron uses this metaphor in *Angel's Town*. When the family photo works for you, you use it. You're proud of it, display it. At some point you might want to opt out of identifying with the family. So you might stress individuality. Everybody can play that game. But what I'm saying is that if you went from the Hard Shell Baptist Church in Georgia and then go to the Northern Hard Shell Baptist Church in New York City, there's a strong commonality. I don't know if it's the same thing if you're a Dominican going to Cuban Miami or a Cuban going to Dominican New York.

Swearingen: From my perspective of an outsider, I think there's more of a sense of commonality among African Americans than there is among Hispanics, Chicanos, Latinos, etc. In the latter case, there are much more diverse points of origin. That's one of the issues.

Gilyard: And the fact there's often a strong sense of national origin. Black folk generally don't have a sense of a national origin located in Africa. You might have a shot at that if you get one of those DNA tests as Oprah did. But historically, to the extent that any of us have wanted to identify with Africa, it has been a continental identification as opposed to a national one. In contrast, Puerto Ricans have a strong sense of Puerto Rico, Dominicans of the Dominican Republic. There's a clear sense of place beyond, say, New York City. And I've observed this in New York. We have a Puerto Rican parade and Dominican parade. Both great events. But there's no Latino parade.

Swearingen: Tucson's complex that way. Lots of San Salvadorians and Guatemalans, not just Mexicans. Lots of different identifications. Texas has an elite, educated, upper-middle class that goes back to the days of the republic. And those are Spanish people, you know, not Mexicans. They never were Mexicans. They were Texans from the very beginning. So they're very proud of that and even look down on the Chicanos and the farm workers' union and the people with Indian blood, etc.

Gilyard: But I don't really mind the "largest ethnic minority group" rhetorical construction. It suggests a coalition, and if the coalition can make progress in terms of improved services and increased access to goods, it's doing what a good coalition should do. On the other hand, I wouldn't want the label to lull people into thinking they don't have to work on the coalition. And I would want the coalition to be politically progressive. But let me shift gears again to cover another controversial topic important to you: rhetoric and religion. As you know, the subject of religion is increasingly being discussed in our professional spaces. Would you comment on rhetoric and religion as related to your concerns with theory and pedagogy?

Swearingen: Several different points interest me right now. One of them is the history of rhetoric in early Greek religion. One of the points of origin of rhetoric as a discipline was the practice in early Greek religion and other religions globally of training priestesses and priests to speak or sing stories that tell the story of the community to the community. And the fact that there was formal teaching of this, how to speak the story of the people, is one of the ways rhetoric began before it became political rhetoric. I think it's very interesting to look at the structure of the earliest Greek political speeches, the funeral orations, because they are still quasi-religious. They invoke the ancestors; they invoke the gods; they advise the people to honor the dead by living their lives well. They're very priestly, and I think it's interesting to look at how that became gradually secularized and turned into prose and turned into political oratory. So that's one aspect. Rhetoric originated in the practice of priestly discourse, and I don't think we should ever forget that because it still tries to have that power of exhortation and inspiration, and should, I think. Another issue is the rhetoric about religion that we are subjected to almost every day. The academy, the liberal academy, has to its disadvantage ignored and not taken religion seriously and not studied religion as an intellectual activity. It is ignorant of smart, conservative, religious people. And I think we ignore them at our peril. But critical skepticism, critical thinking, is also a form of faith, a set of beliefs. If we're not able to see that we operate according to a set of beliefs just as what we call religious people operate according to a set of beliefs, then that's pretty stupid. I hope we can get more in line with reality on that front. This does mean that we should not study the abuse of certain forms of religious rhetoric in our political culture, a very important subject for rhetorical study. On a related point, I am interested in the influence of college students' religious background on their learning patterns. If you've grown up a Baptist or a Catholic or whatever and you have a certain hermeneutic practice and have been taught how to talk about a texts and issues in certain ways, this can be reflected in classrooms. I sometimes ask my students whether it is okay to have different interpretations in Bible study groups in which they participate. I ask if the goal is to come to a consensus and agree on the correct interpretation of a particular scripture or whether the group goal is to talk about everybody's different understandings of the passage and accept them all as okay. I think that difference is really important to know about when students come into a classroom. And then a third alternative is that they don't have open discussion groups at all. They listen to what the minister says. The priest tells them what to think and they're fine with that.

Gilyard: As you say, it's important to know their hermeneutic practices. They're going to read texts up against those practices. They're doing what we teach people to do. You can't reasonably dismiss that as only stubborn and inflexible.

Swearingen: By the same token, I'm interested in learning more about their attitudes towards learning in general. How are they relating to the process of becoming educated? Do they see higher education as something that might be threatening to their faith? Are they resisting it? Are they open to change? Getting them to think about that is very important.

Gilyard: I've been curious about your thinking as you described it in your essay "Rhetoric and Composition as a Coherent Intellectual Discipline: A Meditation." This is one of the reasons I wanted to interview you; you've hit so many notes over the years. As I understand it, you describe a state of affairs wherein there was a feverish attempt at working through the challenges of postmodern rhetorical theories as they related to conceptions of language, community, and curriculum, and even department structure. I have wondered if you thought your descriptions were widely applicable or restricted to venues such as research institutions and scholarly journals. Are the tensions that you describe, say between critical theory and rhetoric, applicable to only a small range of institutions or did you see that as discipline wide? Moreover, I'm now interested in your current assessment of the field. Are things getting better or worse or both?

Swearingen: I think anti-intellectualism has always been a kind of thread in CCCC among compositionists of a certain stripe. We just want to teach; we don't want to have to do all this big theory. At the other end, rhetoric is seen as really theory, so we're going to affiliate ourselves with Paul de Mann, with Adorno, and do the higher Gucci theory end of things. Those are the two extremes, and I think in the middle is where most departments are. I want to consider more the relationships among rhetoric, culture, and history. I think some practitioners of cultural studies today are talking about rhetoric and culture together but moving away from history. They're doing an ahistorical or even anti-historical model of culture where somehow it's almost incorrect in terms of theory to look at a historical development because it's a master narrative or because it's an old-fashioned way to look at things. That's a pretty dangerous way to construct cultural studies. It's okay to be synchronic as opposed to diachronic, but it's best to alternate between the two. You see one set of things one way and you see another set of things the other way. But if we're going to get rid of the notion of development and historical sequences entirely, then I don't know what we're going to do. You can't just talk about culture in a vacuum or without a purpose. So this rhetoric and culture connection is interesting to me. Eventually, what I would like to see happen in, say, Chinese rhetorical studies or African rhetorical studies, is to find out what the internal names are for all kinds of tropes. We use the equipment we got from Aristotle. But within Chinese rhetorical culture, what do they call ethos, what do they call argument, what do they call persuasion? Because, in the Chinese tradition—if I understand LuMing Mao and others correctly—they don't really do persuasion. But they do stuff like it and they have names for it. So I want to know what do they call it, their labeling system. And with the Zulu chieftains, for example, how do they talk to each other about their formulaic speaking? What are their words for it? How do they teach it? How is it valued aesthetically? So we just need to know more.

Gilyard: Sure. I'm thinking about the study of those traditions and about your earlier comment about Mandela. Studying Mandela in depth would be interesting, situating him with respect to various traditions. I like the idea of that kind of systematic and historical inquiry making connections between earlier and later rhetorical production. For example, if you look at Harriet Jacobs' *Incidents in the Life of a Slave Girl*, you can see what I call the victim's gambit. It's a question of ethos. It's always a risky move: "I did this immoral stuff. But I'm banking that when I give you the context, you'll understand that my immorality is a misdemeanor in the context of the major felony of immorality that slavery is." And so that's an ethos-building move that you see repeated in, say, *The Autobiography of Malcolm X*, you know, when Malcolm says something like, "I was a ghetto-created nigger, and so I did a lot of things such as being a petty hustler, drug user, and thief. But up against the major immorality of racial oppression, I'm trusting my reader to accept me and understand that what I'm saying overall is worthy."

Swearingen: The confession.

Gilyard: That's right, exactly. Of course, the narratives I mention are not the only narratives that make these moves. As you indicate, you can go all the way back to Augustine. But there are these intertextual moves that we can see that help to make the case for history.

Swearingen: I'm very interested in whether, in its own time, Douglass' narrative, in those places where it was read aloud, functioned as a kind of script and was teaching people how to tell their stories, how to talk. It seems it was like scripting their self-understanding.

Gilyard: So rather than just writing to the world, was it a form of rhetorical instruction in its verbal enactment?

Swearingen: Because he describes going back into the slave plantation cultures and secretly having these Sunday meetings. I don't know whether the narrative itself was also circulated and read aloud and whether it functioned as a kind of talking book, as a script, as a teaching device.

Gilyard: Well, we know that David Walker's *Appeal* was circulated. We're clear about that one.

Swearingen: And that kind of reading something aloud goes all the way back to my interest in dialogue, Plato's dialogues. People before Plato did not do dialogues; they didn't know how to do that. So when Plato wrote his dialogues, that was instruction: "Here's how you do this. This is how you talk about stuff, justice and truth." It's like watching a play, with the purpose of the play being to teach people how to talk like that if they never had done that before. I find myself doing that with students now who don't know how to talk very well. So I'm having to just really script the class discussions and say, "Well, here's my question; what is your answer?" They might say, "I don't know what my answer is!" And also I'll say, "What do you think?" And they'll give me a quotation and I'll say, "That's a quotation. What do *you* think?" Push. Push. Push.

Jaime Armin Mejía, a native Tejano from the Lower Rio Grande Valley, has been teaching at Texas State University, San Marcos, since 1991. Throughout this time, he has worked to merge the interests of Rhetoric and Composition Studies with those of Chicano/Chicana Studies. His work has appeared in such venues as *Latino/a Discourses* (2004) and *Rhetoric and Ethnicity* (2004). He continues working on developing a theory for Chicana/Chicano rhetorics and plans to produce a book-length book on this topic soon.

The Conversation

Keith Gilyard: Throughout your career, you have sought to merge Rhetoric and Composition with Chicana and Chicano Studies. Obviously, you are not bothered by any notion that Cultural Studies represents an imposition on Rhet-Comp. Could you say more regarding your own journey as an academic and about your continued effort to effect a merger of disciplines in your work?

Jaime Armin Mejía: I began teaching as a TA at Pan American University. At that time, around 1981, I took a class in Mexican American literature. I had a background in literature as an undergraduate, and back then I thought of the discipline of English only as literary studies. So I took Mexican American literature, and it was the first time I'd ever known, to be honest, that such a body of literature existed. That discovery of Mexican American literature in the early 1980s coincided with my being trained to be a TA at a university where the student population was predominately Mexican American. By that time upwards of ninety percent of the student body was Mexican American, and, of course, it was my home turf, south Texas, in the Valley. This was after spending most of my undergraduate career at North Texas, which was predominately Anglo.

Gilyard: University of North Texas?

Mejía: It was then known as North Texas State. Every school I've ever attended has changed its name. In any case, what was happening down in the Valley was that I was hired to teach basic writing and had no experience in teaching whatsoever or any knowledge of how to do it. I was confronted in the classroom with nothing but Mexican American students who ranked in the bottom percentiles in terms of ACT scores.

Gilyard: Yeah, I read where you wrote that once.

Mejía: That was an interesting moment for me, to be standing before students who clearly were hungry and seemed to desire any help in terms of just getting past that class.

Gilyard: So the Rhet-Comp piece and the Mexican American literature piece were new at the same time.

Mejía: They were both new at the same time. As for Rhet-Comp, I had no training at all. TA training classes started in the fall, and I began in January. So I had to wait until fall for that training. In January, I was basically given a room number, a textbook, and a roster, and was told by the chair to go get 'em.

Gilyard: That might have been to your advantage. (laughing)

Mejía: It might have been to my advantage, but...

Gilyard: It's rough, though.

Mejía: It was very rough, and I remember at the end of the semester being across the street from the university at a Pizza Hut with other TAs. I declared that I had been a failure and was very depressed, very sad about that because I definitely took it very personally and saw it very much as a brown thing.

Gilyard: What happened? What did you base it on? Test results or other outcomes? Why did you have that sense of failure? Did the students feel that way? I mean...

Mejía: Well, you know, maybe it was because of the pedagogy. That is to say that they were basically being asked to write paragraphs. And I think the pedagogical approach was extraordinarily limiting and restrictive and unimaginative. And it might have been my failure in recognizing that the pedagogy was really not a very good pedagogy. I must have felt confined.

Gilyard: You felt complicit in that you didn't challenge it?

Mejía: I wasn't able to challenge it. I didn't know what the possibilities were. The following fall I did take the TA training class with the director of the TAs, a young Mexican American woman, a brand new Ph.D., who had gotten a background in Rhetoric and Composition at Texas A&M. While I took the class, we started reading Mina Shaughnessy. I remember reading an article by Edward P. J. Corbett. You know, it certainly improved my understanding of how to teach and what expectations there were. At the time, I was very impressed with Shaughnessy in terms of *Errors and Expectations*, in terms of how she described her students. And I believed that our students at Pan American were comparable students. Later that year, I took a graduate level sociology class called The Mexican American People in which my main project ended up being a survey of basic writing and first-year composition classes to try to determine if the profile indeed coincided with the kind of profile that Shaughnessy described for her basic writing students. It was a research paper that I wanted to expand into a thesis project, but there was no support for that. There was a nibble, but it just didn't happen. But I remember that there was a day I walked into a professor's office and was handed an issue of *College English*, I think it was, and there was an essay in there by Richard Rodriguez. This essay preceded the publication of *Hunger of Memory* and ended up being in the book.

Gilyard: Right, right. I know the piece.

Mejía: It was one of those interesting things. Many Mexican Americans have told me how that essay by Rodriguez really sort of captured their reality. They identified with the essay. Little did we know that in the book he would basically be anti-bilingual education, anti-affirmative action.

Gilyard: Anti-teaching Mexican American literature, too. At least in terms of his doing it.

Mejía: Probably. But I didn't conceptualize it that way. At any rate, I took a class with Patricia de la Fuentes, who spoke with a British accent. She was the daughter of a British ambassador to Argentina. She came to the United States and ended up being an aficionado of Chicano literature, one of the early proponents of Chicano literature. We read poems, plays, short stories, and novels. As I neared the end of my master's degree, I chose to take an area exam in Mexican American literature. This professor then gave me a very extensive list of what had been published in Chicano literature. It so happened that the library had almost everything. I remember during that summer I was reading everything on the list and everything that was in the stacks. I was reading maybe as many as five to ten books a day because they were small books. That's how I became acquainted with some of the leading minds in Chicano literature.

Gilyard: So when you thought about teaching any kind of course after that, there was always going to be a merger. You were never going to see a clear divide between Mexican American literature, which functions as a rhetoric, a representation about different kinds of lives that weren't given any kind of play within academe, and the field of Rhetoric and Composition.

Mejía: Well, you know, the process of actually conceptualizing the merger of the two areas would take time. I would have to take required courses. But I was beginning to think that students like to write about what they know, and what they know is sometimes predicated on what they read. And if they were reading, you know, Mexican American literature, they could thereby develop their literacy skills better. This seemed to me a reasonable equation, particularly with respect to the students I saw at Pan American. But then I would leave Pan American and go to Ohio State, where there were no Mexican Americans to speak of, for doctoral study, partly because Corbett was there. I knew two things when I went to Ohio State. I knew that I was going to write a dissertation on a Mexican American author, and I knew that I was going take rhetoric and composition classes to develop myself as a better teacher of composition. One of the first classes I took up there was a rhetoric class in which we read Kenneth Burke and Wayne Booth. I remember trying to do a rhetorical analysis of novel by Tomas Rivera—a Mexican American novel. While the professor may have known Burke and Booth, she didn't know what to do with a Mexican American novel. And that presented a serious problem in many respects. That is to say that for some reason these professors couldn't stretch or extend themselves beyond their mainstream sensibilities to include people of color, at least Mexican Americans like me. I think the underlying assumption was that you come to this school to assimilate and you come to this school to learn what we have to teach. What you introduce may be exotic, but it's going to somehow have to be shaped to fit. And if it doesn't fit, then it's not our problem. It's your problem.

Gilyard: This brings me to another question. I know that you had a strong reaction, one that you expressed at CCCC last year, to a suggestion by Anna Devere Smith that ethnic minorities should leave "safe houses of ethnic identity" and enter the "crossroads of ambiguity" represented by the public sphere. I wonder why we just can't search for a crossroads of clarity. Why does it have to be the crossroads of ambiguity? At any rate, you pointed out that ethnic identity houses are not necessarily safe and that the way that power and privilege accrue in public is not all that ambiguous. Could you expand on those remarks given your latest observations?

Mejía: So far as the crossroads of ambiguity, I think one of the things that dawned on me while I was thinking through what I thought Anna Devere Smith was saying was that it seemed to be a call for only minority students to sort of leave their culture and enter this other crossroads. It doesn't seem to be a call for people from the mainstream to do the same thing. That's where certainly our views diverge. Her arguments don't make sense to those of us who live in areas where so-called ethnic minorities constitute the majority population. We need to understand the historical context. We need to develop pedagogies, predicated upon historical realities important to us, that would work toward creating college students educated to serve communities that are no longer predominated by mainstream or white people. But that's a power situation. Who has the power to determine curriculum? Who has the power to determine pedagogy? We haven't come to the point where Mexican Americans in these geographical locations have the power to determine curriculum and pedagogy. But I think those days are coming very soon. But it's going to be a fight, and I see this as a big fight. And there's nothing ambiguous about the fight. I think I've mentioned to you before that Linda Ferreira-Buckley had been placed on a sort of governor's committee that was really created by legislative act to develop concepts for determining the college readiness of high school students in Texas. It was very clear from her perspective that conservative elements in the state wanted to control the curriculum and the pedagogy behind what constitutes college readiness. From her perspective---and it's one that I can easily see---they were conducting a last ditch effort to maintain control over curriculum and pedagogy in Texas schools as well as using that as a way to exert control over college curriculums. But, you know, the days are numbered for those efforts. What is problematic, though, on our end as Mexican Americans, is that we really have to make decisions about what we're going do with Spanish in terms of curriculum and pedagogy. That's a very important consideration for Rhetoric and Composition, which has exclusively been nothing but English. We have to contend with bilingual education.

Gilyard: How might that play out in different ways? In other words, what's the difference if it went one way as opposed to another way with respect to making a decision about Spanish?

Mejía: If bilingual education is considered simply a tool for assimilating students to learn English to the exclusion or at the cost of losing Spanish, that's the status quo, and I think it's problematic economically as well as socially because Spanish is not going away. The media, especially the Spanish-language media, are way ahead in terms of marketing and news reporting. The American mainstream media are beginning to catch on. But American curriculum from K-16 represents indecisiveness, and Rhetoric and Composition Studies is going to have to engage the question of rhetorical dynamics when Spanish is a major part of the mix. There's also the possibility that other indigenous languages, whether they be from Mexico or the United States, also have to be considered as part of this whole dynamic. Of course, contention will exist. A lot of Mexican Americans consider assimilation to be pragmatic, an unquestionable direction. They sometimes see the acquisition or practice of Spanish as lower class, tied to immigrant groups. Government, for its part, has instituted perhaps at the federal and certainly at the state level, you know, documents that are bilingual. And it is a very expensive proposition to be able to translate every legal document into Spanish, and there's great resistance from the right to even doing that. Government has done things like that because it's been mandated to do so. But we're simply not finding schools to be very hospitable places. It's just an amazing thing. I don't think it's entirely the school's fault, the parents' fault, the family's fault, or society's fault. But when we know that there are certain pedagogical approaches, curricular approaches that can at least maintain the interest of certain students in school to develop the kind of literacy skills, critical literacy skills, that will get them through school and give them the possibility of obtaining more jobs and living better lives and paying more taxes to fund more needs, then we have to step up to the plate and take care of that. It's complex, but I'm hopeful.

Gilyard: Up to this point you've been talking about Mexicans and Mexican-Americans, and I know that at several points in your writing you have echoed the fairly popular claim by now that Hispanics or Latinos constitute the largest ethnic minority group in the United States. Yet, the assertion, one might even say trope, certainly can be contested. In fact, you argue in your written work, "Latinos who do not define their ethnic identity as Chicanos or Chicanas clearly come from different houses which hold to different sets of beliefs about our place in the United States. The variants of these sets of beliefs can sometimes vary widely, so widely, in fact, that one of the reigning principles over who we are as an ethnic group is that we are not one monolithic group." I don't suppose we'll smooth out this one, but I'm interested in what you see as the purchase of the largest-ethnic-minority-group trope. What work does it do?

Mejía: I think the origins of some of my thoughts over this question, over this trope, as you call it, go to my involvement with a documentary project that had to do with the Mexican American legislative caucus in Texas. A team went out and interviewed former and current Texas legislators to tell the story of the history and development of the Mexican American legislative caucus in Texas. I was asked to write the narrative and edit the narrative for the documentary. Obviously, that involved my viewing and studying these interviews. All of them talked about education being very important for Texas and certainly for Mexican Americans in Texas. Many of them brought demographics into the picture. They referred to a fellow named Steve Murdock, a demographer, who for more than a decade has been presenting at various organizational meetings across the state his projections for demographic growth in Texas. Unequivocally, Texas is going to be predominately, if it isn't already, Mexican American. I know that whites constitute a minority in Texas already. And Mexican Americans constitute a majority in public schools today. I've seen the maps that he's drawn and the broad swath across Texas that's going to be predominately Mexican American. Insofar as the currency of the largest-ethnic-minority-group idea, I think there is a lot to be gained. While we come from varied cultural experiences, I think when we have common goals that our varied political experiences and our various cultural experiences will come together and we'll move together if we seek certain common goals like education.

Gilyard: But let me tease this out, though, because when you talk about the demographic work, you're saying Mexican Americans again. Before you were saying Latinos. I'm trying to keep this from slipping. When you describe the majority population as Mexican American, I understand that as more concise and neater in terms of thinking about difference. So I got that part about Mexican Americans in Texas. But you're also making an argument for Latinos being the largest ethnic minority group in all of America.

Mejía: Well, Latinos for a long time have not been happy about Mexican Americans constituting the majority in this group.

Gilyard: In the Latino group?

Mejía: Right. And so far as us having differences within our camp, under the broader Latino umbrella, and so far as there being differences— political, historical, certainly sociological, economic, cultural…

Gilyard: But you still call it an ethnic group despite all of that?

Mejía: I think broadly speaking we hold ingredients that tie us together. Differences exist, but I think in many cases most Latinos remain without intimate knowledge of the cultural distinctions that mark each group as different. If one were to go to many Mexican Americans today and ask them to define or to just simply state the distinguishing characteristics of Puerto Ricans, of Puerto Rican history, of the politics of Puerto Rico, most would not know at all what the historical dynamics of Puerto Rico are. I would say the same thing about Puerto Ricans relative to a question about Mexican Americans in the Southwest and the differences among Texas Mexicans and Arizona Mexicans and California Mexicans and New Mexico Mexicans. I think Puerto Ricans don't know what are the distinguishing marks, cultural marks, that separate us. Nonetheless, I am suggesting that cultural spaces exist where all the differences are transcended and there is some semblance of cohesion. I think those spaces are primarily found through the media. Spanish-language media, particularly television but certainly radio and entertainment modes like CDs and videos, are able to capture an audience that crosses different cultural distinctions. There is a Latinidad that exists across all of these different cultures. In that respect, while we do represent different markets, I think in certain media boardrooms they are advancing the notion that there are common strands or elements that tie us all together.

Gilyard: But do you think Cuban-American controlled TV and radio, say in Florida, are promoting commonality as their message?

Mejía: Well, the biggest show on Spanish-language TV in the United States is the *Sábado Gigante* show with Don Francisco. That comes out of Miami. Previous presidential candidates went to this show and presented. These presidential candidates were speaking to all Latinos, not just to the Cubans. Televisa and Univision are responsible for developing this sort of cross-ethnic, cross-national, transnational identity. There are problems related to Don Francisco and *Sábado Gigante.* Maybe too much focus on sexy babes dancing in front of Don Francisco and making no bones about it. But there's melodrama---he connects long lost family members---and there's clowning and there's a carnival atmosphere. And there's also a very serious side to this show. That is by no means the only show like that, but it represents almost a touchstone and a model that many others have attempted to emulate, both regionally and certainly across the country.

Gilyard: I want to walk you through this because it gets confusing. I have to refresh my memory from time to time when considering these designations or ethnic descriptors. You have *Latino, Hispanic, Texan, Mexican,* and *Chicano.* Take me through one more time relative to the difference between designating oneself as a Texas Mexican or Chicano, not Hispanic. You identify as Chicano?

Mejía: I do identify myself as a Chicano. For some years now, I have fallen back on a definition I found in a book by Paula Moya, who is a professor of English at Stanford University. She provides a succinct definition of what a Chicano is. She basically positions that term against the other terms. Mexican Americans are people of Mexican cultural descent who are U. S. citizens. *Hispanic* is effectively an umbrella term that according to Richard Rodriguez was coined in effect by presidential decree by Richard Nixon but remains as a sociological term that stands in contrast to Latino/Latina, which is also another umbrella term that seeks to cover all the different groups. *Mexicano* is another term that among Mexican Americans carries a lot of valence, resonates a great deal. Her definition situates Chicanos, at least Chicanas, as understanding that there are inequalities and injustices against people of Mexican descent, that is, Mexican Americans in the United States. Chicanos and Chicanas, however, stand apart by working and fighting against the injustices in the United States. However, people use the terms Chicano and Chicana in different ways. People will go to a school in certain parts of the Southwest, for instance, maybe an elementary school, and they'll say, "Look at those little Chicanitos or Chicanitas." By Paula Moya's definition, it's hard for me to be able to do that.

Gilyard: You couldn't do that.

Mejía: I couldn't do that because I don't think they have the political consciousness to label themselves that way. Moreover, I think that in a lot of elementary schools today we have kids who are being raised in immigrant homes and have yet to assimilate or identify themselves as Mexican Americans, much less as Chicanos and Chicanas. As you well know, the 1990s brought in the biggest influx of immigrants from Mexico and Central America in all of U. S. history. So terms are sometimes difficult to work effectively, but what are our choices? Some people have said that either we choose our terms of self-identity or we have them imposed upon us. I think Chicanos have correctly chosen to resist other terms, although I don't believe our resistance is to the idea of Latinos or the term *Latino* or *Latina*.

Gilyard: At times you have kept a keen eye on the output, indeed the cultural rhetoric I would argue, for our purposes, being produced by the Chicano and Chicana artist community. Is that still the case and, if so, what have been the most notable recent developments?

Mejía: In1991, when I returned to Texas and came to central Texas, certainly there was a lot of energy among local artists and musicians. It was the beginning of a high point in Tejano music, certainly, and literary arts. A feminist wave was part of that, and artists like Carmen Lomas Garza were attaining a status and level of visibility that was unprecedented. At the University of Texas at Austin, at the University of Texas at San Antonio, and to some extent here in San

Marcos, you had Chicano and Chicana scholars, many newly minted
Ph.D.s or graduate students, who were very much engaged in the
study of Chicano and Chicana culture, which included art, music, and
literature. We in central Texas had a pretty good vantage point to see
the rise of popular culture in the arts and to see the legitimation of
our art. I think that continues. I think we've continued to grow and
expand in terms of publication and media productions. Media outputs
through public television and some mainstream media exist that
weren't available to us fifteen, seventeen years ago. So in response to
your question about what are the most recent developments, you know,
it's the continuing engagement of popular art and the dissemination of
it and the commercialization of it in different places. That continues
unabated. That is to say that there are efforts today by an increasing
group of scholars, artists, and musicians to make connections to our
past, to fill in gaps. I'm reading, for instance, a novel that was published
about five years ago by Sandra Cisneros named *Caramelo*, and it's
interesting to discover now that the novel is about a family genealogy.
It's a history of a family that goes back three or four generations into
Mexico, and it's a recuperative novel. It's addressing gaps in our past
that are very important for our understanding who we are. It's not the
only effort of its kind; there have always been such novels. But I think
it's interesting to see her doing it in this particular novel in such detail
and in such expansive ways. It reflects tremendous amounts of energy
and imagination to capture exactly the realities that were going on
before the turn of the 19th century, the 20th century: the Revolution
in Mexico, the causes for people immigrating out of Mexico into the
United States, the economic and political circumstances that drove
them out and brought them to the United States, how people were lost
and others not lost, how people in terms of the past and today in some
respects haven't changed in terms of their humanity or their lack of it.
I see efforts by many scholars and artists to capture, to use your term,
tropes that extend beyond the border. They are making the connections
not just to Mexico but all of Latin America. More and more scholars
are seeing that there are connections among all Latino groups not just
U. S. Latino groups. So we're stretching beyond the Mexican border we

generally think of and past the other Mexican border and even further south. That's going to continue.

Gilyard: Could you give a description of the course you're beginning to teach on Chicano rhetoric? I forget exactly what the title is, but I'd like you to talk more about that because I think that's a concrete response to the question of what might be some of the curriculum changes we might effect in rhetoric pedagogy or composition pedagogy to build a bridge to Mexican American students. But I think a course like this isn't really just for Mexican American students. I think everybody should take a course like this. So how did you conceptualize it? I don't think there's another course like it. I've never seen a course designated Chicano/Chicana Rhetoric. So how did you conceptualize it and what are some of the things you're going to be reading?

Mejía: We have a new M. A. program in Rhetoric and Composition Studies. One of the tenets is to bring ethnic considerations into rhetorical studies. I was teaching a composition course last spring, and then at the end of the semester, I was informed that that course would be killed as part of the curriculum for the M.A. program. I personally took exception to that, and out of a compromise I was put on rotation to teach another course. I remembered that there was a tenet to the conceptualization of the program that involved, you know, ethnic rhetorics. So I spontaneously, and I'll say this really honestly, I very spontaneously said: "Why not teach a class on Chicano and Chicana Rhetorics?" So this is what the class is called, Chicano and Chicana Rhetorics. I couldn't believe that they had actually put it on the schedule. The course was put up for pre-registration a few weeks ago, and it started off with a dismally low enrollment. I was thinking, "Well, it's not going to make." But I only needed eight students. And since it's a relatively new program, it might even run with less than eight students. Today I have ten students. So I think there's no question that the class is going to run.

Gilyard: Would you take all of them over to Kreuz [bbq] and bribe them to stay in? (laughing)

Mejía: No. (Maybe thought hard about it, though.) That's an expensive proposition.

Gilyard: That's true.

Mejía: But one of the things I should say is that the composition pedagogy class I taught last spring had three or four Chicano and Chicana students who had taken my Chicano/Chicana literature class. I also had Anglo students, more than half the class. In the end, the Mexican American students were more able to take issues concerning composition pedagogy and theory and show how certain curriculum and pedagogy can have deleterious effects on people. Some, not all, of the Anglo students were very resistant to engaging pedagogy or theorizing pedagogy with respect to the same kinds of problems. That is to say, it seemed to me that minority students, Mexican Americans, having taken a Chicano/Chicana literature class, were more adept at being able show how literacy itself, the acquisition of it, is political---that and there's power involved in terms of who decides that certain people should be literate. It seems interesting to me that minority students understand the politics of literacy whereas, for some reason, probably very good reason, Anglo students do not consider that an issue.

Gilyard: They're in an unmarked position. It's not as pressing an everyday matter for them.

Mejía: Which is a problem for me. I informed them that if their goal is to pursue a career in teaching composition in Texas and if the demographic trends continue, it's likely that the students they're going to have will be predominately Mexican American and of a culture different from theirs.

Gilyard: No question.

Mejía: They will have to develop pedagogical approaches, curricular approaches that bridge or extend a bridge of understanding to those students. And if the Anglo students are saying that is not important or not critical, you know, then I think there's a problem with them and this situation. However, it's interesting to see that my Mexican American students understood this situation, this dynamic, perfectly.

Gilyard: But that's why I said the class is not just for Chicano students. That's why I said the class is for everybody.

Mejía: While the class is for everybody, it was the slowest graduate rhetoric class in terms of getting students. Anyway, I have thought a lot about the selection of the books that I would use. The books to me are the foundations on which the course will be built.

Gilyard: I might argue that Anzaldúa's book is a gesture that way because it is a book about rhetoric.

Mejía: I think there are a lot of books that are a gesture in that sense. I thought about a lot of books that I could make serve a course in rhetoric. There's a book by David Montejano called *Anglos and Mexicans in the Making of Texas*. He's called the foremost Texas-American historian in the U. S., and he's teaching at Berkeley. I thought, well, lots of these students haven't read a good history of Texas, from a Texas point of view. David's book is a landmark and definitely reflects a certain rhetorical perspective. In fact, my written description of the course basically follows what Terry Eagleton said about literary theory and literary criticism, that it's all rhetorical. On that basis, I then could say that I could use books of Chicano and Chicana literary criticism and from those books teach students how to conduct rhetorical analysis. Initially, I had chosen a book by each of the Saldívar family, José David Saldívar, his brother Ramón, his sister Sonia Saldívar-Hull1. I had a book for each of them on my original list, but when I finally ordered the books I knocked off the brothers and left the female, who has a book called *Feminism on the Border*, because you cannot do anything relating to Chicano and Chicana studies today if you don't include women. You just can't do it. And while the brothers have good books, I had to be very careful. It's a very interesting family. The Saldívar family has three Ph.D.s; they're all very distinguished scholars. The book that Ramón published most recently on Américo Paredes is just an absolutely magisterial book. And Jóse David has a couple of books that I considered, one in particular titled *Border Matters.*

Gilyard: You're trying to develop a strong historical component.

Mejía: I think all the books do that in some respect.

Gilyard: Art is so prominent in it. I really like that.

Mejía: Well, let me read off the books.

Gilyard: You could...

Mejía: We're using *Culture and Truth* by Renato Rosaldo, an old book; *Angels' Town* by Ralph Cintron. I'm intentionally introducing these two together. They engage in a sort of anthropological-rhetorical approach. Then I'm bringing with them a book by a guy named Pablo Vila called *Border Identification,* which also in a sense is ethnographic, an anthropological border study of El Paso. So there is that element to it, but these works will be working against each other rather than with each of other. So far as the books on art, I knew about Alicia Gaspar de Alba's book called *Chicano Rhetoric,* which is essentially a critique of an art exhibition called CARA, an acronym for Chicano Arts: Resistance and Affirmation. She does a pretty good, stinging analysis of a very good art exhibit that did produce a book, which I do own. Alba's book is basically a feminist analysis with a gay element in it. But it cuts down Chicano ideology. But more recently, just in the last few weeks, another book has come out called *Chicana Art* by Laura E. Pérez that does a much more extensive feminist analysis of Chicana feminist art, and it also includes many plates of art in it. These two books I'm coupling together so that students can understand that when they look at images by Chicanos and Chicanas, there's a method and a grounding from which to develop a rhetorical analysis. Today's world, at least for our students, is a very visually oriented one. What better visuals to analyze than Chicano and Chicana art?

Gilyard: I agree.

Mejía: There are some images in these books as well as in the art exhibits that are truly fantastic, and the analyses that students will learn from are just amazing. The images, again, are very indigenous to Chicano and Chicana realties.

Gilyard: Students will get a strong grounding in the practice of visual rhetoric.

Mejía: The papers they write will include images, something that I've been doing for several years anyway in my classes. Let me move on. Another book that I'm using is *The Impure Imagination: Toward a Critical Hybridity in Latin American Writing* by Joshua Lund, which deconstructs the concept of hybridity in ways that I think are very important. While the book is not centered in Chicana/Chicano realities, a great deal of it is centered on Mexico, and certainly on other parts of Latin America. Lund goes after Néstor García Canclini, who wrote about hybridity theory back in the 1990s. I plan to couple Lund's book with *Mestizaje: Critical Uses of Race in Chicano Culture*, which also engages the issue of hybridity. I think my students need to be able to attack anyone that uses the label *hybrid* to describe anything, especially things that concern Mexican American culture. There's going to be a bridge to that because the book by Pablo Vila, *Border Identifications*, also conducts this sort of deconstruction of hybridity along the border.

Gilyard: What's your specific issue with the term hybridity?

Mejía: Well, Lund's title suggests it. The impure imagination is what is hybrid. This is set against the pure imagination, which is always white and European. That is problematic. We have to acknowledge the fact that there's a relationship between racism and what is considered high art and low art. Néstor García Canclini dropped the ball on that, and that's basically what Lund nails him for. I think my students deserve to have exposure to one of the most exciting new developments in theory. This notion of hybridity and the critique of it are important for rhetorical studies. One has to understand who is being described by hybridity, what audience the argument works for, and what people think the term should mean. I'm going to be jumping, playing off of that idea with Renato Rosaldo's *Culture and Truth* and Ralph Cintron's *Angel's Town*. From *Culture and Truth*, they should be learning about the place of the ethnographer or the place of the anthropologist, how much it's impossible for them to maintain complete distance from whatever subjects or objects they study. I think it's a critical warning to those who are engaged in ethnographic studies about the fact that they have biases that they bring to each study.

Gilyard: Well, they're part of the rhetorical situation, right?

Mejía: Also the class will be reading a book called *Mascaras*, which is an edited collection of essays by Latinas, many of whom are Mexican Americans. The essays are about writing, what compels the authors to write, what the rhetorical circumstances are. It's interesting how female-centered most of the essays are, connecting the impetus for writing to a mother, grandmother, or other strong female presence. But it's also noteworthy that Sandra Cisneros, probably the most prominent writer among them all, writes her essay about her father. In a sense, she has always stood apart this way. Anyway, I've used this book in other classes, and it's a good book that is a keeper, especially because it covers a lot of different Latino and Latina groups, not just Chicanos and Chicanas. It's good for Chicanos and Chicanas, especially in Texas where we rarely have contact with other Latino groups, to see how others operate at least partially. So I'm coupling this book with *Feminism on the Border* by Sonia Saldívar-Hull, which is sort of a literary survey as well, but it contains literary criticism and theoretical viewpoints that my students need to have. So with all these books I intend to see what I can get, what the students can get. They will be conducting rhetorical analyses on art, literature, communities, or events in the community. That's sort of the game plan.

Gilyard: Sounds superb.

Mejía: Well, it's going to be an experiment like every class is an experiment. We'll see how it goes.

Michael Bérubé is the Paterno Family Professor in Literature at Pennsylvania State University. He is the author of six books to date: *Marginal Forces/Cultural Centers: Tolson, Pynchon, and the Politics of the Canon* (Cornell University Press, 1992); *Public Access: Literary Theory and American Cultural Politics* (Verso, 1994); *Life As We Know It: A Father, A Family, and an Exceptional Child* (Pantheon, 1996; paper edition, Vintage, 1998); *The Employment of English: Theory, Jobs, and the Future of Literary Studies* (New York University Press, 1998); *What's Liberal about the Liberal Arts?: Classroom Politics and "Bias" in Higher Education* (W. W. Norton, 2006) and *Rhetorical Occasions: Essays on Humans and the Humanities* (University of North Carolina Press, 2006). He is also the editor of *The Aesthetics of Cultural Studies* (Blackwell, 2004), and, with Cary Nelson, of *Higher Education Under Fire: Politics, Economics, and the Crisis of the Humanities* (Routledge, 1995). Bérubé has written over a hundred and fifty essays for a wide variety of academic journals such as *American Quarterly*, the *Yale Journal of Criticism*, *Social Text*, *Modern Fiction Studies*, and the *minnesota review*, as well as more popular venues such as *Harper's*, the *New Yorker*, *Dissent*, *The New York Times Magazine*, the *Washington Post*, the *Nation*, and the *Boston Globe*. *Life As We Know It* was a *New York Times* Notable Book of the Year for 1996 and was chosen as one of the best books of the year (on a list of seven) by Maureen Corrigan of National Public Radio. Bérubé is a member of the Advisory Board of the Penn State Center for American Literary Studies.

The Conversation

Victor Taylor: Could you describe the intellectual context for your early work? Are there key figures from that time who still strongly inform your thinking? Fade into the past?

Michael Berubé: The immediate context of my first book on Melvin Tolson and Thomas Pynchon was, of course, the great Canon Debates of the 1980s, to which I was trying to make an original and counterintuitive contribution. Most of the debate to that point had focused, understandably enough, on women and writers of color who'd been overlooked by the gatekeepers of the academic literary canon. I wanted to examine the academy's *contemporary* role in literary gatekeeping, and to place it in the context of the rest of contemporary literary culture—the apparatus of publishers and reviews and anthologies and course adoptions. So, for example, it wasn't sufficient (for me) to note that Melvin Tolson was a really interesting African-American poet who fit neither under the rubric of the Harlem Renaissance or the rubric of the Black Aesthetic; the same could be said of people like Owen Dodson and Robert Hayden, as well, though only Tolson staked his career on long poems in the mode of Eliot and Pound. Instead, I wanted to look at the institutional context for the reception of African-American literature: when, for instance, was the first MLA paper devoted to African-American writing? (1953—Blyden Jackson, a talk on the dilemma of the Negro novelist.) As you might imagine, answering that question involved paging through decades of MLA convention programs. And I wanted to look at the history of anthologies of African-American writing, especially but not exclusively poetry, not only to see how Tolson was anthologized but also to track the production and publication of such anthologies (and their longevity), especially with regard to the extraordinary boom in anthology production from 1965–1972 (and the equally extraordinary bust from 1972 to about 1995).

Then, by juxtaposing Tolson to Pynchon, I tried to take aim at that aspect of the ideology of the avant-garde that construes canonization as death. (See, e.g., Adorno's musings on the relation between museums and mausoleums.) A corollary of this account of reception is the idea that great work is always misunderstood and/or neglected when it first appears, because it is such a violation of the "horizon of expectations" (in Hans-Robert Jauss's terms) for a new work of art. Thus, for instance, I found people trying mightily to demonstrate that *Gravity's Rainbow* met this criterion—even though it won the National Book Award, was the first American novel published simultaneously in cloth and paper, and sold an extraordinary 800,000 copies. And I found (no surprise) that Pynchon became part of the contemporary American canon almost from the moment *GR* appeared—even as his leading academic critics (like George Levine and David Leverenz) apologized to him for putting together a book of essays on his work.

The Tolson/Pynchon contrast, then, allowed me to explore different kinds of gatekeeping and different kinds of approaches to canonization. It wasn't just a matter of arguing, "hey, the Cultural Center is being dismantled just as the writers of color show up," though there was that too. Instead, it was a way of asking about the various cultural functions of institutional literary criticism. I don't think it's had much influence on anything, though. It seems to have been a bit too weird a contribution to the canon debate, and perhaps too late an entry, as well.

Since then, the work of Bruce Robbins has only become more important to me in about eight different ways, and Richard Ohmann and Paul Lauter have stood the test of time well. Jauss has all but disappeared from sight, fading far into my past, and I don't have much use these days for Althusser (who popped up intermittently) either. On the other hand, when I was writing my chapter on pornography in *Gravity's Rainbow* I was introduced to the feminist porn/antiporn debates of the 1980s, and those seem to have had quite a long shelf life indeed. Feminist film theory is no longer a wholly-owned subsidiary of Lacan Enterprises, to be sure, but those debates over sexuality and representation have only gotten more intense in the last twenty years, particularly after the queer turn. I haven't contributed to those debates since then, though. Instead, I wound up trying to ask about the functions of "institutional" literary and cultural criticism in the public sphere by writing criticism in more "public" venues. And that turned into a career in itself.

Taylor: I'd like to pick up on the idea of "institution" in your response. There is, as Derrida says, "the institution of literature" and the institution in which literature exists. Sometimes they collide and sometimes they are in agreement. I'm more interested in institution itself. How do institutions in the sense of canon and academic forum accommodate change? It seems that the "institution of literature" somewhat "naturally" allows for change while the wider forum is quick to shut it down. So, it is one thing to write about postmodern novelists for a journal and quite another to offer a course on postmodern novelists or even write a dissertation on the topic.

Berubé: OK, now this question takes me back. In my very first MLA interview, twenty years ago, Linda Shires of Syracuse opened the proceedings by asking me what I meant by "institution." It caught me so by surprise—we had been told to expect the first question to be, "tell us about your dissertation," and to rehearse one-, two-, and three-minute answers—that I must have babbled on for about ten minutes. I'll try to do better this time.

I was trying to argue that (as you suggest) there is not one but a variety of institutions at work in the "institution of literature," and that they tend to accommodate change either by (a) defusing it, which, in the late 1980s, was the fear of deconstructionists and New Historicists who were ambivalent about the extent and the rapidity with which the American academy absorbed and even celebrated their work; or (b) practicing a kind of "strong reformism" in which the formerly excluded, once included, change the terms of inclusion in the future. (A), no surprise, was the dominant attitude of Pynchon critics toward Pynchon's embrace by mainstream literary culture and the academy; (B) was Tolson's approach, as evidenced not only by his attempt to crack the citadel of high modernism but by the text of *Harlem Gallery* itself—for instance, in the poem's narrative of the black stevedore who enters a formerly segregated diner, asks for chitlins, and when rebuffed by the waitress, says, "I've always said you white people weren't ready for integration." Which is not only a nice piece of détournement in its own right, but a canny suggestion that you can't suddenly admit the people you've been excluding and expect to serve the same menu. The lessons for the "canon" should be obvious, and I believe this was in fact Tolson's point. Or so I argue in *Marginal Forces.*

So I was, and am, rather more humanist about institutions than your average poststructuralist; yes, institutions and discursive formations determine what can be said by whom, but they can change with changing demographics and protocols. I use *determine* here in the sense Raymond Williams developed in "Base and Superstructure in Marxist Cultural Theory"—in the sense of "setting limits." But like Williams, I think those limits are negotiable by individual agents.

You mention the difference between the acceptable canon for refereed journals and the canon for dissertations or courses. One of my frustrations with the "canon debate" way back when stemmed from my realization that there is a staggering array of canons and institutional contexts of literary reception operating in the profession and in the broader culture—from the syllabus to the anthology to the citation index to the Modern Library to the Library of America to the Harvard Classics to Cliffs Notes to the public library magazine-ad One Hundred Greatest Books (leather-bound of course). The most important of these, I argued, is the category of books in print because once a book falls out of print it is very, very difficult to revive it. Hurston's *Their Eyes Were Watching God* is the most spectacular example of recovery-from-oblivion in our time, and in the years since my book came out, the Dalkey Archive Press has emerged, and now specializes in bringing back works like Djuna Barnes' *Ryder* as well as novels by more recent writers like Paul West, Gilbert Sorrentino, and Clarence Major. But as a general rule, it takes a major research program like the one launched by the social movement known as second-wave feminism or the recovery projects initiated by people like Cary Nelson to put forgotten works back on the map *permanently*, in an institutional sense, so as to enable ongoing critical conversations about them. Actually, I think the profession is pretty flexible about courses and dissertations on postmodern or otherwise obscure writers; the institution only becomes "confining" in a coercive sense when you hit the sluice gates—the most important of which is of course the institution known as the job market. (I was forbidden from doing Thomas Pynchon as my major author for my Ph.D. orals, but apres moi, le deluge—and it came not from postmodernists but from feminists. Within years, guess what? The major author exam itself was relegated to the ash heap of history. So change does happen, even in hidebound institutions, when the demographics of change reach critical mass. Whenever that may be.)

Taylor: I have some perspective on Shires' question since I was a grad student (not her grad student by the way) at Syracuse in the late eighties. "The Postmodern English department," as it was called internally, was at war (theory war) with "institution." All the conflicts that you've discussed were part of a daily combat zone. There were, as Donald Morton more or less described it, the "paleo-traditionalists," the "neo-traditionalists," and the "theorists," which included the deconstructionists and the Marxists. The "paleo-traditionalists" were defending "author," "period," and "explication" exams based on the canon. The "neo-traditionalists," mid-career scholars trained as new critics or historicists, were defending the same categories but advocated for a revised, expanded canon. The "theorists" were ready to change it all. The problem was that each group was after curricular hegemony. The "neo-traditionalists" won since there were able to placate the "paleos" and deny tenure to the "theorists" or marginalize the established "theory" faculty within the space of departmental policy.

So, after that micro-history, isn't the problem of institution really the problem of hegemony? I mean we like to think that the academy is a space of debate, but curriculum is the "weapon" of choice when you want to form a hegemonic sphere, right?

Berubé: Oh. My. God. *That* Syracuse? *Then?* Yep, that was about hegemony, all right—that wasn't just a question about Pynchon as "major author;" that was an attempt to redo the English department altogether. Wasn't the new term "textual studies?" I remember when

I got news of the proposed revision, I thought, "holy shit, this place is actually going to take theory seriously in an *institutional* sense." In fact, Syracuse was my #1 choice as a result. But I blew the interview, partly because of that question…

Anyway, I think my point still holds. I mean, it's not like I forgot about power/knowledge, now. I wasn't suggesting (or didn't mean to suggest) that the institution we inhabit is simply a nice space for a debating club. In the Gramscian universe—that is, the one we live in—agents do go around trying to build historic blocs, win consent, and so forth. I posted something on this in the course of writing a three-part, something-like-10,000-word series of posts on Williams' "Base and Superstructure" (http://www.michaelberube.com/index.php/weblog/comments/1038/). And the line of argument I trace there is basically what I'm getting at by calling myself more humanist than poststructuralist with regard to institutions.

And what happens in departments, particularly when things happen on the scale of Syracuse in the 80s, really does enable certain discourses and marginalize (or banish) others. That's one reason I put so much pressure on the concept of "neglect" in reception history. I think it's way too sloppy and undertheorized. At the same time, I didn't agree entirely with Cary Nelson's concept of "repression," and I spent a few pages in the intro to *Marginal Forces* trying to parse the difference between passive neglect and active repression, while acknowledging that once X has been effectively repressed (kicked out of the department, the canon, the institution), everyone from that point on can go ahead and safely neglect X…

Taylor: Syracuse, as I remember it, was "superficially radical." Yes, "textual studies" replaced English, but the infrastructure and superstructure stayed the same, paleo/neo-traditionalist … only the "vocabulary" changed. The problem with Syracuse at the time was not that it went "theory," but that it did NOT go "theory" enough. Or, more accurately, it went "theory" just enough to meet the career aspirations of certain faculty. The institutional problem was, in fact, "neglect" and "exclusion." Your "friends" are your "friends" and your "enemies" are "ensembles of social relations." This seems to be universally true—Syracuse 1980s and small teaching colleges 2008. So, today, could you give a new faculty member a preview of what to expect if he or she is on the "margin" in academia?

Berubé: Hmmm. Although I knew of Syracuse's attempt at departmental transformation from afar, I didn't know the parties and players well enough to be able to comment on this level of detail. Not that you're asking me to comment on Syracuse, but your question raises the very difficult metaquestion of the degree to which institutional change does or doesn't hinge on the actions and aspirations of specific parties and players.

So I don't have a generic preview of what to expect for new faculty members, be they at research universities, small teaching colleges, elite liberal arts schools, or regional comprehensives. I can, however, try to describe a few forms of marginality I've seen over the past 20 years. Starting with the most hopeful:

One: the margin that, like academic feminism since 1970 or multiculturalism/postnationalism in American studies since 1980, actually has a chance of moving to the center and redefining what "access to the center" will henceforth mean. To new faculty in those kinds of margins, I think the best advice is simply to keep doing your work, expect and endure the slights (though you don't have to suffer fools gladly), and know that time and history are on your side. That would have sounded insanely Pollyannaish in my field with regard to feminism in 1970 or multicultural/postnational American studies in 1980, when the field was basically all white guys all the time. But lo, look what a couple of decades with enormous demographic and intellectual shifts can do. Patience, hard work, thrift, etc., just like that Ben Franklin said.

Two: the margin that will likely remain a demographic/identity margin, as when you're the only African-American on the faculty or the only Latina scholar for many miles around. You know the drill: you will be asked, upon the moment of your arrival on campus, to serve every kind of "diversity" function for students, colleagues, and administrators alike. You have to refuse all invitations (and there will be many) to be the token X for every function, the go-to person for all students of color, and the Representative of All Your People. Especially in rural locations, this can be exceptionally difficult. But your status on the margin is partly a corollary of the fact that your institution doesn't have a critical mass of X, so it's crucial—for the institution, and for your own survival—to build a critical mass of X.

Three: the margin that will remain a margin for intellectual/ideological reasons. Political theorists in political science departments, Continental theorists in Anglo-American analytical philosophy departments, Marxists in economics departments (if there are any left). For you, I fear, in many departments there is no hope. And the smaller the department, most likely, the dimmer the hope: there aren't many political science departments under 20 that believe they need *two* theorists. You will always be outvoted on curriculum committees, strategic planning committees, and (most important) search committees. There may not be more than one or two people in your department (though there may be less) who have the faintest idea of what you're talking about. And you don't have the option of people in Marginal Category Two, because there is no realistic chance that your institution will ever attempt to build a critical mass of X. My advice to people in this position is to develop many professional and personal friendships with colleagues at other institutions—by way of conferences, conventions, Internet, whatever. Find ways of staying sane and getting good feedback while knowing that you'll very likely inhabit the margins of your own institution—and, if possible, find good fun ways of owning and inhabiting that margin. Easier to do after tenure than before, needless to say.

Taylor: The concern for the margin and marginalized is consistent in your work. In the 1980s it was a fight to have Pynchon included in the canon.

Berubé: Actually, Pynchon was already in, by most measures. He may not have been a Major Author in the Chaucer-Shakespeare-Milton sense, but he was the leading contemporary American writer until Toni

Morrison published *Beloved.*

Taylor: Today, the margin is occupied by more than writers. "Letting in," as it were, other literatures is "letting in other people." Could you talk about the rhetorical problem of inclusion? For instance, imagine this scenario: Carrie, a 23 year old with Down Syndrome enjoys music and painting. She decides to take Art 101: Art Appreciation and MUS 101: Music Appreciation at a local college. She completed a GED, but doesn't have any prereqs for college and the dean of admissions says, "Sorry, but you can't take those classes. Please feel free to attend the College's music and art events throughout the year, however." How would you make a case for her, especially to a dean who actively seeks to recruit, as he says, "the best and the brightest"?

Berubé: Actually, as Barbara Herrnstein Smith argued (however obliquely) in *Contingencies of Value,* the project of bringing in other writers can't be neatly separated from the project of bringing in other people. But to the larger point you raise, I would point that dean to Penn State's LifeLink program, which brings students with intellectual disabilities onto campus and enrolls them in appropriate college-level courses. I would also point him (or her!) to the University of Maine's pilot programs that do the same. I vividly recall a conference I attended in November 2007 at which someone spoke about Maine's program to me and said that she defends it from skeptics by insisting that even if some students with intellectual disabilities wind up being unable to do the work, *everyone deserves the chance to fail.* It may not sound like the most inspiring bumper sticker in the world, but I found it oddly moving. I would follow that point, of course, with the argument that some nondisabled students will fail, and some students with Down syndrome might not: it was Jamie's eighth-grade history of art/music class, after all, that taught him the distinctions between medieval, Renaissance, classical, baroque, Romantic, and modern periods (distinctions he understands quite well) and gave him his current fascination with late Italian Renaissance painting.

Taylor: Is this directly connected to your next project?

Berubé: *Disability and Narrative* will build on my work in disability studies—specifically, my 2005 *PMLA* essay of the same name. In this book, I will examine the complex relations between narrative and cognitive/developmental disability, not with regard to how cognitive/developmental disability is represented in fiction but with regard to how narratives—including certain "experimental" narratives—are influenced or structured by ideas about cognitive/developmental disability. The book will discuss writers such as William Faulkner, Maxine Hong Kingston, Richard Powers, and Mark Haddon along with popular films of all genres (from Disney to serious drama to science fiction). And it will, I hope, constitute a fresh direction for disability studies in the humanities, as well as for the study of narrative, insofar as it will show how disability affects the actual texture of narrative itself—especially when, but not exclusively when, the narrative involves (or purports to be composed by) people with cognitive/developmental disabilities.

Mindedness is so obviously a necessary condition for self-representation and narration that it should be no surprise to find narratives in which various forms of damaged mindedness serve neither as moral barometers of individual persons nor as invitations to pity or horror but as meditations on the very possibility of narrative representation. One might think here of the way that the trope of short-term memory loss is used to comic effect in *Finding Nemo* or *Fifty First Dates*, to suspense-thriller effect in *Memento*; or of the way that varieties of artificial intelligence and human intelligence—in neuroscientists, novelists, people with Alzheimer's, adults with Capgras syndrome, and children with Down syndrome—weave the thread of the narrative of Richard Powers's novels *Galatea 2.2* and *The Echo Maker*. My hope is not only that *Disability and Narrative* will offer a study of disability and narrative, but that it will also further our understanding of how narrative illuminates (and proceeds from) some of the functions of the human mind. I'm hoping to finish it in the next couple of years.

Haivan V. Hoang is an Assistant Professor of English and the Director of the Writing Center at the University of Massachusetts, Amherst. With wide interests in college composition and literacy studies, her scholarship centers on issues of race, literacy, and ethnography. She is now finishing a book called *Rewriting Injury: Asian American Rhetoric and Campus Racial Politics*. The study, which explores Asian American students' activist rhetoric during the historical counterpoints of the early 1970s and early 2000s, seeks to mine the students' political texts for broader lessons about rhetoric, campus racial politics, and higher education.

LuMing Mao is a professor in the Department of English at Miami University of Ohio. He teaches and researches Asian/Asian American rhetoric, comparative rhetoric, Chinese and European American rhetorical traditions, pragmatics, and critical discourse analysis. He is author of *Reading Chinese Fortune Cookie: The Making of Chinese American Rhetoric*. He is co-editor, with Morris Young, of *Representations: Doing Asian American Rhetoric* and, with C. Jan Swearingen, of *Double Trouble: Seeing Chinese Rhetoric through Its Own Lens,* a special symposium to be published in the June 2009 Issue of *College Composition and Communication*. He is also co-editor, with Robert Hariman, Susan Jarratt, Andrea Lunsford, Thomas Miller, and Jacqueline Jones Royster, of the forthcoming *Norton Anthology of Rhetoric and Writing*.

The Conversation

Keith Gilyard: LuMing, I'll start out by asking you a simple and devious question, devious because I know your work. Where are you from?

LuMing Mao: That is an interesting and meaningful question. I did my graduate work at the University of Minnesota and spent five-and-a-half years in Minneapolis and St. Paul. Then I went to Oxford, Ohio and started my teaching and research career at Miami University. To go back a little bit further, I was born and bred in Shanghai and grew up actually in Shanghai as well. So I spent my formative years in Shanghai, and that certainly has had and continues to have an impact on what I do and how I do my academic work here in the U. S.

Gilyard: You know why I asked you that, right? (laughing)

Mao: Yes! Yes! Yes! (laughing)

Gilyard: You consider that to be able to answer that question is in some sense the practice of Chinese American rhetoric.

Mao: Exactly, because I have always been torn between the need to give an answer that is more situated and complex in terms of history and spaces and the need to provide an answer that responds to local expectation, that is, an answer that is direct, immediate, and "right to the point." I often feel inadequate or dissatisfied when I sense the pressure to give an answer that is more immediate, more local than it is more contextualized.

Gilyard: How are you defining Chinese American rhetoric these days?

Mao: These days, I see Chinese American rhetoric as an example of how Chinese, Chinese Americans, and even other non-Chinese Americans to some extent use language or other symbolic means of communication to effect social, cultural, and political changes in ongoing sociopolitical contexts.

Gilyard: In some ways, you speak to the next question when you talk about people other than Chinese Americans employing certain kinds of communication techniques. I'm interested in how you deal with the question of rhetorical uniqueness when you consider Asian American rhetoric.

Mao: Actually, in my book and in some of my essays I try not to claim uniqueness for Asian American or Chinese American or for other ethnic rhetorics, for that matter, partly because I strongly feel that they may overlap in terms of discursive features and appropriation. Once you claim uniqueness for one particular ethnic rhetoric, I think you put yourself in a very difficult situation when you find similar features in other discursive traditions or practices. A rhetoric is Asian American or Chinese American not because it is unique but because it has a cluster of features that necessarily and sufficiently point to or speak to and nurture or advocate a particular sense of consciousness, collective or otherwise, and speaks to a particular cause or identity that we can claim to be Asian American or Chinese American. That is how I'm trying to negotiate between the desire to make a claim for uniqueness and a need to give this thing an identity. To claim uniqueness is an attempt to give an identity to a rhetoric that hasn't been recognized or sufficiently categorized. I don't want to suggest that this tension is to go away. Rather, I say we need to be mindful of the tension and, at the same time, pay attention to what I lately call "occasions of use."

Gilyard: How do you deal with that Haivan?

Haivan Hoang: It's interesting because the question of whether there's a unique Asian American rhetoric is aligned in some way with the question of "where are you from?" When asked that, I say California to mess with people because I know that they're thinking, "Oh, she's from Vietnam; she's from some nation in Asia." This is where the question of uniqueness comes in. What they're looking for when they ask me the question, usually, is whether there is some kind of ethnic authenticity to which I'm laying claim. And I would say no. In my own work, I'm more interested in the subject positions from which Asian Americans speak due to *historical formations* of Asian Americans.

Mao: There's almost an analogous discussion in an essay on feminist rhetoric that I read within the last several weeks. The essay asks to what extent we can use woman as a category to represent a particular individual. To what extent is such use over-generalizing? Basically, what does *woman* represent? Does it point to gender or to a set of what this author calls "structural constraints" that sets limits to what a woman is expected to do or not do.

Hoang: Joan W. Scott addresses this issue in writing about women's histories and points out how histories often take as self-evident the category of *woman*. She believes the question should be why the difference is being enunciated in the first place. To destabilize the categories is what she sees to be the project for feminists. But you need to maintain some semblance of a category in order to destabilize it.

Gilyard: Right. LuMing, you know I've followed your work for years, but I haven't had the chance to speak with you about your recent book *Reading Chinese Fortune Cookie: The Making of Chinese American Rhetoric.* Would you explain how you decided on the fortune cookie as a governing analogy for your work and how you see the metaphor continuing to operate in investigations of culture and rhetoric?

Mao: I think there could be two answers. One is that I have always been fascinated by this cultural artifact that is on display every time I go to a Chinese restaurant here in North America. You don't see that in Europe or in Asia at all. I've been interested in people's comments about the fortunes they receive. Sometimes they laugh, and sometimes they complain. I began to pay close attention and that led me to explore the history behind the formation of this thing we call the Chinese fortune cookie, an artifact that represents two distinctive traditions. One, as I said in my book, is the European-American tradition of eating dessert after dinner; the other, from ancient China, is the practice of communicating covertly by sticking a piece of paper in a pastry, often times in moon cakes. The co-existence of these two traditions in this nifty thing really has been fascinating to me, especially how their co-existence doesn't erase the distinctive traditions. We have the cookie as an example of dessert and we have the fortune inside the cookie that speaks to a particular slice of history that started in the fourteenth- and fifteenth-century A.D. in China. That is the first part of my answer.

Gilyard: Yeah, but the main thing is—I just have to say this—is that you and I went to a Chinese restaurant while I was on one of my trips to Oxford, and you didn't explain any of this to me.

Mao: (laughing) I guess I wanted to protect my secret at that moment. Now, the second part of my answer, what I'm fascinated by most of all, is the fact that the fortune cookie represents this hybridity, this togetherness in difference, the phenomenon that these two traditions now co-exist in a third. But their co-existence doesn't mean that their differences are now being discarded or erased. Rather, their co-existence in some ways preserves the difference and also produces new forms of meaning and new forms of identity, and this analogy I continue to believe is guiding me in thinking about issues and studies in our investigations of culture and rhetoric. Simply put, togetherness is the mode of the day. That is, we are together whether we like it or not. On the other hand, togetherness represents both opportunities and challenges in how we theorize, how we conceptualize different forms of togetherness, and how these different forms continue to yield new forms of meaning and new forms of identity.

Gilyard: Exploding stereotypes with respect to, say, face, individuality, and directness, is part of your mission. This effort seems to have political dimensions beyond an academic concern with describing a particular rhetoric. Was this always your intent?

Mao: To be honest with you, I don't think it was my initial intent. My initial intent was really to uncover the narratives that I believe are shaping or contributing to the meanings of these concepts. As I began to look into the history of these particular narratives, I began to see the connection that they have to the political, to a space that is beyond academe. So these days I'm more mindful of the connection of this kind of rhetoric to the political and to the social, and, indeed, I really want to see to what extent this kind of rhetoric can have a positive, transformative impact.

Gilyard: Haivan, as we specifically mention politics, I think of your writings about solidarity rhetoric. Of course, the notion of solidarity isn't simply an Asian American concern, but I like how you bill yourself as a Vietnamese American rhetorician and then animate the concept of solidarity rhetoric to talk about or at least allude to political efforts whether they be Vietnamese American efforts, Pan-Asian, or otherwise. Would you talk about your theorizing in this regard and how such theorizing relates to notions of identity, cultural difference, and race?

Hoang: Before I answer your question directly, I should say that my thinking about solidarity rhetoric has changed a little in that I think that my dissertation's construction of solidarity rhetoric could use a more critical edge. Specifically, at the time I was writing this dissertation and thinking of this project on solidarity rhetoric, I was frustrated by what I saw as appeals to resistance without a defined end goal for that resistance. I was frustrated also by the negative subject positions that Asian Americans and other racial minorities are constructed as holding, where we're always arguing *against* rather than struggling *for*. I also confronted the difficulty of not having much to work with in terms of secondary literature on Asian American rhetoric. Morris Young had sent me the page proofs of his book, which was coming out the year that I was finishing my dissertation. Of course, I had read earlier articles by him as well as by LuMing, also some articles on Asian American literature within Asian American studies. But I looked primarily toward rhetorical theory, specifically regarding questions of division and connection, so Bakhtin's notions of centrifugal and centripetal forces were important.

Also Rorty's conception of humanist solidarity and the connection that all humans have. In drawing from rhetorical theory without attending to a historical construction of Asian American racialization, I think I was overly idealistic in the possibility of solidarity rhetoric. So in answer to your question about how solidarity rhetoric is employed in political efforts and how that relates to identity, cultural difference, and race, I would say that solidarity rhetoric can have very different instantiations depending on the political exigence of the moment. A clear example can be found in the Third World Liberation Front strikes at San Francisco State in 1969, where different racial minority students' organizations came together and actively decided to build a coalition for the purpose of self-determination and having control over ethnic studies and their higher education. I think this was especially important among the three Asian American student organizations that signed the strike demands. PACE, the Filipino organization, was concerned with economic issues in the Mission District and other economically depressed areas where Filipino people were living. The group also desired to mentor youth who would come to the university. The Chinese American student organization seemed to be very concerned with Chinatown and the issue of ethnicity. The Asian American Political Alliance, a third group, was mostly Japanese American but chose actively to label itself Asian American.

But a different instantiation of solidarity rhetoric can be found in the 1990s when a lot of students again were organizing and striking for Asian American studies and other ethnic studies programs in universities that hadn't institutionalized and adopted and embraced such programs. But by reinstating the same kind of solidarity rhetoric, they weren't necessarily using it to the same effect and sometimes not even effectively. Their calling up notions of identity, cultural difference, and race were sometimes decontextualized because they were drawing from the context of the 1960s rather than the 1990s where the conditions had changed significantly within higher education, where ethnic studies courses had been offered even if there weren't widespread and fully functioning programs and departments. The 1990s were also a time Asian American student enrollment was increasing at a rate that was unprecedented in the U. S. There was certainly antagonism against that as you can see from the activism protest around Berkeley admissions in the mid-80s.

Gilyard: I see.

Hoang: Their situations were very different. Solidarity rhetoric was employed to different effects. The question is not necessarily the relationship between identity, cultural difference, and race, but the question is why are these called up in different ways in relation to the contemporary social structure and situation within which students find themselves.

Gilyard: I think so. In line with that, as I listen to you talk about those movements and the questions of ethnicity that come up, I think about the degree to which people see things these days in terms of class issues. How would you speak to the issue of ethnic differences via-á-vis class solidarity based on your work?

Hoang: I think that's really difficult because ethnicity and race are clearly cultural constructions. Discussions of class solidarity are different, depending, of course, on how you define class. If you're defining class in very material ways, which would be my inclination, those aren't necessarily cultural constructions where cultural production can change one's position in a classist reality. So I think class solidarity raises different questions.

Gilyard: This is part of what comes up all the time, in recent work by Walter Benn Michaels, for example.

Hoang: He came to speak at the University of Massachusetts a couple weeks ago, and I was very frustrated by the talk for many reasons. In response to Michaels, class and ethnic difference largely go hand-in-hand. And I should say racial injustice, not just ethnic difference. He's right that we do need to look at who is benefiting from the efforts to address past racial injustices. One of the compelling arguments he made, for example, about affirmative action was that affirmative action as it's usually employed benefits middle-class and upper-middle-class racial minorities. A very typical argument, one that has led me to think the policy needs revision. But Michaels seems to think the policy should go away altogether, which doesn't really make sense to me. Secondly, he is treating race in very simplistic ways, the ways that universities treat diversity in terms of static categories. They dehistoricize such categories, and that's why he can critique race the way he does. But if he took up the way that race scholars are looking at race, he would have a very different project.

Specifically, in relation to Asian Americans, the issue of class solidarity is difficult because you think of class solidarity in multiple ways. Class solidarity could be thought of in terms of the very material realities that people experience. If you have Southeast Asian refugees and you have world travelers from Hong Kong, those are very different populations although they're placed in the same racial subject positions. So that's one dimension of class solidarity we first need to identify. What are those material realities and how do they break down and then around what are we identifying? But a second issue of class solidarity that I've been thinking about more recently is something—it came up from a book I'm reading by Colleen Lye called *America's Asia*. She talks about the "yellow peril" and the issue of "model minority" as both being a part of the same conceptualization of Asian Americans in terms of an economic trope. We are always seen as an economic threat. That has to do with the racialization of Asian Americans. It allowed, for example, one of my peer graduate students to say, "Well, why do you need your paycheck? Don't you have enough money?" I thought, "I get paid the same thing as you. Don't you need your paycheck?"

Gilyard: That's crazy.

Hoang: There are definite assumptions about economics when it comes to Asian Americans due to this long history of "yellow peril."

Gilyard: You know, I think you should have several book contracts yourself by now.

Hoang: I wish.

Gilyard: I think the book I might want to read first would have you talking about Asian American rhetorical memory because I find your discussion of that to be so insightful. Would you talk a bit about memory as rhetoric and how you might grow this project I'm talking about?

Hoang: In relation to solidarity rhetoric, memory was one of my chapters within the dissertation. I saw memory as one of the sites around which the Vietnamese American students in my study were identifying. For me, one of the most interesting parts of my research was an interview with a student who also was a poet. And he was very poetic and rhetorical in his characterization of what happened when protesting Senator John McCain's use of the word *gook* to refer to his Vietnamese prison guards. And he remembered this incident in several different ways. First, he spoke about persuading his peers to challenge McCain's characterization of the North Vietnamese prison guards. Second, he talked about this in relation to a peer who was very resistant against him. Third, he talked about this in relation to intergenerational perspectives. But he didn't talk about the utterance of this slur in terms of direct opposition against McCain, which I thought was interesting because this wasn't really about McCain. This was about the community the student thought himself to be a part of, the Vietnamese American community.

More recently, I've been reading some of Joan W. Scott's work, who I mentioned earlier, and one of the terms she uses really resonates with me. She calls this—the kind of solidarity rhetoric I'm talking about— fantasy. She's interested in history as what she calls "fantasy echo." So the solidarity is always a fantasy and it's the echoes that can destabilize the fantasy. In terms of writing the book, what I need to do is to resist writing a singular narrative that would say, "This is what Asian American student rhetoric is about." And I think by utilizing the kind of fantasy echo or copiousness or shadows on the cave walls—however you want to phrase it—as a structure for the entire book, I can actually employ the kind of memory I'm talking about. That's my goal at this moment.

Gilyard: How is your research informing your course offerings and classroom practice?

Hoang: I'm teaching a graduate class called "Writing and Race," and I had a lot of trouble with the syllabus because I wanted adequate representation of different racial minorities' histories. But I didn't want students to see these histories as discrete. It wouldn't make sense to have two weeks on Asian Americans, two weeks on African Americans, etc.

Gilyard: Right, right.

Hoang: So I decided to move somewhat chronologically and place side-by-side articles and books that weren't normally read together. For example, when we got to the early and mid-1970s, I put "Student's Right" next to an article on *Lau v. Nichols* next to articles on basic writing. When we began the class, I put sociologists Omi and Winant's book *Racial Formation* next to critical race scholar Ian F. Haney Lopez's *White By Law*, next to an article by Amy Zenger from *Rhetoric Review* that talks about the official move to make English the medium of composition instruction. I am asking my students to think about the intersections, how the works speak to one another. Intersectionality grounded in particular histories and particular social structures can be really revealing in terms of our disciplinary history.

Gilyard: Definitely. That's a great textual conversation you put together. The hope is that it would stimulate an equally great conversation in class. Your talk about intersections reminds me of something to ask LuMing. How do you respond, LuMing, to the criticism that your theorizing about Chinese American rhetoric sees it as only a product of Chinese and European American traditions? I suppose I should just own this as my criticism. Chinese American experience in the United States has been characterized by prolonged contact with several ethnic groups. I have participated, for example, in literary celebrations of the Asian American-African American connection. Musician Fred Ho perhaps is a paradigmatic example of Asian and African American political and cultural mixing. Younger folks, as exemplified by hip-hop journalist Jeff Chang, seem to indicate that all the mixing—no pun intended—in hip hop is going to make discussions of rhetorical traditions even more complicated. "A" can identify with "B" in a Burkean sense but also with "C", "D", "E", "F," and so on. How would you respond to that?

Mao: I am mindful of this concern or criticism. But I do want to continue to use the name Chinese American rhetoric to describe this set of practices deployed or employed by Chinese, Chinese Americans, and non-Chinese Americans. On the other hand, by using the name Chinese American to describe this rhetoric I do not intend to suggest that such a rhetoric has not drawn upon other rhetorical or discursive traditions or practices. That is I think what Jeff Chang is talking about: the paradoxical nature of naming. When you perform a speech act of naming something, you are giving it a category because your intention, or my purpose or our purpose in this case, is to give value to and give an identity to a discursive practice that hasn't been given proper attention. But once you do that, you are circumscribing a boundary, as it were, to the extent that it could exclude other inferences and other traditions. So I see that as a challenge, as a kind of necessary tension that is going to attend to or that has been attending to the description of Chinese American rhetoric or any other ethnic rhetoric. Think of the name English, for example. During the early modern period or middle ages, the term English described a particular language to give it an identity and distinctiveness. This was in association with rise of the nation-state of Great Britain. But in saying that, certainly it doesn't mean that English is only Anglo-Saxon. In fact, it has and continues to draw upon other linguistic inferences. So I do see a tension that is necessarily embedded in naming.

Gilyard: So you have focused to be able to get some work done?

Mao: Yes. But I appreciate this criticism. I think it calls attention to both the difficulty involved in doing this kind of project and the necessity in giving something a name.

Gilyard: Well, it stays complicated. I mean, I understand the argument against claiming uniqueness. But you can be distinctive without necessarily being unique. You've more or less said this before. But you still seem somewhat reluctant to name distinct linguistic features that mark Chinese American rhetoric. Yet, to speak Chinese American rhetoric is to speak something concrete and definable in a given time and place, no?

Mao: Yeah, yeah.

Gilyard: So there are some features, right?

Mao: I think I've been motivated by the following, which led me to do what I did in the book and in some of the other things I've written so far. By using the singular for the word rhetoric in Chinese American rhetoric, I actually do want to ascribe an identity to this rhetoric in order to contest the dominance of the dominant. But, on the other hand, I know that there are many kinds of rhetorics for Chinese American rhetoric; in other words, folks who practice Chinese American rhetoric deploy a variety of features and characteristics that are a part of their rhetoric. To the extent that is the case, I actually want to lay emphasis on each and every specific occasion of use to see how a particular set of features is being utilized to effect particular social, linguistic, and political purposes. I'm kind of playing with the singular on the one hand and also calling for immediate attention to the specific practices that folks participate in.

Gilyard: I'll have to think about this more. Let me get to another aspect of your work. I appreciate how you complicate notions of contact zones, borderlands, third space, and multiculturalism. These ideas are of course easier to discuss than to operationalize. Contact can be very rough; some borders are heavily guarded; some folks are stuck for various reasons in first space; multiculturalism can be so elastic a term as to lack significance. But you are very careful in how you approach these concerns. What is your latest thinking in this regard and how does such thinking relate to how you function in classrooms?

Mao: I have been thinking a little bit more about borderlands and third space as of late. In particular, I think of the complexity we need to accord to how third space both presents an opportunity and a challenge. In my own classroom practices, I have tried to share with my students both the need to advocate both the importance of third space, where transformative work can be attended to, and the realization that third space can also present problems, challenges, and complexities. I sometimes use the analogy to conversational dynamics. That is to say, who gets the floor and who selects the person next to speak, as it were, and how turn-taking gets dealt with in general present a set of serious issues for all of us who participate in the work in third space.

Gilyard: Let's go from the classroom to the community because you've mentioned that you've drawn inspiration from the Chinese American community in Cincinnati. This suggests that your scholarship and vision are grounded in everyday communal experiences, and that something substantive is at stake. You indicated earlier your desire to do transformative work. Would you elaborate upon how your relationship with that community or any community has spurred you to practice, as you have maintained, a different rhetoric?

Mao: In part I want to nurture and present a different kind of identity. Part of the inspiration you speak of has to do with this daily or weekly tension I experience: the tension between the desire not to be recognized and the desire to be recognized. This dual desire has a lot to do with the ongoing social, cultural, and political contexts. This tension has motivated me to articulate a discourse to talk about and, indeed, to further contribute to this participation by the Chinese American community in developing this American story.

Gilyard: What do both of you see as the work before you as you continue to explore questions of culture and rhetoric?

Mao: (to Haivan) Go ahead. You go first.

Hoang: (laughing) Studies of Asian American rhetoric are really just beginning to come into the conversation. But maybe my answer to what's needed is an extension to what you asked about memory earlier. One of the big gaps that I find in my own research is that I need more histories of the structural mechanisms that reinscribe race for Asian Americans. Some things are very basic common sense, like, in my ethnographic case study, one of the students I interviewed said that Asian Greeks, the fraternities and sororities, are not the same as the "real Greeks." At first, I thought, "What is he talking about?"

Gilyard: Where are the real Greeks?

Hoang: Right! The real Greeks. He was talking about how the Greeks have a lot of power in student government in terms of making decisions about the budget for undergraduate students. Of course, his comment about real Greeks makes sense if you think about how recently racial minorities have been in many universities and how old fraternity and sorority systems are. So some of the structural mechanisms that reinscribe race have become more subtle, but they're still there. We need more historical accounts of how these structural mechanisms are still in place, especially in less overt ways. This relates to your earlier question about memory because I think what memory allows us to do is to look at an actual cultural site and the layers of memory there. What Asian American rhetoric is in that instance is the response to that lived site and all those retentions.

Gilyard: Right.

Hoang: So, one, there's need for more historical work on structural mechanisms that reinscribe race. Two, we need more identification of how these memorial sites persist.

Mao: I want to echo what Haivan just said.

Gilyard: Prompt her to go first, then echo. Slick.

Mao: Let me just add two more points to make it symmetrical.

Gilyard: Okay.

Mao: (laughing) One has to do with the issue of representation. Lately, I've been thinking more about representation, whether its re-presentation as well as representation. And especially re-presentation of Asian American rhetoric and how such a speech act is imbued with politics, identity issues, and then discursive practices. I want certainly to do more work on this particular issue in relation to our current project called *Representations: Doing Asian American Rhetoric.*

Gilyard: This is a collection?

Mao: Yes.

Gilyard: That's great. I've been asking for this kind of stuff for a long time. If you remember, we were on a panel and I was asking for it from you.

Mao: You have been one of the motivating forces behind all of this work. So that is one. The other thing I have been thinking about, in the connection with third space, is exploring the product that comes out of third space, the product that often—like ethnic rhetorics, Asian American rhetorics—has been seen as something that mediates between the first and the second. I want to complicate this notion of mediation. I think it is more than mediation. Perhaps it messes things up. Perhaps it actually disrupts the first and second rather than mediates. The Latin term *tertium quid* means "the third." And tertium quid has often been constructed as a mediating force. More specifically, the term tertium quid, I think according to OED, is a third chemical that mediates the first and second chemicals. I want to mess up this tertium-quid implication and examine, instead, the extent to which the dynamics are disruptive.

Hoang: For significantly more work to be done in Asian American rhetoric, more students will need to see the value of English studies and the humanities and social sciences as a whole. I talked to a graduate student last week who was interested in American Studies initially and now thinks she's interested in Black English and Rhetoric and Composition. I told her that these are not mutually exclusive things. Just because disciplines define themselves in certain ways doesn't mean that we can't draw from different streams, and, in fact, we should. If we're talking about racial minorities, for example, and following the work of most historians of composition, who tend to look within the university, we can only go back so far. So on the Rhetoric and Composition side, we need to encourage students to explore other areas within English and within the humanities and social sciences. There seem to be a lot of graduate students who've expressed interest in Asian American rhetoric during meetings of the Asian/Asian American caucus at CCCC. It's hard for me to tell whether they're going to do research in this area because it's hard for graduate students to come to conferences every year. I haven't seen enough of them come regularly that I would be able to guess. But I am glad that some of them are interested in Asian American rhetoric and have asked people like Morris and LuMing questions about what their sources are.

Gilyard: All of us really just have to mine this potential, take advantage of the interest. Not just any particular small group of scholars but the whole field

Hoang: Can I ask you a question?

Gilyard: Sure.

Hoang: A few years ago, you responded to a panel that LuMing, Morris, and Terese Guisantao Monberg were on.

Mao: That was five or six years ago.

Gilyard: Maybe at CCCC in Denver

Mao: I think 2001.

Hoang: You asked the question—

Mao: You remember? (laughing)

Hoang: You asked the question of whether Asian American rhetoric was about the rhetoric that came out of Asian American bodies or if Asian American rhetoric was a distinct system analogous to the linguistic system of Black English. That question has been confounding me for a long time.

Gilyard: It's like the question of what African American art is. Or of what Chinese art is. You can always say it's what Chinese artists produce. But we can also look at characteristic—though not necessarily unique—forms or traits that have evolved in a particular context and determine with a relative degree of assurance that it's Chinese art. It's the same way I can listen to a stranger talking on the other end of the telephone and make pretty good guesses about ethnicity. Like the guy that does those studies about racial attitudes and changes his accent while on the phone.

Mao: John Baugh! His work on linguistic profiling.

Gilyard: Right, John Baugh. If I pick up the phone and pay attention to semantics or phonology, I can make some educated guesses about, say, whether an Asian American is on the other end of the line. I also can get fooled because linguistic forms and what some members of an ethnic group speak do not exist in a precise one-to-one correspondence. In any event, the forms vs. body argument can go on forever. I stay away from absolute claims about bodies and focus on cultural forms. Of course, culture travels. Because you produce a form doesn't mean you own it forever. But that's just the way I like to get conversations going. Can we look at some forms? It's just circular reasoning to say Asian American rhetoric is what Asian Americans speak. LuMing is resisting me a little bit on this. But some of my questioning, including in Denver, is an attempt to push on the question of forms.

Hoang: Specifically, in relation to African American English and African American rhetoric, you have a linguistic system versus a rhetorical system. A linguistic system, as I understand it, seems to be a description of a grammar that is pervasive, right, a system that is alive every day among many people. The cultural forms of a rhetorical system are usually more of the most valued forms, not necessarily the ones we use every day. It's an art.

Gilyard: That's one way we can look at it.

Hoang: So I was wondering if you saw that distinction as well or—

Gilyard: I guess the model I had in mind—I believe I mentioned it on the panel—was Geneva Smitherman's *Talkin and Testifyin*. I was wondering if it were viable to look for an Asian American parallel to that work. In continuing to think along those lines, I find useful your distinction between linguistics and rhetoric, though I'm not sure how far I want to push that distinction. But it certainly can be productive to talk about linguistics as that which speaks to the question of entire verbal systems and rhetoric as that which has to do with which elements of the system will be used strategically or, as you say, artfully. But you folks are turning the table on me, questioning me.

Mao: Hey, we have you here

Gilyard: I remember somebody from the audience remarking that forms could be recorded and specified but that it wasn't clear that it should be done. I don't remember the possible objection, what the explanation was. However, it made sense at the time.

Hoang: Well, I guess it depends on what form that recording would take. I mean if you look at the traditional rhetorical tradition, the early texts that we go to were written as sort of instructional rhetorics, right?

But then, it gets complicated if we say, "Oh, here's an Asian American rhetorical treatise. Now you do it." I guess that would be complicated. I don't know how I would handle that.

Gilyard: Well, you don't have to handle it right now because we're out. I want to thank you folks for hanging out with me in my hometown of New York City at yet another CCCC.

Bronwyn T. Williams is a professor of English at the University of Louisville. He writes and teaches on issues of literacy, popular culture, and identity. His publications include *Tuned In: Television and the Teaching of Writing* (Boynton/Cook), *Identity Papers: Literacy and Power in Higher Education* (Utah State Press), *Popular Culture and Representations of Literacy*, with Amy A. Zenger (Routledge), and *Shimmering Literacies: Popular Culture and Reading and Writing Online* (Peter Lang).

The Conversation

Keith Gilyard: In your work, especially *Tuned In: Television and the Teaching of Writing*, as well as in your collaboration with Amy Zenger, *Popular Culture and Representations of Literacy*, you help to demonstrate how literacy proliferates as a trope in film. You see literacy functioning in film as an indicator of social phenomena, as a marker of individual identity, and as a statement about power. You also indicate that how audiences perceive these representations is uncertain to you and is an area of study worth pursuing. Could you summarize your thinking on these matters and project ahead in terms of the research you envision might be done?

Bronwyn Williams: I'm always wary of seeing popular culture as a totalizing thing and only in terms of binaries—that it either overdetermines and people have no control over it or that people can resist it completely. Margaret Morse, in her book *Virtualities: Television, Media Art, and Cyberculture*, uses the metaphor of a membrane. A membrane is permeable. The effects of popular culture come through but that doesn't mean that everything comes through or that people then don't find ways of adapting what comes through into their own lives. Dominant ideologies are sometimes reproduced, and yet people also resist them if they don't make sense to them in their own situations. I have used films to get at issues of patterns and power, and students have responded in interesting ways. For example, I sometimes have students write literacy narratives. They do some initial writing about their experiences along with watching some clips from *Shakespeare in Love* and *Office Space*. They see some of the different ways that authorship and power play out. I ask them, "Okay, in these movies, who gets to read? Who gets to write? And in your own life who gets to read and who gets to write?" The hope is that they bring a more critical—

Gilyard: Who gets to be the author? Who gets to be published?

Williams: Right. I hope they become more critical in their literacy narratives. I want them to move past their initial formulations, which often run along the lines, "Well, I liked writing because this one teacher liked me." There is also a set of cultural influences that were and are operating.

Gilyard: One can sometimes grow weary, you know, looking for literacy metaphors. Even I get tired of that at times, but I think that ultimately your work has enriched my movie watching. Now I'm wondering, given your interest in film and television, if you think of devoting particular attention in class to films *about* films and *about* television. *Network* would be an obvious example. I'm also thinking of *How I Got into College*, in which video is used to displace test scores and the admissions essay. Also *Crazy in Alabama*, in which the main character is driven by the desire to be a television star, and *White Men Can't Jump*, which was on television just this past week. I was channel surfing and saw it once again. Much of the plot revolves around preparations for an appearance on *Jeopardy*. I'm assuming you saw or heard about these films.

Williams: Yes. And your point is interesting. I think I introduce elements of what you're talking about as I go along, but I haven't done it as a complete course.

Gilyard: You probably wouldn't want to do it as a complete course. People would probably get sick of it by the end of the semester. It was just an idea. You had me thinking so much about literacy and film that I just started thinking of films about literacy and films about film.

Williams: And one can observe the mediating influence of television. For example, in *White Men Can't Jump*, the identity of the Rosie Perez character is partly shaped by the quiz show. The show really rewrites her identity within the romantic relationship and for us in the film as we watch it. Another interesting thing I see happening in films—*American Beauty* comes to mind first—is kids shooting videos. The project I'm working on now is about participatory online popular culture and the kinds of literacy practices that people are doing.

Gilyard: Well, I want to talk more about that later.

Williams: *American Beauty* seems to me an interesting move toward that, and it's not the only film I've noticed that features kids with cameras.

Gilyard: Well, a recent example is *Disturbia*. The kid is under house arrest because of various mischievous adventures, so peeking into other people's windows and lives with his video camera becomes his primary social outlet. Then he shoots up on something suspicious, even horrible.

Williams: And, thinking more about television, I'm reminded that there is indeed an interesting genre of television shows about television shows. You know, "The Mary Tyler Moore Show," "Sports Night," and the recent ones like "Thirty Rock." Now, of course, like most shows, these are more about relationships than about television. Still, though, there are interesting issues of representation and reality, the kind of stuff that could be fun to work with in a class.

Gilyard: Did you see *How I Got into College?*

Williams: I have not seen that one. I got a sense of what it's about--

Gilyard: How about *Crazy in Alabama?*

Williams: Yeah, I did see that.

Gilyard: That's a crazy movie. Melanie Griffith is a true nut in that one. I want to get your take on a couple more literacy-film connections. These are favorites of mine that I never thought of in terms of literacy until I read your work. The first is *Heat*. I don't know why *Heat* came to me, but I recalled that the Amy Brenneman character, Eady, hangs out in a bookstore, a fact that gives her credibility with the audience, or at least I suppose you would theorize that. Then the De Niro character shows an interest in her work, which blocks her from reading him well, though the audience already knows the gangster that he is. She's not attuned to that because he takes an interest in what she's doing, which is connected to print literacy.

Williams: Yeah, he's reading when they meet at the bookstore. He's reading an architecture book or an engineering book or something like that, right? So it's not like he's just reading *Playboy* or a NASCAR book. I mean, she makes class assumptions about him based on how he's dressed but also based on which bookstore section he's in. But gender identifications factor in as well. She's in a bookstore with him as opposed to some other kind of business where they could have been. She's not a waitress, you know. So we read her as educated in a certain way. We read her as a member of a certain class. And she's in an acceptable profession, not a criminal like him. Moreover, he's reading for instrumental means, how to blow open a bank vault. And one gets the sense that literacy for her is a job, yes, but also her passion. She's a graphic artist or something like that. I forget. But literacy for her is a state of grace. It makes me think about Sylvia Scribner's piece on literacy in three metaphors. We get the sense that literacy reveals Eady's inner character in some way. When I think of that scene, I think of gender roles and class markers, which is how I think literacy so often gets used in movies, really quick class and gender markers based on what kind of reading and writing the character is doing.

Gilyard: You're very clear on that. I mean you and Amy Zenger are all over this. But it reminds me of when I started looking at literacy themes in African American fiction years ago. It messed up my reading of African American novels for a few years. It was like learning about Freud. You start kicking over every chair or upturning every rock and you see the psychoanalytic principles you're already looking for. It was like, "Aw man, when am I going to get through this period?"

Williams: Well, I had the boys helping me do this, too.

Gilyard: The twins!

Williams: They'd come home and say, "Dad! Dad! *Spiderman 2*! He's reading poetry."

Gilyard: Then there's *The Godfather*, Tom's literacy when he's the consigliere. Because he is literate in the legal system, especially the aspects most relevant to the Corleones, he rejects Kay's letter. You know, they have this scene in which she says, "Can you give this to Michael?" And she represents the good literacy, schoolteacher, right? And she wants him to pass along the letter to Michael. So literacies clash there. Literacy doesn't signify one particular thing in that scene.

Williams: I was thinking about *The Godfather* and the way literacy operates in *The Godfather* and *Godfather II*. You don't see literacy when they're dealing with the family. You know, even with the five families, they get together and meet around a conference table face to face where they embrace and they can look each other in the eye. But they use literacy when they're dealing with the outside institutional world, with law, when Michael says, for example, "He's a crooked cop. We got some newspaper reporters on the payroll that would like that story." In *Godfather II*, when Michael's in front of a Senate committee, he starts reading his written statement. It seems to me that literacy is one way they try, Tom also but Michael particularly, to establish legitimacy. Michael is always talking about taking the family legitimate, and he seems to understand that if he's going to be taken legitimately that these institutional literacies are a part of how that happens. He has to have those mastered.

Gilyard: I didn't dig that deeply. I only thought of one scene. You got the whole *Godfather* mapped out, and *Godfather II*, probably *Godfather III* also.

Williams: It's my favorite movie, you know. But you don't see Vito thinking about literacy like that. The one time he does, the one time that I can think of, is when they raise the sign on the store, which is, again, their move towards legitimacy. You put up a sign that announces that you have a legitimate business. That might be taking it a little too far.

Gilyard: I don't think so.

Williams: Anyway, that's where I went with that. It would be interesting to see if literacy works similarly in other crime films relative to the question of establishing legitimacy. And another thing about Kay, she's a teacher but we never see her actually teaching.

Gilyard: Right. And then Tom's literacy trumps hers when she came with the letter. She couldn't get anywhere with that.

Williams: That's true. And I think it also points again to the gender split. Hers is a letter of love, right? Hers is establishing relationships. His literacy is about business. Business, not personal. He likes Kay, but that's not going to interfere with his need to do business.

Gilyard: And when you think about the scene over in Sicily—you're talking about the legitimizing move—Michael is trying to teach his wife English. She's actually practicing when the car blows up, in addition to trying to learn how to drive. There's probably a whole lot more. I watch *The Godfather* at least twice a year, so I'll probably find some more stuff the next time I see it.

Williams: And it's also true, I think, that part of the reason Tom's literacy trumps Kay's is because she also understands the institutional power behind it. She doesn't really argue with him.

Gilyard: No.

Williams: She protests mildly, but she doesn't say, "Oh you're wrong. You can't do this."

Gilyard: He wins that one, no question. I want to move on to another feature in your work. You connect literacy to individualism, I focused on that point in your writing a couple of times. I see literacy as one possible expression of individuality, and, of course, I'm making a distinction between individuality as productive self-fulfillment and individualism as an expression of selfishness. Would you hold to your thoughts about individualism or might you expand that argument?

Williams: I think that's an interesting distinction. I guess I see individualism as an ideological force. When people are trying to make sense of the world, individualism says they should look after their own needs first. They should do what they want to do. Sort of the cliché of American singularity, you know, "I can do what I want to do; I can live where I want to live." That kind of thing. So that's how I think of that term. And about individuality, I think you're right. I mean, there's that empowering sense of literacy and I think that I would see that as a different, a connected phenomenon but a different one, maybe the other side of the coin. Individualism is some kind of limiting sense of what one needs to do at the expense of what the community needs, at the expense of other people.

Gilyard: That's what I'm saying.

Williams: Okay. But the other side of that is that I do believe that people should express themselves. I mean, I'm a writing teacher.

Gilyard: That's why I make the distinction. For me, individuality is that self-expression. You can connect it to an Emersonian sense, an Elbowian sense, whatever. And that's what democracy does or should do—guarantee the right of everyone to develop and express his or her individuality. But it seems to me, if I think in Deweyan terms for a minute, the expression of individuality is always to be done with reference to a community. The community shouldn't dictate all the actions of individuals, and the idea people often speak about of rugged individualism is to be applauded at times. But sometimes people champion individualism as though community never has to be considered.

Williams: Yeah, I can see that. The way that plays out in films sometimes is that there's a distinction between the film about the literary author and the film about the teacher. The author can be much more individualistic. He or she has to go off alone. He or she may have other relationships, but at some point the person goes off by himself or herself and is inspired. And it's often presented as happening at the expense of other relationships. It often seems, you know, really destructive almost or a selfish act. The teacher films are different. The triumphs there—the teachers', the students'—are as much about relationships between people as they are about literacy. In *Il Postino*, where you see the relationship between Pablo Neruda and the postman…

Gilyard: I love that movie…

Williams: Or in *Dead Poets Society*, where the idea is how do you make people more fulfilled, how do you make them richer as people? Or *Finding Forester*, where it's about how do you let this young man discover his gifts? In those films there is that kind of individual and yet relational kind of thing you're talking about.

Gilyard: Did you see *Akeelah and the Bee?*

Williams: I haven't seen that yet.

Gilyard: It's a noteworthy film with a community perspective. Akeelah's preparations for the National Spelling Bee take a dramatic turn for the better when the entire community gets involved. The concept is that five thousand teachers are better than one. So folks begin hanging up words all over the community. I think for your analyses you'll like this film. You'll want to look at it anyway.

Williams: Part of the reason I think the teaching movies are more about communities, more about relationships, is that the message is that anyone can succeed this way with the right support. The literary author films are often much more about their authors' distinctiveness, how much they're unlike the rest of us. I think that's why they may feel to me much more about individualism. The authors are set apart and they can do things that regular people cannot do. The focus is on that magical, romantic author.

Gilyard: Let's tune in to *Tuned In*, which is a valuable book. I really enjoyed it. You argue that writing is a powerful tool for learning but that it holds no monopoly over the enterprise of critical meaning making. The case for an exclusive focus on print literacy cannot be made on strictly rhetorical or interpretive grounds. However, linguists would argue, and I tend to agree here as well, that there does exist a privileged relationship between reading and writing. Elements of the written code, many of which are not taught explicitly, even an ear for the written code, are acquired through reading immersion. It seems that this linguistic consideration has to be accounted for in a thorough discussion of print literacy and writing curriculums.

Williams: I don't disagree with any of that. What I think I'm arguing in *Tuned In* is two things. One is that we don't usually present the case to our students explicitly enough about what print literacy is, what it does, and what it does differently than images, visuals, electronic literacy. Two, we don't think enough or talk to students enough about what they do rhetorically and semiotically with popular culture. There are rhetorical ideas to examine, particularly in terms of concepts such as audience, genre, and narrative. What we need to do more of—and I guess you know I'm piggybacking on what Cindy Selfe says about affordances and what Kathleen Welch says about electronic rhetoric and delivery—is discuss with students the composing choices they make with films and images. We can talk about the particular effects, and the reasons for those effects, that certain choices are likely to produce. So we can discuss those things and also talk about those visual choices in relation to print language, what different media allow. When I'm talking to first-year students, I sometimes indicate, broadly speaking, the difference between exteriors and interiors. What images allow you to do is juxtapose exteriors in ways that create sign systems and interesting ideas. What print can do differently is move you inside, move you into interiors recursively and slowly. It allows you to slow down, and slowing down is very important. So, again, I would not disagree with your comments. Part of what I'm arguing is that if we better understand how students are using images and electronic media, we can better make the case for some of the things we want them to do with writing.

Gilyard: I think you have the right take. We need better than knee-jerk opposition to using popular culture, particularly film and television, in the classroom. People point to the interpretive and rhetorical abilities developed by writing. But you can develop those abilities through film and television, so that cannot be the only case you make for writing. That's the reason I bring in the linguistic angle to strengthen the case for writing, though I don't think the profession as a whole does it enough in theoretical terms.

Williams: No, and the scholars of popular culture generally don't consider enough the literacy that popular culture requires. Television isn't without writing, you know. There are all kinds of print being used in particular ways. We're not engaging with that very well and showing the way that print is different. For example, take the little crawl at the bottom of CNN. We could get students to think about what that does or doesn't do for them compared with the kinds of assignments we are asking them to do for class. What is the difference for them between the words they are seeing on the screen and what the person is saying on the screen? I'm certainly for strengthening, as you are, the practice of print literacy. But I also think, sort of going back, as you mentioned, to Dewey and certainly through Freire, we just don't engage students enough about their experiences. We have to be more productive in that sense. We can't settle for merely rendering the critique, "Well, yes, that was your experience and weren't you a fool for doing it?"

Gilyard: Near the close of *Tuned In*, you assert that teaching that ignores popular culture supports capitalist oppression. I underlined that because that assertion begs for elaboration.

Williams: Did I say that?

Gilyard: Oh, it's there.

Williams: Well, that's what happens near the end of a book when you start bursting into song, as it were. I think what I was trying to get at with that statement, in that section of the book, is to some extent what I was just talking about. I mean, I am influenced by my wife, Mary Brydon-Miller, who, as you know, worked with Paulo Freire when she was in graduate school. So I approach from a Freirean idea of trusting that people have knowledge of their own experiences and have worthwhile things to say about them. Teachers bring their own experiences and expertise but can learn from students as well. It has to be a genuinely dialogic process, not superficial. Unfortunately, I think what happened to Freire in composition pedagogy—and to Donald Murray and some others—is that some of the disciples gained fervor and lost nuance. So you have to be careful to ensure genuine dialogue. Moreover, I think composition in some sites is still dominated by the idea that instructors, in the first-year classroom in particular, have to get students into academic discourse, get them into a particular way of thinking and writing. And I certainly think that you need to be getting students to understand the way literacy and power interact, the way institutions set conventions, the way to understand those conventions rhetorically in terms of the literacy practices. At the same time, though, I think if the message to students is that their prior experiences as readers, whether of print or popular culture, are going to be shut out of the classroom and left unexamined both from rhetorical literacy perspectives and from a cultural studies and materialist perspective, then, in fact, taking this sort of academic higher ground allows the dominant ideology to reproduce itself, and that does reinforce social inequalities and capitalist oppression. I probably just wanted to use the term *capitalist oppression,* you know. Power to the people and all that. But, seriously, I'm thinking in terms of dialogue and critical education, of a collaborative and respectful effort with students.

Gilyard: Earlier you mentioned the new work. You're going online?

Williams: Yeah.

Gilyard: What are you doing there?

Williams: I did the research for *Tuned In* about ten years ago. A few of the students were going on the Internet doing stuff involving popular culture, but not many at all. Now so many watch clips online; they're in discussion forums; they're writing fan fiction. You know, there's an "About Me" section on a *MySpace* page that is probably the least important thing on the page. Most of the rest of the content is popular culture: lists of favorite movies, images of Orlando Bloom or Johnny Depp, songs. So on these social networking sites they're creating these collages of identity through popular culture. They also go on *Television Without Pity* or other fan-forum sites and engage in long print debates about popular culture. And there's an increasing body of work about participatory online popular culture and the way that's really shifting. We've gone from a popular culture of quilting and square dances to a mass popular culture—from a means of production so heavily capitalized that you had a mass audience and very few people producing to this interactive thing where young people are expecting to be able to participate in a variety of ways. Very often they appropriate popular culture texts, write back to them, mix, sample, just do all the kind of stuff that's now possible because of technology. At the same time, it seems to me that we've done a lot in Rhetoric and Composition and literacy studies about what happens when people read and write online. All of this is to say my project is at the nexus of the work on popular culture and the work on online writing. How is popular culture influencing the online literacy practices that these young people are engaged in outside of the classroom primarily? The global nature of how pop culture is being written about and redistributed is also really intriguing to me. Twenty years ago, you watched a television show at night and maybe talked to the guy next door. Now you can be talking to somebody in Australia or Kenya or Italy.

Gilyard: Your mention of Australia reminds me of how by using e-mail I began to pay attention to the way time has collapsed in a sense. Sending messages and almost instantly receiving responses from around the country had become mundane, so I had some sense of the phenomenon. But then I wanted to contact this scholar who worked at an Australian university; I thought of that as so far away. I e-mailed her—and had a response within fifteen minutes. So I have a different frame of mind now. But that's just an aside. I want to touch on the conversation about how to characterize the textual output on *IM* or *MySpace*. Some would say it's more orality than it is literacy. It seems to be a sort of in-between discourse. What's your view?

Williams: It's in-between and it also varies. If you look at something like instant messaging, text messaging, or some of these massive multi-player games like *War Craft* or *Second Life*, the language is as close to orality as you can make print—the abbreviations, the lack of punctuation—because people are trying to type as fast as they can talk. But not everything is like that. When you look at some of the fan forums for movies and television and so on, the writing is much more conventional—punctuation, sentences. There's slang, but it's more like the way people used to write letters to one another. And they're really often engaging. I mean these forums go on and on for pages. Writers are cutting and pasting another person's comments, refuting them, taking a lot of care with argument. You can tell that they really composed the message and that it's not just off the top of their head. So some online writing is like orality but not all. I think that in itself is what's interesting, the way the context is shaping or changing the performance of self and the way that's getting reflected in the conventions and in the rhetorical positioning of people.

Gilyard: What are some other aspects of your project?

Williams: The other thing I've been particularly interested in is the way the work I do in literacy and identity and popular culture just keeps getting closer and closer together. At first, the areas were sort of separate to me. But now people can do more of the different kinds of performances of identity online, and *multimodality* is sort of the word of the moment. So instructors are having students make films in class and post them on *YouTube* and things like that. But I think it's often done without thinking deeply about the pop culture tropes that these students have learned about film and the identity parts of that. In other words, if you're not talking about film and about television and about class and race and gender to students as they're putting together a film for class, then they're not really doing a very critical piece of work with respect to those issues. Then the instructor is really horrified or surprised because the student project lacked an expected critical content and was merely imitative of some movie. But where do you expect them to go for their models?

Gilyard: I haven't looked much at the identity work concerning online communities, but you know one of the issues is that online participants don't have to deal with face-to-face parameters as they would in some other identity-negotiating situations. They can just appropriate an identity and drop in on chat rooms. So what's real and not real? It's like the white guy who wrote the slave narrative. He studied the literary and rhetorical conventions, and by the time the hoax was discovered he had raised enough money and was over in England, I think. Paid and out. Slave narrative or not? But in any case not a slave's narrative.

Williams: Right. I sometimes wonder, as I think about what I write, how much I could go online and appropriate other identities. I think I'm a pretty good liar, but I don't really know how good a liar I am. Would something seem wrong if I tried to write as a woman? Would I give myself away rhetorically or linguistically at some point?

Gilyard: But novelists create these performances all the time.

Williams: I know they do.

Gilyard: Male novelists like Al Young write first-person narratives with the main character being female.

Williams: So the question I have now is whether we are going to have a generation of people who know how to do that even better? What is really happening when they go on *Second Life* and become a rabbit or something? Are they learning rhetorical ways of repositioning their identity? The other part of it, though, is that I think a lot of times people keep going to the sites that don't challenge their identity but reinforce it. I mean, who's going to *BlackPlanet* in general and posting or who's going to a NASCAR site? Sometimes the online site is a reinforcing mechanism. Sometimes it's a place where people are doing some of these more playful things. But even on *Second Life*—you can be anything you want to be there—people tend to make their avatars fairly close to themselves in appearance, age, etc. That's what the early research seems to be indicating. I wonder why people do that. Why, if you can be anything, would you choose to be the same person? I haven't done any work on that, but to me that's an interesting question.

Gwendolyn D. Pough is an Associate Professor of Writing, Rhetoric, Women's and Gender Studies at Syracuse University. She is the author of *Check It While I Wreck It: Black Womanhood, Hip-Hop Culture, and the Public Sphere* as well as numerous essays and articles on black feminism, hip-hop, critical pedagogy, and black public culture. She has co-edited a special issue of the journal *FEMSPEC: an interdisciplinary feminist journal dedicated to critical and creative works in the realms of science fiction, fantasy, magical realism, surrealism, myth, folklore, and other supernatural genres*, and she has co-edited the critically acclaimed *Home Girls Make Some Noise: A Hip-Hop Feminism Anthology*. She is the Assistant Chair of the Conference on College Composition and Communication. In this four-year term on the officers' team she will move from Assistant Chair to Associate Chair to Chair and finally Immediate Past Chair. She writes romance fiction under the pen name Gwyneth Bolton. She has eight novels and a novella published to date and has won several awards for creative writing.

The Conversation

Keith Gilyard: *Check It While I Wreck: Black Womanhood, Hip-Hop Culture, and the Public Sphere* is an important book, the first expansive statement in Rhetoric and Composition about hip-hop by a member of the hip-hop generation, one whose connection to hip-hop goes back virtually to kindergarten. Your own history, your sense of history, and your grasp of public sphere theory make for a compelling mix. I think you oversell your point at times. For example, black women are not always *the* reason, as you suggest, that a so-called black prince is able to shine in the public sphere. But I do get your point about the crucial and sometimes overlooked role of African American women in the freedom struggle. As that struggle continues, I'm interested in whatever expanded or updated comment you might make about the *rhetoric of wreck,* a concept you developed wonderfully in your book and is a construct related, as you point out, to ideas of talking back, going off, turning it out, throwing a niggerbitchfit, and being a diva. You suggest, partly following Jill Nelson, that these discursive strategies can be important ways to effect change. Could you point to specific instances?

Gwendolyn Pough: Being able to really measure the work that wreck or acting out or talking back has done in the larger public sphere becomes somewhat difficult, but I think we can indeed point to instances. In the book, I point to Queen Latifah and her song "Ladies First" as an example of bringing wreck. I think contemporary examples exist. Michelle Obama could be an instance, though I haven't yet figured out how to theorize her. I sense she's bringing wreck but in a different way than I usually discuss.

Gilyard: Well, the media wouldn't let her throw anything close to a niggerbitchfit without crucifying her.

Pough: They won't let her have a niggerbitchfit. I don't know if she *would* have one. But I think that what she represents, the way she carries herself, brings wreck to all of those stereotypical notions of black womanhood.

Gilyard: So that suggests there are additional categories of *wreck* because she, her disrupting quality, won't fit into one of the categories you previously indicated. It's interesting, though, because some wish they could force her into one of those categories. They want to say, for example, that she's turning it out, in a sense, when she makes comments about being proud of the country for the first time. They take the comment out of context and construct her as having some sort of fit.

Pough: They want to paint her as this angry black woman whose words, therefore, cannot be trusted. This would mean, of course, that *she* cannot be trusted. But she won't hold still for that type of stereotyping.

Gilyard: But she's doing *something.*

Pough: Right. As I say, I have to theorize to see exactly how she relates to the ideas I have had about *wreck*. I certainly would love to conduct research about Michelle Obama.

Gilyard: Sticking with the idea of stereotypes for a moment, I am reminded of a presentation that characterized Queen Latifah as a mammy figure. This contrasts to your claim that she brings *wreck*, disrupts stereotypes.

Pough: Well, some of her movie choices give support to the mammy thesis. In *Bringing down the House*, she plays the recently released prisoner who is taking care of the little white children. But even in that film, with its high level of buffoonery, there are moments in which she is critical, like when one of the white characters wants her to sing an old Negro spiritual. I look at Queen Latifah in terms of her overall contribution, which I think is clearly positive, especially with respect to the music.

Gilyard: This makes me think again of Michelle Obama. I haven't heard about her musical preferences. I know Barack is mainly an old school, Gladys Knight and the Pips guy, with some Jay-Z thrown in. I've heard him talk about this. He's pumped steady Stevie Wonder on the campaign trail.

Pough: I've never heard her talk about her musical preferences.

Gilyard: She's forty-four, right?

Pough: Yeah, she's hip-hop generation. Both of them are.

Gilyard: For your theorizing about her persona, it would be interesting what connections you could make to hip-hop, including her possible embrace of some of hip-hop's critique. Now all she's giving us is the dream. You know, I come from these humble origins in Chicago, value education, and love America. Don't go by what I said before.

Pough: I know. I always loved America. *Been* proud. But, I mean, so what if she didn't? So what if she hasn't been? So what?

Gilyard: She has a perfect right to be indignant and disappointed at times, and we don't always have to read her remarks all that literally. You can't come with the hard press all the time. I mean, the idea that she and Barack are some kind of undercover terrorists or terrorist-sympathizers is ridiculous. What you see with Barack is pretty much what you get. He's all right, even a corny dude sometimes. After Michelle spoke at the convention, he told her she was cute. Of all the things he could have emphasized at that moment? Come on, Barry!

Pough: Yeah. (laughter)

Gilyard: I recall a question you posed in your essay "Personal Narratives and Rhetorics of Black Womanhood in Hip Hop." That was for my collection *Rhetoric and Ethnicity*, and you spoke similarly in your own book. You asked, in effect, "How can one develop a rhetoric of black womanhood against the contemporary and historical representations of hip-hop culture?" I see that question as still relevant, and I wonder what your present answer would be. Of course, part of the answer is the nearly 500-page anthology *Home Girls Make Some Noise*, which you edited with Elaine Richardson, Aisha Durham, and Rachel Raimist. In your introduction to that volume, you asked additional questions that you yourself may be among the most qualified people to answer. In other words, what should be the agenda or agendas of hip-hop feminism and how do such relate to Black feminist or womanist initiatives not expressly connected to hip-hop?

Pough: It's funny that you say that I should be the one.

Gilyard: Well, you sent out the questions.

Pough: When we sent out the call for papers, I had, of course, some sense of what *I* thought the agenda should be. But I really wanted to start this larger conversation. Although that conversation was good, some of the key points, to me, of a hip-hop feminism or black feminism weren't included. We didn't have a lot of people talking about HIV/AIDS, for example. That's the most pressing issue right now for any black feminist because of the alarming rates at which black women are succumbing to this disease.

Gilyard: That's not just a hip-hop concern.

Pough: Nope! Not just a hip-hop concern at all but definitely one that I think the hip-hop generation is particularly prone to because of some of the messages in the music.

Gilyard: Some of the artists are cognizant of the problem and are trying to address the issue in their art.

Pough: Some are. I mean, you have "Wrap It Up" campaigns that a lot of hip-hop artists are involved with. But you also have songs like "Bust It Baby" and "Superman Dat Ho." This is all going on at the same time.

Gilyard: Could you lay out more political items for a hip-hop agenda?

Pough: In other words, what does a hip-hop political agenda *really* look like?

Gilyard: I've been trying to find this out for a long time.

Pough: Yeah, what *does* it look like? Can there really be an expressly hip-hop political agenda? Or is it the case that an agenda is constructed that some but not all members of the hip-hop generation support? What I've seen so far is get-out-the-vote stuff. "Rock the Vote."

Gilyard: At least "Rock the Vote" is coded advocacy. When you hear Wyclef talking, he's really saying vote for Obama. That's how the commercial functions. But when we've heard Russell Simmons or LL Cool J talk along the lines of "Get out the Vote," they have often refrained from endorsing candidates. Their focus has been on getting youth to exercise their franchise. And that's cool. But a politics has to have opinions and platforms. A politics is about who is going to get what access to goods and services. What are the strategies or structures in place or that you will advocate for that affect how goods and services will circulate among the populace? This is basic. A political agenda addresses these questions specifically. I don't hear anything articulated that I could call a hip-hop politics.

Pough: I agree. And when people throw around terms like *hip-hop mayor*—we heard that a lot in connection with Kwame Kilpatrick—what does that mean besides the fact that some candidate or office holder is in his or her thirties or forties?

Gilyard: That's all I can see that it means so far. Maybe hip-hop agenda is not the way to look at things. You know, as I've said on other occasions, folks didn't talk about the soul music political agenda. It was the Civil Rights Movement because it was a response to a specific lack of civil rights.

Pough: That's another thing. You had strong political efforts going on simultaneous with major cultural movements. You had Black Arts along with Black Power. We need a stronger cultural-political connection. Now you do have activists, maybe feminist activists, working on issues like HIV/AIDS or reproductive freedom. And some of them are using hip-hop in their activism, but the focus is, say, reproductive freedom—

Gilyard: With a hip-hop twist—

Pough: Yeah. But the activism is there. And you have critique in some of the music—Mos Def, Talib Kweli, Dead Prez. A lot of artists that have messages in the music still. But critique alone is not a political agenda.

Gilyard: Dead Prez claim to be socialists.

Pough: They claim a specific political identity, the others not so much. You can't have a politics about social justice if your primary message is about getting paid.

Gilyard: If that's your first principle, and sometimes only principle, you have no critique in service of social justice. Anything can be justified—artistic taste, misogynist lyrics, why you signed with a particular label, why you released a certain CD—by expressing the primary imperative to get paid. Maybe talk about artistic freedom goes along with that, but folks often trade in the artistic freedom for getting paid. When your main principle is money, and that money is connected to artistic production, you won't see or hear much social criticism in that artistic production. You have no moral ground on which to stand to criticize the slave master. Ol' Massa was doing what he was supposed to do.

Pough: Massa got paid.

Gilyard: Folks packing all those dark bodies up and flipping them to the other side of the big pond. The slave trade. The traders had to get paid! You have to undergo a rigorous personal critique to develop a rigorous social critique for the purpose of achieving social justice. You can't get too far along that journey if the only idea that matters is getting paid.

Pough: I think some people are still looking for the second coming of Martin Luther King, Jr. That may or may not ever happen, but I'm pretty sure such a person won't come from a pool of rappers trying to sign with major labels. Rappers want to get signed, want to make money. We can't expect Jay-Z to be the one to lead us. (laughter)

Gilyard: Right, but he *told* you that. He's exclusively about money. So you have to count on him to be him. I think your mention of King is interesting, though. I think people, especially black people, talk a lot about, maybe wish for, compelling, charismatic leaders. But that creates unrealistic expectations when they try to map the possibilities inherent in a preacher-activist like King on to, say, an Obama. He's trying to become Chief Executive, applying for a job within a certain structure and within certain structural limits.

Pough: King didn't work with an official role in that structure. He could say lot of things that Obama is not going to say. Some people want Obama to be this merger of King and Kennedy and maybe even Malcolm, but it's not going to happen. And a lot of people would be and maybe are going to be disappointed.

Gilyard: He's a politician.

Pough: This doesn't mean he can't make a difference as president.

Gilyard: Well, I'm pretty sure he's not the type of person who would drag us into a war on a pretense about weapons of mass destruction.

Obviously, he would try to influence the courts in a certain kind of way. So there are differences he can make. But he's not going to critique capitalism as the latter King did.

Pough: He'll talk some about economic justice but not too much. *It's not like all of a sudden we gon get reparations for real-for real.* His positions will always be somewhat moderate.

Gilyard: And the politically wise know that. But let's turn from politics to pedagogy, or at least from presidential politics to the politics of teaching. In talking about the value of hip-hop as related to pedagogy, a connection you maintain we all should recognize, you speak of the classroom as a training ground for discussions of diversity and citizenship. What are some of your more recent experiences with the pedagogy you describe in *Check It While I Wreck It?* How have your classes been operating? What have you done? What have you seen?

Pough: Since *Check It While I Wreck It,* I've been able to teach a series of classes focusing on women's rap and hip-hop feminism. This occurred at the University of Minnesota and is continuing at Syracuse University. So that's been good. And the classes have become varied in terms of the student population. The first time I taught a class like this, back at the University of Minnesota, there were only women on hand except for one guy. This one lone white guy who loved Eminem. He advocated for Eminem throughout the whole class. The classes at Syracuse have been mostly women, but there has been a little bit more of a mix. And it's been interesting trying to get students to take on certain conversations, having them look at homophobia, for example. I get them to look at hip-hop lyrics and try to make connections to the larger community and the homophobia that exists in the larger community. I get *guys* in the class to really think about sexism and sexist lyrics in different ways. I think one thing I really like about the teaching I'm doing now is that I'm getting students to think about diversity with respect to the group projects that I use in the class. They're working together around these issues, and it sets the scene for what they can do outside of the classroom. I've added activism projects.

Gilyard: What kind of projects have they been doing?

Pough: I have had students go around campus to conduct interviews with other students to find out their stances on a range of issues. This is an awareness-building activity. My students also have been involved in letter writing campaigns to magazines. All kinds of cool stuff.

Gilyard: Well that does sound cool. What has been the reception of *Check It While I Wreck It* in Rhetoric and Composition?

Pough: I don't think a lot of people in Rhet/Comp are aware of the book. It's used a lot in Women's Studies and African American Studies. But I haven't seen it a lot in this field, maybe a few people. I know some folks at Michigan State did use it, however.

Dr. Lee?

Gilyard: Maybe we can talk it up more. And talk up Gwyneth Bolton.

Pough: Gwyneth Bolton!

Gilyard: You know I have to get in some conversation about Gwyneth Bolton the romance novelist. How did that come about?

Pough: I always wanted to be a writer. As an undergraduate, I majored in writing. I was going write fiction. That's all I ever wanted to do.

Gilyard: That was in New Jersey, right?

Pough: Yes, William Paterson College. I was planning to be a fiction writer as well as a hip-hop artist, a rapper.

Gilyard: Oh you were going to be a rapper, too? We may get a CD from you down the road.

Pough: Like Cornel West. (laughter) Yeah, I might drop my CD. But I always wanted to be a writer, a fiction writer primarily. I write a poem every now and then, but I'm not really a poet. So fiction writing was always the major goal. But I also knew I wanted a job because the starving-artist idea didn't appeal to me. So I said I'll be a teacher and I'll teach college, not knowing all the preparation involved in getting to teach college. Once I went to graduate school and later took an academic post, I kind of forgot about creative writing because I just didn't have the time. I didn't have time in grad school, and I didn't have time on the tenure track. When I finished *Check It While I Wreck It,* I realized I could write a book and remembered that I had wanted to write a novel. So I decided to write a romance novel. That's how my series of novels began.

Gilyard: I read two. Not surprisingly, given who you are and who I am, I saw links to your academic work in Rhetoric and Composition. For example, *If Only You Knew,* which I enjoyed, says something about communication or lack thereof. Saying or, more accurately, what does not get said between Latonya and Carlton is a central theme in that book. You go to the other end of the spectrum in *Divine Destiny.* Telepathy, or optimum saying, is at work there, and negotiations go on about how to guard one's speech against intrusion. Moreover, in your collective narrative, which is how I'm thinking about these two books, you embed commentary about racism, oppression, and female agency. I don't imagine one sees that a lot in romance novels. So, as I read, I couldn't help but think of the author, Gwyneth Bolton, as Gwen Pough using the romance novel in a self-consciously rhetorical way.

Pough: I think some of it comes out thematically just because of who I am, but I don't think I'm trying to do Rhet/Comp stuff self-consciously. I met a woman who does academic work on romance novels. She read my novel *Sweet Sensation,* and she started explaining to me all these different things about language that she sees in the book. I thought, "Well, I guess I am a rhetorician, so..." Your comment reminds me of that. You know, I do literary analysis also. Every time I'm dealing with someone's literature now I'm thinking about whether the author is aware of the patterns. I'm thinking, "Okay, this person probably doesn't know." I don't think writers do. You're a poet.

Gilyard: Poets definitely know about patterns. And sometimes they also use poetry didactically. They do write to teach. I think if I wrote a novel now, and novelists know about patterns and tropes too, my motivation would be to teach. I would be consciously rhetorical for better or worse. Some folks would definitely say worse.

Pough: With *Divine Destiny*, I knew I wanted to do something about revolution. You know, I'm all about the Black Panthers and all—have always had that interest.

Gilyard: Right. And so much of the struggle involves language battles. Darwu attempts to control his partner Kara's thoughts, her dialogue with herself. She's trying to ward that off, trying to hold on to her own inner language. The meta-linguistic dimension just struck me as I read. That's why I wondered if you were purposely using the prose vehicle to make comments about language and power and identity. But from what I'm hearing you were just writing your novel with a revolutionary struggle in mind and the language angle just came out. I didn't read *Sweet Sensation*. It's hard for me to stay current because you publish so prolifically. You sent me postcards announcing three new joints! When do you write and how much of your time do these novels take? You spinning them out like crazy.

Pough: I write mostly late at night, and I try to write a little bit every day no matter what. I want to be constantly in my story. I tell myself I have to write 100 or 200 words per day. Usually, once I make myself sit down to my computer, I end up writing more than that. But if I don't sit at the computer, then I won't do anything. So I make myself sit down every day.

Gilyard: Sometimes the day that you don't write much is the price you pay for the days you manage to flow. You ultimately benefit from the discipline. I used to be disciplined like that.

Pough: Seems you still produce a lot of work.

Gilyard: But I'm obsessive-compulsive with it. I'm not getting in front of the computer every day. But I can also write for fifteen, sixteen hours at a time. Then I have to hang out, be the old guy at the club or something. The way you work, though, is a good model, a better model for graduate students. One student was asking me the other day about the discipline. I said, "You need to get some, you know. Write every day."

Pough: That's the best chance to finish that dissertation.

Gilyard: Did you write the same way then?

Pough: With the dissertation, I went on campus every day during the summer and just made myself sit there as a job. 9–5 every day.

Gilyard: You're just a pro. What does the future hold in terms of textual production for—I don't know what to say—Gwen or Gwyneth? I'll just say G. What is G planning to do?

Pough: G is gonna be on hold for a minute doing work for CCCC.

Gilyard: I forgot to mention that. Congratulations on your election to the officer rotation of CCCC. You'll handle it.

Pough: I would like to push forward some more on my scholarship, though. I'd like to finish my project on book clubs.

Gilyard: Is that archival or historical?

Pough: They're contemporary book clubs. I have been talking to book clubs across the country.

Gilyard: So you have a file that you have been compiling?

Pough: Yes. I did a survey, interviewed people.

Gilyard: You can't write eleven novels a year, do a monograph on book clubs, and get ready to be Chair of CCCC.

Pough: I'll have to put the novels on hold for a minute.

Gilyard: You can't put the novels on hold.
Pough: Gwen Pough is 'bout to take over. (laughter)

Gilyard: Really, you gon put the novels on hold? I was wondering how you were gon juggle all that. You can't put the novels on hold, though.

Pough: I think I'll have to. I can't figure out how else to do it.

Gilyard: You got to keep firing. Where do you get your ideas?

Pough: For the romance novels?

Gilyard: Yeah.

Pough: So far they've just been coming to me. I don't know how else to explain it.

Gilyard: Do you have a plot in advance or do you work the plot out through the writing of the story?

Pough: With the first two novels, *I'm Gonna Make You Love Me and If Only You Knew*, I worked out the plot as I went along. Then with *Divine Destiny*, the idea came to me and I started writing a bit and then I plotted it out. So it depends. Usually I can write about halfway through a novel; then I have to plot out the second half. But now since I am more moved to get a contract first, I have to write out the proposal and the synopsis before the contract.

Gilyard: How easy was it to get on? Easier than the music world, I think. You had better be glad you chose novel writing over the music.

Pough: Yeah, but the music world gives you more money if you hit. But in the romance novel industry you don't have to have an agent. You can sell without having an agent. So it's a little bit easier to get in. On the other hand, because it's such a large industry that produces so many books, the contracts are kind of boilerplates. You're not going to get rich writing romance novels.

Gilyard: But it's what you want to do, and that's important.

Ernest Stromberg is Associate Professor of Rhetoric, English, and Communication at California State University Monterey Bay. He has published journal articles and book chapters on American Indian literatures and rhetorics and is the editor of *American Indian Rhetorics of Survivance: Word Medicine, Word Magic* (University of Pittsburgh Press, 2006). Additional research interests include composition theory and pedagogy and embodied ways of teaching and learning.

The Conversation

Victor Taylor: We are beginning with the beginning. Describe the intellectual and academic context within which you decided to study rhetoric?

Ernest Stromberg: I began graduate school in the early 1990s at the University of Oregon. I had completed my Bachelor's degree in English in the mid-eighties and then left school to earn money and to figure out what to do with the rest of my life (an experience probably not that uncommon among English majors). My decision to return to school for graduate work was precipitated by my participation in a summer classics program in Greece. Led by a philosophy professor, the program encompassed six weeks of travel and study across various locations in Greece. Surrounded by students either still in their undergraduate programs or freshly graduated from a range of schools, including UCLA, Harvard, Yale, Humboldt State, and the University of Nebraska, I found myself back in an arena where questions of ontology and epistemology were considered vital and primary. This experience reawakened my own passion for ideas and learning, and I knew I needed to return to school.

Shortly after returning from that study abroad experience, I began applying to graduate programs in English with frankly little understanding of what graduate school was about. In hindsight, I can see that the gap of time between the completion of my undergraduate degree and my decision to pursue graduate work may have put me at something of a disadvantage from those students who apply for graduate programs directly out of their undergraduate program in that I was now in a context with no mentors to guide me in the process of applying and only the vaguest sense of what I wanted to study. As I work with undergraduates planning to pursue graduate work in the humanities and note how competitive the process has become, I consider myself fortunate to have been accepted into a Ph.D. in English with only a very vague project in mind on the study of American Indian literatures.

My interest in American Indian literature was sparked by a class on "Ethnic American Literature" that I took as an undergraduate. On a side note, I find it somewhat encouraging that many of the texts we studied in that class now, twenty years later, are regularly included in the standard survey of American literature class. In that class we read several American Indian texts, including Leslie Marmon Silko's novel *Ceremony*. *Ceremony* shook and undid the framework of my intellectual world in terms of how I understood history, ethics, the meaning of race and race relations, war, environmental issues, and perhaps most importantly the role of narratives in creating reality. *Ceremony* is a rhetorical tour de force and one of the most important novels of the twentieth-century. In the opening pages, Silko provides an indigenous articulation of the rhetorical function of narrative:

> I will tell you something about stories,
> [he said]
> They aren't just entertainment.
> Don't be fooled.
> They are all we have, you see,
> all we have to fight off
> illness and death.

While I was not familiar with Kenneth Burke's work at the time, I would later come to see an alignment between Silko's articulation of the power of stories and Burke's notion of "literature as equipment for living." Both Silko and Burke highlight the social and rhetorical dimensions of language and more specifically the rhetorical function of stories to shape how we understand the world, how we understand ourselves, and how we understand the ethical premises upon which we base our interpersonal and social decisions. As Andrea Lunsford puts it in the title of one of her books, "Everything's an Argument."

When I began graduate school in an English program, I knew two things: I loved literature, and I wanted to focus on American Indian literatures. What I did not know was critical theory (I very intentionally avoid the term literary theory as theory is hardly confined to or even necessarily oriented towards "literary" texts). Initially, I balked at theory. But by the end of my first year I became a convert, seeing theories as lenses to look at texts that allowed for multiple readings. It also became clear to me that theory has everything to do with the "real world" inasmuch as various theories bring into focus possible relationships between language, texts, labor, capital, power, and psychology. Postmodern challenges to what Lyotard terms "metanarratives" were especially liberating. The deconstructive undoing of notions of "western civilization," "progress," and, more specifically, "manifest destiny," aligned with the rhetorical work that I saw and see American Indian texts performing on how those of us coming from and indoctrinated within mainstream social systems understand the world. As texts that write back from the margin to the center, American Indian literatures perform powerful rhetorical work in influencing how we see, think, feel, and act.

Still, at the start of my graduate studies, while aware of the constructed nature of social reality and while I was reading literary texts in terms of the cultural work they performed, I had not yet aligned my engagement with literature in explicitly rhetorical terms, nor had I conceived of myself in disciplinary terms as a participant in the field of composition and rhetoric. My introduction to rhetoric and composition as a field came, as it does for many of us, in the context of teaching first-year composition. As with most graduate programs in English, the University of Oregon offered me the opportunity to teach first-year composition. However, unlike many programs, the University of Oregon required all first-year graduate students to undergo training in the teaching and learning of writing prior to being granted the privilege of teaching an actual class. The training included a version of the practicum in Composition with readings from the field and practical guidelines for teaching writing with a focus on the teaching of written argumentation. Additionally, we were all required to undergo an apprenticeship in which we were paired with an experienced teacher whom we shadowed throughout the term and in this context were provided the chance to teach some classes under our mentor's supervision. This is the context for my introduction to rhetoric and composition as a field of study.

I went into graduate school with a passion for my subject of study and a desire to become a teacher. The graduate coursework in composition and the apprenticeship showed me that there was so much more to effective teaching than simply standing in front of a room and delivering a lecture. We explored and debated questions of pedagogy, how to lead a discussion, how to place learning at the center, the role of the teacher among other topics. Along with readings on the teaching of writing, we also focused on written argumentation and rhetoric. It was in the context of learning about the teaching of writing that I was introduced to the works of Aristotle, Olbrecht and Tyteca (*The New Rhetoric*), and Kenneth Burke, among others.

Taylor: Is rhetoric, past, present, and future, necessarily interdisciplinary and/or theoretical?

Stromberg: This question, by its nature, requires a theoretical answer. On the one hand, to borrow from William Covino, if we consider that rhetoric as an activity, object, or performance might include "everything," or at least all forms of human communication, then it is of course not only interdisciplinary, it transcends the very notion of disciplinarity. At the same time, all rhetoric as a human activity is not theoretical and not necessarily theorized if we take theory to be the act of developing a meta explanation for how communication works and/or an overarching set of guidelines for how to communicate ethically and effectively. I need to pause here to say that one of my own operating assumptions is that underlying all discourse conventions exist "theories," perhaps unstated, of how one should communicate, what can and cannot be said, proper modes of communication depending on the context and audience, all the rhetorical elements. However, in terms of having been theorized in the sense of making the rules explicit and the assumptions and reasons underlying these rules understandable, all rhetoric is not theoretical.

If by *rhetoric* we mean an object or subject fit for academic study, then the answer to these questions shifts. The study of rhetoric as the study of human communication is, to repeat my earlier assertion, inherently not only interdisciplinary but trans-disciplinary. At the very pragmatic level, teaching rhetoric in a first-year composition or communication course means, at the least, exploring with students how different disciplines and different contexts have different communication conventions. In this sense, the teaching of writing as the teaching of rhetoric is teaching communication flexibility. To teach writing is not simply to teach rules of grammar or elements of a style; it is to cultivate and deepen students' existing understanding and ability to assess the elements of rhetorical context and to cultivate an understanding and ability to determine and apply the appropriate communication approach to the rhetorical contexts. Here the word *process* comes to mind in that you cannot give students "rhetoric" as a set of discrete skills. Rather, rhetoric becomes more a matter of knowing how to ask relevant and useful questions and the dispositions and skills to adjust and adapt communication to those situations. Teaching rhetoric, in its most practical manifestation, becomes the creation of a training space, a dojo if you will, for practicing the ways of rhetoric.

So my response is a bit of a yes and a no. In the Western tradition and in other cultural traditions, rhetoric, while emphasizing skills in persuasive communication, has long been a theoretical subject. Aristotle's *Rhetoric* certainly offers a theory of rhetoric in that it not only explains how to communicate effectively it provides the rationale or "theory" for understanding what makes effective communication. Prior to Aristotle, Isocrates articulated a theory of rhetoric that we might identify as "constructivist" in the sense that absolute truth is not available and that "oratory is good only if it has the qualities of fitness for the occasion." In various ways, if more implicitly and explicitly, Aristotle and Isocrates offer understandings of rhetoric as epistemological. We use rhetoric to arrive at decisions, if not absolute truth. More recently, Thomas Kuhn and Stephen Toulmin, neither of whom would identify nor have identified themselves as rhetoricians, have further articulated the ways in which rhetoric produces "knowledge."

All this is to say that while in the past rhetoric as a field of study may have had a practical or praxis emphasis, it seems to me it has always either been theoretical or contained significant theoretical implications for understanding how we know and what constitutes knowledge.

Scholarship in the area of rhetorical studies continues to be rich with theoretical insights, and if we consider what some have called the "rhetorical turn" in a number of disciplines, the interdisciplinarity of rhetoric will only continue to grow. I deeply appreciate the work Andrea Lunsford is doing, to give just one example, to re-engage rhetoric and composition with performance studies. In a similar vein, the program where I teach at California State University, Monterey Bay does not offer "writing classes." Rather, we offer courses in English Communication that integrate the teaching of written and oral communication with critical thinking. Frequently these courses also integrate a lower division requirement in ethics. So, in a sense, we have gone back to our interdisciplinary past, reuniting writing, oratory, and philosophy from the assumption that rhetoric is interdisciplinary and that effective instruction calls for interdisciplinary integration.

Taylor: How does the American Indian rhetoric of survivance, to borrow your book title, fit or not fit with rhetoric's openness to other disciplines?

Stromberg: The concept of "survivance," a concept I derived from the work of Gerald Vizenor, defies the limitations of disciplinarity. For Vizenor, as with scholars such as Vine Deloria Jr., or Edward Said, western disciplinarity manifest in fields such as anthropology or sociology carry and have perpetuated the West's legacy of colonial dominance. In his scathing indictment of anthropology, Deloria asserted, "The fundamental thesis of the anthropologist is that people are objects for observation, people are then considered objects for experimentation, for manipulation, and eventual extinction.... The massive volume of useless knowledge produced by anthropologists attempting to capture real Indians in a network of theories has contributed substantially to the invisibility of Indian people today." Deloria made this observation in the 1960s, and I know that anthropology as a discipline has taken its own version of the rhetorical turn, becoming more reflective of its practices and discourse. Nevertheless, I refer to Deloria's position as a way to highlight how approaching American Indian rhetorics requires a great deal of openness both to the limits of one's own knowledge and an openness to other ways of knowing. An openness to other ways of knowing by definition means an openness to insights and approaches from other disciplines. Furthermore, to engage with American Indian rhetorics means, to me, an openness to keep open what we mean by rhetoric. In the Western tradition, as Patricia Bizzell and Bruce Herzberg note, rhetoric "was first and foremost, the art of persuasive speaking." With alternative epistemologies, ontologies, and conceptions of time, American Indian rhetorics contribute to the rhetorical turn toward new conceptions of knowledge.

On a more practical scale, the publication of *American Indian Rhetorics of Survivance* speaks clearly for the field of rhetoric's current state of openness to other disciplines. Contributors to this study include scholars from the areas of Rhetoric and Composition and English studies as one might expect, but in addition we have contributions from the fields of History, Sociology, Legal Studies, and American Indian Studies. I truly could not imagine doing this kind of work without the perspectives from these disciplinary areas. I also deeply appreciate the University of Pittsburgh Press's willingness to publish such an explicitly interdisciplinary book in their series in Composition, Literacy, and Culture. I think the book's publication illustrates how the areas of composition, literacy studies, and of course the study of culture are interdisciplinary.

When I initially imagined the collection, I hoped it might serve more than an academic audience and certainly more than an audience limited to the area of composition and rhetoric. My larger ambition, mostly unrealized, was to create a text with both academic and practical value. I hoped that for people belonging to and working with American Indian communities, the collection would be of use in understanding the dynamics of rhetoric in ways that might be useful in getting rhetorical work done that would be of service to Indian people. This is one of the challenges of academic work--bridging the gap with the world outside our academic disciplinary circles. That being said, I don't mean to devalue our academic work. Much of what we do has so-called real world applications, and especially in the area of rhetoric and composition where so much of our work directly informs our teaching, the applications are fairly direct. Still, I had hopes of creating a text with the potential for more direct community application. Even within the academy, there is room for more dialogue between scholars in the field of rhetoric and composition and scholars in communication studies. Given this current period of intense multimodal technologically driven communication and multiple sites of "writing" practices, this is the future.

Taylor: I like the way you've brought together your own intellectual journey and the movement of the field. Clearly, you have found a unique synergy across disciplines. However, what about the points of divergence? For instance, you mention theory and Lyotard's comdemnation of "metanarratives," but rhetoric, at times, seems to become a so-called "meta-narrative." When Native Americans, for instance, appropriated the discourses and rhetorical conventions of the "Whites," was this succumbing to a "metanarrative" or does the appropriation re-rhetoricize (if I can coin a term) the prevailing communication system? Either line of inquiry could lead to serious debates about the role of rhetoric in politics, ethics, and power relations.

Stromberg: In terms of whether rhetoric functions as a "metanarrative," if we look at the study of rhetoric only through the lens of the Western European tradition and to the extent that we only accept as effective rhetoric which conforms to the principles of Western European rhetorical traditions, then yes, it does function as a "metanarrative" or a "metadiscourse." And in many ways that is how rhetoric has been taught and continues to be taught. The divergence you mention has in part to do with a history of a proscriptive rhetoric that was part and parcel of colonialist and imperialist endeavors. The teaching of rhetoric as one aspect of the "white man's burden" to "civilize" the less enlightened. Clearly we have not transcended that legacy, and those of us who teach rhetoric and composition or communication courses need to be mindful of this complexity.

At the same time, we confront the reality that the discourse conventions based primarily on Western European traditions continue to be the discourse conventions of power. As a teacher at an institution charged with serving first-generation and low-income students, I feel a responsibility to teach communication skills that will enable them to pursue as many options for their futures as possible. This means preparing them to address the prevailing rhetorical expectations. At the same time, there are ways to teach inclusively that honor the resources students from a variety of backgrounds bring to the class. In other words, rather than seeing the conventions we teach as the superior approach and intended to replace what the students already know, we might more effectively teach in ways that suggest multiple registers and acknowledge multiple literacies. I also realize that this is much easier in theory than in practice.

As for the study of rhetoric, I think recent scholarship on women's rhetoric, comparative rhetorics, and cultural rhetorics operates from assumptions of "local rhetorics" and counter-hegemonic rhetorics. Within the context of the United States alone, we might identify a wide range of alternative rhetorical traditions, many of which draw upon and alter aspects of the Western tradition to create something new and distinct. For example, we might consider African American rhetorical practices that synthesize Christian rhetoric with African rhetorical traditions and have been shaped within the crucibles of slavery and resistance to systemic oppression.

I would say contemporary American Indian rhetorical practices reveal similar patterns of "re-rhetoricizing" prevailing communication practices. This of course is not a neutral pattern given the history of military subjugation and then educational programs designed to assimilate American Indians to Western European culture. The initial encounters with Western rhetoric were clearly oppressive impositions on American Indians. Yet the term *submission* implies a surrender or abandonment of culture that has not occurred. American Indian rhetorical practices continue to evolve. Of course, this is a complex and problematic evolution given economic conditions and ongoing assimilation efforts among other contextual elements. We might identify this ongoing resistance and insistence on cultural autonomy in the ongoing class action suit filed by American Indians against the Bureau of Indian Affairs for mismanagement of monies held in trust for Indian tribes. This is a case, like many others, where American Indians have had to make use of all the "available means of persuasion" to protect their interests.

On another note, the contemporary communication situation raises fascinating questions for rhetorical studies in terms of the influence of new technologies and new mediums of communication. We have what some are calling the "net generation" for whom the Internet, cell phones, personal computers and other technologies are part of the cultural landscape they are born into. In ways that I think we are only on the cusp of understanding, these communication technologies are reshaping the rhetorical landscape.

Jack Selzer, a graduate of Xavier University (BA) and Miami University (PhD), has taught at Penn State since 1978. He and his colleagues have built respected graduate and undergraduate programs in rhetoric and composition, and over the years he has served his university and his profession as Director of Composition, Director of Graduate Programs in English, Associate Dean, President of the Association of Teachers of Technical Writing, and President of the Rhetoric Society of America. On his own and in collaboration with colleagues he has edited *Understanding Scientific Prose* (Wisconsin, 1993), *Rhetorical Bodies* (Wisconsin, 1999), *Tambour* (Wisconsin, 2002), and several textbooks. And he has written *Kenneth Burke in Greenwich Village* (Wisconsin, 1996), *Kenneth Burke in the 1930s* (South Carolina, 2007; with Ann George), *1977: The Cultural Year in Composition* (Parlor, 2007; with Brent Henze and Wendy Sharer), and the textbooks *Good Reasons* and *Good Reasons with Contemporary Arguments* (with Lester Faigley). He is currently taking aim at a third Kenneth Burke book and one on the rhetoric of the civil rights movement.

The Conversation

Keith Gilyard: As you know, I recently read *Kenneth Burke in the 1930s*, the wonderful book you co-authored with Ann George. It brings together two favorite topics for me: Burke and Depression-era cultural politics. It also prompted me to look back over some of Burke's writing, which, in turn, reminded me of the old joke about the woman who was finally persuaded to read Shakespeare. She said his work was full of clichés. That's how it is with Burke. Language as symbolic action? Literature as rhetorical? Entering a conversation in a parlor? Terministic screens? What overworked ideas. Although no interview can do full justice to Burke's many contributions, I do want to take up a few of his ideas with you with an eye on contemporary times. Of course I want to talk about how you view your own intellectual project. Perhaps we can start with that, with what set you on your present course.

Jack Selzer: I began my career, as you know, with an interest in scientific and technical writing. I was hired here in 1978 to teach technical writing and naturally became interested in the rhetoric of science as a result. But here at Penn State I have always been fortunate to be surrounded by a bunch of very serious rhetoricians. Some were in what was formerly called the Speech Communication department, now Communication Arts and Sciences. Others, like Marie Secor, Betsy Brown, Anne Herrington, and Jeanne Fahnestock, were in the English department. Jeff Walker came in, and Sharon Crowley joined us for awhile. Then Cheryl Glenn and you. So I have always been in a rich environment for doing work in rhetoric and have had people giving me a good rhetorical education. As my career evolved, therefore, I was not a technical and scientific communication person in a narrow sense; I always had this broader rhetorical perspective, and thought more in terms of the rhetoric of science. With a number of like-minded colleagues, I published a book entitled *Understanding Scientific Prose*, a project focusing on methodologies for critical reading. In a sense, the book summed up my rhetoric-of-science phase.

When I was considering a new project for an upcoming sabbatical, I needed something that would keep me in State College. My wife teaches American literature here, and we had two little kids at the time who were starting school, so leaving town wasn't an option. I had always heard that there was this archive here of Kenneth Burke Papers—this is partly a story about luck, which I have always had a big supply of—but no one had ever been in there to poke around in a serious way. Because of my *Understanding Scientific Prose* project, I was into doing rhetorical analysis, so I figured I might do a rhetorical analysis of Kenneth Burke: I knew that I along with many others had a hard time understanding Burke, and my thinking in reading Burke was that I just couldn't figure out very well to whom he was talking. I thought, as a rhetorician naturally would, that if I could just figure that out and apply some of my methods of analysis, everything would click into place and I could bring some new understanding to works by Burke. I later learned that it was not quite that simple, but the idea did get me over into that archive.

Gilyard: Why were Burke's papers deposited at Penn State?

Selzer: You would have to ask Sandy Stelts in Pattee Library to know for sure, but my sense of the story is this: Burke had been teaching at Bennington College and was forced to retire when he turned sixty-five years old. He had always saved his papers and files, but now he didn't have an office anymore. Just at that time Penn State invited him to do a visiting professorship, during which he said something to the effect that he had all those papers and no place to put them. I think Henry Sams, the department head at the time and a man who was a friend of Burke and had met him in Chicago, suggested that Penn State would take the papers. There wasn't any real competition. Burke wasn't a famous character. He was then kind of out of favor, especially in literary studies.

Gilyard: That would have been in the early 1960s.

Selzer: Yes, KB would have turned sixty-five in 1962. So I fell into this storehouse, this treasury of materials. My original idea was to produce a single book containing one chapter on each of his major works, setting each one within a rhetorical situation.

Gilyard: That's funny.

Selzer: Yes, I was pretty naïve about what I was getting into; I had no idea how interesting Burke's career was or how extensive those archives would be. The projected first chapter alone turned into a book. The person who was running the Kenneth Burke Papers at that time was a wonderful guy named Charles Mann. Charlie Mann is kind of a legendary figure here at Penn State. He ran the Rare Book Room for many years and was a unique character and a tremendously generous guy. He's famous in Hemingway studies for his work with those papers. Charlie had a very profound influence on me because he was so welcoming and didn't mind stupid questions. I was such a novice, but he never treated me like one. He was full of suggestions and put me in contact with other archives. Being able to work with Charlie Mann was another lucky break in my career, and I have ever since then enjoyed bringing others into those archives— particularly graduate students—because of Charlie's example. After Charlie passed away, his successors in Special Collections have continued to be wonderful to me, especially Sandy Stelts, the current curator.

Gilyard: *Kenneth Burke in Greenwich Village* was the first major fruit of that engagement with the archives.

Selzer: Yes. That was really a fun project. It taught me so much, and gave me lots to teach and write about.

Gilyard: One of the things I paid attention to as I read your books, both *Kenneth Burke in Greenwich Village* and *Kenneth Burke in the 1930s,* is how they seem to be so consciously dialogic and dramatistic themselves. How much did you think about this as you composed?

Selzer: A great deal. I'm very pleased that you noticed that. The subtitle for *Kenneth Burke and Greenwich Village* is *Conversing with the Moderns.*

The idea was to see Burke's work as emerging from a set of interconnected cultural conversations that were going on in the 1920s. There was this "Others" group of poets, talking together about what modern poetry was going to be. There was Alfred Stieglitz and the famous 291 art gallery, and the Provincetown Players inventing modern drama, and *The Dial* magazine. All of them had their communities of people, and Burke was working in and out of all of those circles and others. As I wrote, I saw myself as doing very Burkean criticism, something right out of the famous "conversation" section of *The Philosophy of Literary Form*: that is, seeing Kenneth Burke not as an isolated individual, as a solitary great person, but as someone very much in dialogue with others in those modernist circles. It was fun and a great education to follow all the various strands in those amazing conversations and then to see Burke's writing as part of those engagements. Now I see this as my method of reading. (And my method of teaching writing, too, as you can see in my textbooks.) I do thick descriptions of cultural conversations, and then show how the item I'm studying emerges from and further stimulates that conversation. I always try to understand works as pieces of larger dialogues.

So when I was writing it up, I tried to make my writing dialogic also. I added sidebars. I put in letters by other people and letters by Burke. I poured in footnotes. Anything to break up the straight presentation. I try to write more like a conversation than giving a monologic lecture. You can also tell from talks that you and I have had about the discourses of the Civil Rights Movement how I operate. I always want to know who is talking and writing to whom, or what the background or back-story of a specific speech or book (or whatever) is.

Gilyard: Give it the whole surround-sound treatment, yes. You have mentioned to me on occasion that you plan to push ahead with another book on Burke, moving ahead into what we could call his human relations phase. What do you envision as the time frame in the book?

Selzer: Yeah, well, you're asking about the time frame that I'm going to cover. I'm worried about my own time frame. Clearly I have to pick up the pace here! So I think next will be the 1940s, 1950s, and 1960s.

Gilyard: So you'll put three decades together. I'm happy to hear that for your sake because this one-decade-at-a-time move just wasn't going to get it done. I was worried about that.

Selzer: Quite right! So we have *A Grammar of Motives, The Rhetoric of Motives, Language as Symbolic Action,* and *The Rhetoric of Religion.* This time I think I'm going to try to talk about Burke in relation to academic communities. A lot of times Burke has been understood as an outsider, the gadfly who was outside of the academic context. But I actually think that after 1943, when he took that job at Bennington College, most of the people he was close too were in academic settings, and so his circles were largely academic in nature. I'm going to try to pick up on that.

Gilyard: Each of your projects starts at a point of disjuncture. There's a conventional wisdom about Burke, that his early writings were not salient, for example. Then you demonstrate the inadequacy of the conventional wisdom.

Selzer: I'm gaining confidence (laughing). In the first book, I would have been very happy to agree with anyone, but the fact is that nobody had ever really looked all that carefully at Burke in the 1920s. Actually, they hadn't even looked seriously at anything much before 1945. There were references to earlier stuff and an unpublished dissertation by David Cratis Williams that I read when I was finished, but all that was known about Burke's early years was very murky. Things were, then, open and available. The main thing I had to go up against, as I indicated, were some strong perceptions of Burke as an outsider, the Inspired Genius of Andover Farm, independently thinking great thoughts. It's kind of the modernist cliché about writers, the genius locked up in the upstairs room. In the 1920s book and the 1930s book with Ann George, the goal, as I suggested in other terms, was to develop a group portrait, a team picture. Burke is still the key member of the team, but you can't understand him without those teammates.

Gilyard: Well, the picture is certainly helpful. And I agree with you and with Ann that his early work is rich, perhaps as rich as his later efforts. If I were teaching Burke to rhetoric students, I would present, as the heart of his project, "Lexicon Rhetoricae" from *Counter-Statement* and "Dictionary of Pivotal Terms" from *Attitudes Toward History,* along with the introduction to *A Grammar of Motives,* where he lays out the pentad, and the full text of *A Rhetoric of Motives.* Would you comment on that arrangement? How do you typically organize your Burke seminar? And how have your students been relating him to their own projects?

Selzer: I'll answer, but you'll have to also tell me why you like that particular way in.

Gilyard: Because you ground students in the terminology, which can be an important organizing move, which Burke knew. With the lexicon and the dictionary you have clear explanations of terms that students will encounter again and again. If they want to know what Burke means by *symbol*—verbal parallel to a pattern of experience, a formula—they (me too) have a ready reference. His later work draws heavily on those two texts. I just feel that when you give someone the terminological grounding for a project, it helps that person understand the project better. It's like Aristotle's *Rhetoric* in a sense.

Selzer: Yeah, I see.

Gilyard: Then the pentad lays out the dramatism that obviously is his premier metaphor. So we're rounding out the terminological center. And then I think *A Rhetoric of Motives* is just a beautiful analysis in terms of how rhetoric works, how it factors into human motive.

Selzer: It's such a central text.

Gilyard: And I always pay particular attention to, say, the first one-third. He talks about *identification, consubstantiality, terministic screens,* terms you see repeatedly in the professional literature and in student papers as they try to make it into the professional literature. So these are powerful concepts. I know there's a lot of other work, and I certainly don't argue for excluding any of it, but this is my answer to the question of why I would front these four pieces.

Selzer: I'm interested in that. And your approach gets at the major concepts in Burke's work, I would say. Of course, I have heard other people explain how they approach Burke differently.

Gilyard: Of course.

Selzer: Greg Clark was telling me that he starts with the Hell Haven part of *The Rhetoric of Religion.* He starts with this fable because he thinks it gets a lot of the terms out on the table and you can pick them up in other places.

Gilyard: Similar thinking to mine, just starting with different materials.

Selzer: And Greg told me that Kenneth Burke himself told everybody to start with his fiction.

Gilyard: That ain't fair. How was I supposed to know that? (laughing)

Selzer: And one of our former students, Dana Anderson, now on the faculty at Indiana University, thinks the key text to start with is *The Philosophy of Literary Form* because it looks both backward and forward—it picks up the key concepts from the 1920s and 1930s while preparing for the "motives" books to come.

But I generally operate chronologically. I try to help students discover Burke for themselves rather than tell them what the key terms are. I like to teach Burke to undergraduate students as well as graduate students, and the Greenwich Village angle has been a good place to start with those students. When I teach a course called "Kenneth Burke and Greenwich Village," the students already know something about some of the characters. They've read about Eugene O'Neill, E. E. Cummings,

Marianne Moore, Katherine Ann Porter, William Carlos Williams, and John Dos Passos—people like that. So the chronological approach works for them. With graduate students, I am interested in giving them as many research opportunities as possible. I've benefited so much from these archives that I try to convey my enthusiasm for the work and indeed have had success getting grad students in there and giving them a chance to discover projects. Burke's early period presents so many research possibilities that I've just found it convenient to start chronologically with graduate students.

Gilyard: What about the tours? I haven't yet had the chance to go on one of your walking tours.

Selzer: Well, I've walked people around Greenwich Village and around the grounds at Andover. That's sort of an extension of the relationship that I have been able to develop with the Burke family, particularly Michael Burke, his youngest child. They are the most generous and hospitable and interesting group you can imagine.

Gilyard: And you met Burke himself. He was in his nineties.

Selzer: He was about ninety-six. Rosa Eberly, Charlie Mann, and I went out to see him at Andover on a very cold February day. He passed later that year. That visit got me interested in the personal side of the story—Andover and all the family—and led to me taking students and colleagues on tours to Andover farm and around Greenwich Village. It's been fun. Just about a week, maybe ten days ago, I actually met Kenneth Burke's first child, Elspeth. She was born in 1920 and is still going strong, living in Brooklyn and close to her son, the musician Tom Chapin. Elspeth was telling me all about her childhood with her parents and siblings, Burke's early relationships, his later relationships with his children. Inevitably, the story involves all these other characters, all these fantastic people. So the personal and the critical-research end of it are actually very intimately connected, I'm finding. More circles to consider.

Gilyard: It's amazing to grow up like that. Reminds me of how Lorraine Hansberry grew up in Chicago because of her parents' involvement in politics. She might walk in the living room and see W. E. B. Du Bois sitting there.

Selzer: Yeah, exactly. Michael Burke talks about listening to Ralph Ellison read a rough draft of the "Battle Royal" scene from *Invisible Man* in the living room at Andover, before it was published. Michael was twelve or thirteen, maybe even younger than that. And he was sitting around the fire listening to Ralph Ellison. And William Carlos Williams. And so on. There are many similar stories. It was just a remarkable set of associations to which all of the children were exposed.

Gilyard: I love the history and obviously appreciate your work in that regard. But when I reread Burke, I also like to think about the relevance of his work in a 2008 context. I want to get your reaction to some thoughts I've had about Burke as I witness the unfolding of this presidential election season. I've gone to a statement in *Permanence and Change*, which is this: "A red square is like a green square when considerations of shape are uppermost, but considerations of color make a red square like a red circle." I substitute Hillary Clinton for red square, Barack Obama for green square, being a Democrat for shape, and John McCain for red circle. I leave color as is, and this amended statement explains to me a lot of the voting, and probably future voting, though pundits have been talking around the color issue more than taking it head on. They generally frame it in terms of Obama's rhetorical problem. But it's more than that.

Selzer: In viewing election politics, I tend to fall back on the usual stuff from Burke, let's say *dramatism*. Or I like to go to his notion of *identification*. There is a way to understand an election, you know, as a set of arguments going back and forth that can be understood according to what Burke would call the "old rhetoric," the sort of good-reasons approach I've taken in some of the textbooks I've done. You have a traditional argument, in other words, a thesis statement and supporting propositions, with the more successful arguments winning the argument and the election. In an election, it's more or less a set of arguments by consequence: "If I am elected, these good things are going to follow," or "We will avoid some of the bad things we currently have if you elect me." Then there is evaluation going on of the arguments and the candidates. And the whole affair is often fought out through ethos, pathos, logos...

Gilyard: Well, that's what I'm saying. It's about more than rational argument. It's these other things.

Selzer: That's right. But ever since Ronald Reagan and Kenneth Burke, I have tended to look at national elections in terms of this concept of *identification*. I think that Ronald Reagan, fortunately or unfortunately, basically invited people into certain identifications when he was running for office. He did not really so much lay out the consequences that were going to occur if he were elected. Rather, he invited voters to identify with him, to be certain kinds of people. He wrote a script for them. Of course, that idea also connects to Burke and dramatism. So Reagan made the invitation to people to identify themselves in a certain way, and then the people naturally kind of "became Republicans" as they were watching him and listening to him. He didn't so much give them good reasons to favor him as give them an identity that coincided with his own.

Gilyard: So he wasn't an ideologue in the sense we usually think of it, right? He was more savvy than that.

Selzer: Well, right. He actually was an ideologue in some ways, but that's not how he ran for election. Goldwater: now there's someone who ran as an ideologue. That's kind of what I saw during this election season, especially during the Pennsylvania primary. Hillary Clinton was making more of a traditional argument. She was laying out the good reasons for her candidacy, doing evaluations of herself and her opponents, suggesting the consequences that were going to result from her election. You could almost diagram the whole thing according to logos and her ethical appeal and so on. I find Obama fascinating on all sorts of grounds, including the rhetorical. It's not like he refrains from doing traditional arguments; he can do that too. But he also works on people's identifications; mainly I find it interesting that he's inviting people to redefine themselves, to play out a different script. He's playing with people's identifications, inviting them to be certain kinds of people. People who will then naturally vote for him.

Gilyard: You're calling it a Reaganesque strategy.

Selzer: Tactically, yes.

Gilyard: Yeah, that's been said.

Selzer: The other thing I've heard said is that Hillary Clinton ran as if she were applying for a job while Obama is running as if he's looking for friends or asking for a date.

Gilyard: She sometimes ran like she dared you to refuse her the job.

Selzer: Well, we could go there. But getting back to Obama, I think he is also the kind of person that Burke admired when Burke developed his own rhetorical theory—someone with this *comic perspective*, to use the term from *Attitudes Toward History*. Such a person views the opponent as someone making an error, not someone who is inherently evil. So such a person sincerely searches for common ground. The person resists antithesis, using what Ann George and I call a "wheedling" kind of rhetoric. In other words, you stick with people, even when you disagree, and you don't name call. And you also understand as well the role of art, culture, music, these aesthetic discourses, as means of persuasion. That was *very* important for Burke. And it's important to Obama, who is a truly gifted rhetor.

Gilyard: That's interesting. Of course. And you have taken my question as a provocation to talk about what the rhetors were and are trying to accomplish and the means in play. I have no problem with that. But I don't want to lose sight of what I was driving at. I was trying to illumine the flight of white registered Democrats in terms of that point from *Permanence and Change*. We have had no precedence in national elections, but we have seen this phenomenon on local levels, that is, where Democratic strongholds were no longer such strongholds when the Democratic standard bearer was African American. Color (race perception) trumps shape (views). Obama is like Clinton when being a Democrat is important. Clinton is like McCain when being white is Important.

Selzer: I see. I think I misunderstood what you were talking about there.

Gilyard: We've seen that in Chicago, New York...

Selzer: Los Angeles.

Gilyard: Yeah. I got the nomination, now where did all the white Democratic support go? Races have still been won by African American candidates, but have often been closer than you would have thought based strictly on party considerations. It's not always the case, but it's happened often enough to notice. We know that a significant number of white, working class, registered Democrats are talking about sitting out the general election or voting for McCain. It's not a political decision based on their class interests. I know some have portrayed Obama as the elitist and McCain as some sort of populist, but it is hard for me to believe that people really see that as the compelling division between the two. I could be way out of touch on this. But I'm glad you took the question the other way, though. I'm glad you took it in terms of how you see candidates positioning themselves because that's also fascinating from a rhetorical perspective.

Selzer: Present times are not unlike the very combative period of the 1930s about which Ann George and I have just written. Most people on the hard left during the 1930s, people like Mike Gold, saw things as a huge battle between Good and Evil. It was going to be a knock-down-drag-out fight and they were going to win. Use broadsides, demonize the opponent, employ whatever oppositional tactics were necessary to win the class warfare. And Burke was more disposed to try to create a united front. He saw the value in what was known as the Popular Front. Find some friends. Learn how to cooperate. Look for common ground. Think of people as mistaken and not evil. "Bore from within." You're not going to agree always, but find common ground and keep the conversation going. Keep people together: you can see that as the theme of his famous 1935 speech to the First American Writers' Congress. I do think Obama has this comic perspective. He is a uniter. He does look for common ground. He refuses to demonize the other person.

Gilyard: But part of what made the Popular Front possible was the promise of the New Deal. People were generally sharper about rallying around their own class interests.

Selzer: You did have that, and you also had the blessing from Moscow in 1933 or 1934 that would permit the Popular Front. But the key point to make here is that this popular-front mentality is as much Burke's project, if you will, as *dramatism* and *identification*, some of the later terminologies. I think that Ann was right on in seeing in the 1930s work kind of a handbook of rhetoric. People are always wondering, well, what would Kenneth Burke have said? What would have been his practical advice? It's a popular-front rhetoric that he favors.

Gilyard: Again, that's why I would start there in terms of teaching his project. Think, for example, of Burke's explanation in *Attitudes Toward History* of symbolic mergers: "A symbol is a vessel of much more content than is disclosed by its 'face value' as a label." I am fascinated by this concept and have been relying on it a lot lately. Hillary Clinton maybe would not have committed the gaffe about Bobby Kennedy if she were fully cognizant of this reality. She could not control the connection in some minds of Kennedy's assassination to Obama's potential danger. When she spoke of one event, she evoked the other possible event. She contends, understandably so, that her words were taken out of context. But they were only taken out of *one* context and, because symbols merge, placed in a another. To insist that she was *only* talking about timeline is beside the point. The same with Obama's comment, while discussing a political issue, about the septuagenarian McCain losing his bearings. Obama cannot control if some associate "losing bearings" with being a disparaging comment about age. It seems that these general election campaigns could benefit from having some astute rhetoric students aboard, no? Some of these mistakes could be easily avoided.

Selzer: Well, the campaigns could certainly benefit from astute rhetoric students. And I think that political campaigns are always a good opportunity for rhetorical education. So we're looking at the fall, and we're going have the chance for our students to learn a lot—not so much from the debates but from the ads as well--unless the two candidates are too debate-like and only argue with one another, point-counterpoint. The ads are more interesting when you consider fully the imagery, this esthetic element that I was talking about before, that I think that Burke understood as a very important part of persuasion in even very mundane matters. In his talk at the First American Writer's Congress, he was very much into the imagery of persuasion. How do we get people to join us? Let's pay attention to what Hollywood does. So the ads and the imagery are crucial. Of course, you will sometimes in a campaign get a great individual performance, a set piece like Obama's "A More Perfect Union" speech in Philadelphia. I think that we'll look back and see that speech as one of the great oratorical masterpieces of statecraft, perhaps something like Lincoln's speech at Cooper Union.

Gilyard: And what about the acceptance speech coming up on August 28th? You don't think that date selection was a coincidence.

Selzer: Again, he has a great sense of imagery. I think you saw it in his 2004 convention speech, and now he's going to Denver and speak before 75,000 people. I find him astute in just about every way but extremely so regarding presentational matters. He sticks to his guns also: he's actually quite frank and up front. I predict that he will not ever step in and demonize McCain. Here in Pennsylvania we saw Hillary Clinton and Barack Obama had to go at it for six weeks. That was a long period of time, and they poured tons of money in. And Hillary Clinton was, you know, hitting him with every shot she could. But he refused to answer in kind, I think. He's got this comic perspective, and I think he's got this critical perspective that's, um, let's just say that it's very sympathetic to some of the things I think Burke was trying to get at.

Gilyard: You tied Burke in there more closely than I thought you would.

Selzer: Well, I'm always plugging Kenneth Burke. And thank you for the opportunity to plug his early work. I think it's very relevant indeed to rhetorical studies today. His popular-front rhetoric is a great antidote to power politics. His stress on cooperation and communion is important. Yes, symbolic mergers. The full handbook of rhetorical practices that you see in his 1930s work is a nice complement to what students in rhetoric already appreciate in terms of dramatism and identification and performativity, the things for which he's primarily known.

Gilyard: When you talk about power politics, it reminds me of the talk Lewis Gordon gave here a couple of months back. You were there. He made the distinction between a commitment to politics and a commitment to government. If you are committed to government, then you are committed to ruling above all else with no practical regard for the other side. That's not the road to go down. But if you are committed to politics, then you *have* to be committed to the other side. You have to be committed to the other side's perspective because you have to engage it dialogically.

Selzer: Hey, politics is all about the polis, the city, and the rough and tumble of rhetorical exchange.

Gilyard: Which means that you have to have a commitment to the other side.

Selzer: Exactly.

Gilyard: So I think that distinction by Gordon is important.

Selzer: You mentioned to me that you were also interviewing Steve Mailloux. That reminds me of how much I have benefited from Steve's scholarship. I never said to myself, "Oh, I've read Steve Mailloux, so now my work will be a certain kind of work." But at the same time I very much always see myself sympatico with what he's doing. And the more my work has matured, if I'm not overstating that, the more I can understand that what I'm doing is very much what he's calling for in his work.

Gilyard: Well, it's rhetorical hermeneutics, rhetorical pragmatism, and that's the thing. You can talk about Burke in different dimensions, but obviously you can hook him up to the school of pragmatist thought.

Selzer: Indeed. I forget the exact formulation that Steve has about doing rhetoric to do history ... (hesitates).

Gilyard: Using rhetoric to practice theory by doing history.

Selzer: That's it. Ultimately, if you look at how my books have turned out, they're very much in sympathy with the kind of work Steve does. He's been great.

Gilyard: I'll be sure to tell him.

.

James Zebroski is a senior faculty person in rhetoric and composition at the University of Houston. He received his Ph.D. from the Ohio State University in Columbus, Ohio. He has taught in a variety of settings including the public schools. At UH, he teaches freshman composition, advanced composition, creative nonfiction, gay literature, and graduate seminars on a variety of subjects including Vygotsky, social class, critical theory, and pedagogy. Zebroski is author of *Thinking Through Theory: Vygotskian Perspectives on the Teaching of Writing* (1994), the first book-length consideration of Lev Vygotsky's work and its import for the discipline of rhetoric and composition. He has also published over thirty articles or chapters of books on a wide range of topics, including the politics of writing instruction, ethnographic writing, post-Fordism and twenty-first century composition, contemporary composition history, composition textbook advertisements, and response to student texts. Most recently he has published "Theory in the Diaspora" (2005) and "Social Class as Discourse: Mapping the Landscape of Class in Rhetoric and Composition" (2006), both in the *Journal of Advanced Composition*. His current work focuses on social class and first-generation college students and the teaching of writing.

The Conversation

Victor Taylor: In order to begin to provide a context for the rise of composition and rhetoric in the academy after 1970, could you describe what drew you to the field? What was it that intrigued you?

James Zebroski: I started my Ph.D. at Ohio State University in Columbus, Ohio in September of 1978 and defended my dissertation in August of 1982. So I am very much the product of the 1970s as far as my professional, but also personal, identity is concerned. It is challenging to describe that time in terms that will make sense to people who did not live through it. Yet it is important to situate myself in the 70s because I am in composition/ rhetoric in part because I was a first-generation college student in the early part of the decade.

The 1970s are often ridiculed, and sometimes the popular culture and fads of the time were humorous, but in many ways the 1970s was as crucial a decade as the 1960s, in some ways an extension of that decade, in other ways the end of that decade. The end of the Vietnam War in 1973 was crucial to the country, having been for over a decade the source of turmoil and the first illustration of the limits of power, and it was important to me with a draft number of 160 or so. I could have very easily ended up in Vietnam and had already registered as a conscientious objector. But the economic changes of the 1970s in retrospect can be seen as perhaps ultimately the most profound event of the decade—the shift from Fordism to post-Fordist regimes of capital that really began in earnest in the 1970s and that has since pretty much affected all workers' lives since, whether they be professional workers or assembly line and factory workers or service workers. Literally, the way we spend a third or more of our lives—at work—has been transformed in the period that started with the 1970s. Composition and rhetoric's contingent labor problem is only the most recent and obvious sign of those changes. My parents' generation and my students' generation live and work in two totally different modes of capitalism and my generation is the one in which that shift took place.

Entering public school teaching in 1973 and teaching in a junior high, a ninth grade school, and a high school for five years was important in my decision both to continue with my education and to enter a doctoral program in English education. Teaching before high stakes testing took over in public education meant that there was surprising room for innovation; I was lucky enough to be in several places where teachers were encouraged to experiment with the curriculum to make it more "relevant," as we said then, to student needs and interests. This is where the profession got the attitude that students are intellectuals, that they are capable of great things, that they are already knowledgeable and competent language users when they come through the door. Of course, linguistics and sociolinguistics of that day supported these claims, but when we look at C/R the commitment to the student as someone who can and does create knowledge and meaning—a constructivist view— very much comes from the curricular experiments occurring in the schools and being reported and encouraged in magazines like *Media and Methods*. In contrast, in 1978 when I came into a college English department—and if you go back into the Staff Room Interchange section of *CCC* as Marguerite Helmers does, during this time you see the same thing—it was very acceptable and showed one's wit as a professor to make fun of students and students' language use. Bad student writing then was often posted on bulletin boards or passed around. The attitude was condescending. What was new were the people teaching writing beginning to see students as equal partners in the learning process and in academe. That was not the norm in the university English departments at this time that I was aware of.

When I returned to Ohio State to do the Ph.D. there was Ed Corbett in English and that was it. I had the choice then of taking all literature courses and maybe doing a little work on my own in composition, and even that was likely to be classical rhetoric and those historical periods— the Renaissance, the eighteenth Century, the Medieval period—most "rhetorical," that is, most open to rhetoric, or staying in English education and constructing all my coursework around composition. I opted for the latter, working with Donald Bateman in English education who in the 1960s had done research in a Project English Center on transformational generative grammar. Don supported me in my objective of critiquing process theory and reconceptualizing writing as social by encouraging me to take coursework in anthropology, folklore, philosophy, qualitative and ethnographic research, and, from the start pretty much, by collaborating with me in an investigation of the work of Lev Vygotsky and his activity theory. This was propelled by the publication of *Mind in Society* in 1978.

Which leads to my second reason for choosing to work in English education to study composition rather than English. Theory. Don always encouraged theory, saw his work as theoretical, and, as I note in the introduction to my book *Thinking Through Theory*, I identified as a theorist even before I entered the doctoral program. I did some work in reader response theory in my M.A., for instance. But college English departments were no more hospitable to theory of any sort through those years than they were to composition. And they and the journals like *College English* and even *College Composition and Communication* were especially averse to what I might call leftist theory, work that theorizes power and literacy within a capitalist society. While never a Marxist, I have always seen myself and my work in what the Europeans would label the social democratic tradition. I have always seen Marx's analysis as central to my project; it certainly was central to Vygotsky's. But they—the editors of journals and the professors in English—were having none of it. It is true that Richard Ohmann, who in 1976 wrote the stunning *English in America* that I carried around like a talisman—I wanted to do some version of that—was editor of *College English* for a time. But mostly before and after, that journal and certainly *CCC* were not open to theory let alone leftist theory. So I stayed in English education where I could study composition and do leftist theory.

Taylor: How willing was the academy, particularly through English departments, to accept composition and rhetoric as more than a sub-field of a traditional discipline, namely literary studies?

Zebroski: As I have just noted, not very. The academy has for varying reasons always wanted to slot C/R as a skill rather than as practices, a subtle though critical distinction. Skills are behaviors. Hitting a tennis serve is a skill. Composing in this sense is not a skill, not beyond maybe keyboarding. As long as composition is shunted off into what Lauer called the ghetto—as long as it is seen as a skill, as a behavior or, to use current parlance, as an outcome to be assessed—C/R can never take its rightful place in the academy. The revival in rhetoric in the 60s was helpful in this sense; it showed that the work of composing is an art and practice of the highest sort and of the highest import when we factor in power relations and the political. The pressure is still there today in the academy to apply behaviorism no less rigid and rabid than that which Chomsky critiqued in Skinner in the late 1950s. Skinner at the university at least seems to have won; we are surrounded by the dangerous outcomes assessment movement, a corporate takeover of the university but a takeover from the inside, put upon us by our colleagues.

In December of 1983, I was still wondering if maybe I should get out of C/R and get a position in English education in a college of education somewhere, when I was invited by Colleen Aycock, a fellow teacher at Saint Edward's University and a good friend, to go to a party at Steve Witte's house in Austin, Texas. There had just been a reading conference in Austin and a lot of C/R folks were in town to present. I lucked out and met many C/R people through this party—Jim Kinneavy, Louise Phelps, Lester Faigley. I think Beth Daniell was there as a grad student, but I might be wrong about that. Didn't we talk about the Luria study and Sledd's take on it, or was that later? Anyhow it speaks volumes that around this time Witte won the Braddock Award for his research when the English Department at UT was rejecting his tenure application. Some of the literati as Maxine Hairston then called them—she must have been at that party too; at least in my mind she is—saw C/R as the new barbarians who betrayed humanism either through empirical research (maybe they should be in sociology departments or education schools, it was thought) or later through theory. My articles were rejected mostly on stylistic grounds, not because they were poorly written but because they used theory and the language of theory which the formalist, third-generation new critics of the time who had power and ran the disciplinary apparatus could only conceptualize as bad language use. I have those articles and many were eventually published and they were not badly written. They simply were not literature oriented or stylistically literary.

But even before this, it was clear that while C/R was not widely accepted, a small body of determined first-generation scholars were committed to establishing it. I went to 4Cs as a graduate student in 1980 when it was held in Washington, D.C. It was a very humanizing experience for me to have read all of these articles by people—Donald Murray, Linda Flower, Janet Emig, etc.—and then to see them and meet them. The field was small enough then that one could both read everything there was published in it and see these people at 4Cs. But what really impressed me at that conference was a post-conference workshop on research in C/R with Janet Emig, Joseph Williams, Rosemary Hake, Richard Young, and many more. I can very well remember Janet Emig starting the thing off by saying out loud to all assembled something like look at all of these young people interested in C/R and research in C/R—the implication being that this was unusual but satisfying, in fact, wonderful. After the plenary session we divided into groups and my friend and I went to Emig's group. What I remember was not what we said—I think we were asked what our research interests were and I talked about Vygotsky—but how Emig conducted that group. Amazing, artistic, masterful. Everyone spoke; we all interacted. Emig was a wonderful teacher and mentor in that group. I think that is one of the first times I really saw my identity as a compositionist. I began to think one could build a good life in this field, an exciting intellectual life, and being a good teacher like Emig would be an important part of it.

The lack of acceptance of my published work continued even into the early 1990s once C/R had become more accepted and people like Susan Miller, Lester Faigley, Jim Berlin, Linda Brodkey and others were doing theory. My work saw the light of day only through the help of a handful of supportive and like-minded colleagues. Here is a pretty complete list: Nancy Mack, Ann Berthoff, Jim Berlin, Louise Phelps, Peter Stillman, Claude Hurlbert, Michael Blitz, and Lynn Worsham. This is the literal intellectual community that we collectively formed and that, as much as any other, I wrote and did scholarly work for.

Taylor: Could you situate your work in this dynamic? To what extent were you attempting to write for a new or different intellectual community?

Zebroski: There has always been a dialectic, a struggle, between my intellectual project based in Vygotsky and Marx and the discipline which has always tended toward the positivistic, the formalistic, the behavioristic.

So it isn't surprising that in the late 1970s and early 1980s when *individualistic* cognitive process reigned in C/R and *empirical,* quantitative research was the favored form, I was making the argument that *writing is a social relation*—this in 1986 in a published work, earlier in 1983 in my dissertation—not a process, not a social process, but a relation, a social relation, and that theory and ethnographic inquiry were the most appropriate forms of research.

Later in the 1990s when post-structuralist theory of a very specific sort (mostly French) was being pushed in the discipline, I put forward the argument for Russian and Eastern European theory. In many ways, my book *Thinking Through Theory* is a navigation between the Scylla of French theory—or Theory as I name it in the conclusion of the book— and the Charybdis of American pragmatism of the Dewey sort. It must be noted that pragmatism led fairly directly to behaviorism; one might argue that in being anti-theoretical and eclectic at least to a degree, the pragmatists were all to a degree proto-behaviorists and some, like Charles Morris, not so proto. The American pragmatists even during the Great Depression never really accepted an immanent critique of capitalism like Marx's. They still don't because they don't want to talk about the forces—the political economic forces of this mode of production—as determinative in the last instance. The material reality in the flux. Have the American pragmatists ever talked about social class in a very deep way? Maybe they have, but I am unaware of it if they did. One would expect them to see social class, at best, as a cultural and personal identity issue rather than as a systemic effect produced by capitalism.

So now one can see, I am already speaking to the current moment in C/R, which is again anti-theoretical, a development I addressed I addressed in my "Theory in the Diaspora." We are told that theory is over. We are told we are in post-theory moment, an argument that benefits certain people and certain forces. But there is a theory that has hegemony in C/R. The fallback theory in the USA for the last century has been pragmatism, which has some insights to be sure. But I would argue there is a connection between our inability as a discipline to address social class and our acceptance of pragmatism as a theory or anti-theory or whatever.

Taylor: In addition to your scholarship, could you discuss landmark works in composition and rhetoric? Works that helped you shape a new line of inquiry.

Zebroski: During the years 1987–1992 single-authored books came to the fore. I decided I was going to focus on Vygotskian theory, and I knew as friends and/or colleagues, several of the authors whose books had the biggest influence on me. Although I was publishing a good many essays and articles, the most important project during this time was writing my book *Thinking Through Theory*. Three major books impacted me. First, Steve North showed us all how to do this single-person authoring in C/R with his 1987 *Making of Knowledge in Composition*. I always admired that book and how North plays out his argument which can be read (I read it so) as a very materialist Foucauldian argument—that the scholarship and research of emerging C/R comes out of material power relations and the practitioners get short shrift. Knowledge comes out of power. I also admired the way North took some extremely very heavy criticism from the older first generation of C/R folks. Some of the reviews in the journals were pretty nasty and I think missed the point of the book in debates—important ones to be sure—about the details. The fact that the impetus for North's book came out of an unsuccessful graduate oral exam and was essentially about epistemology also showed me that scholarship and daily work could be connected.

Second, Louise Phelps's *Composition as a Human Science* the very next year in 1988 would forever call into question the claim of some literati, among others, that C/R people were not very smart or very serious thinkers or scholars; to have a book published by Oxford is to this day a huge deal. The book is brilliant. But more important for my work, I learned from that book (and from North) to be more careful about making claims about theory and practice and the relations between scholarship, theory, and teaching and, in fact, to theorize this complex set of relations. Louise was a role model of how a theorist—a phenomenological theorist—might do work and function in the discipline. When I knew all of the other work and writing that Louise did and how it related to the published book, I began to get a sense of the relation between a book and the other scholarship one does. So Louise in that book and in conversations taught me how to compose an intellectual project the trajectory of which spans decades. How do you conceive of that? How do you plan for work five years or ten years down the road and still be flexible enough to respond to current opportunities? How do you connect teaching, curricular work, administration, with scholarship? How do conference presentations, and scheduling them, help you to do invention on topics you wanted to investigate anyhow but never would have had the time for? And how do you modulate all of this in some harmonic, pleasing, and sane way? Louise's book and work have taught me these things among others.

The third book was *Rhetorical Power* by Steve Mailloux. Huge impact. We were in the middle of the theory wars at Syracuse in the late 1980s and early 1990s; *Rhetorical Power* came out of that and made a contribution to that dialogue. I never was sure how important rhetoric was going to be in my work until I read Mailloux. Rhetoric as Steve then defined it—it is one of the few things I have committed to memory in the last thirty years ("the political effectivity of trope and argument in culture")—is still amazingly generative for me, as was the entire book. In fact, I remember reading the book one June nearly straight through in one long sitting and then going to bed and dreaming about it. I woke up, went directly to the study, and wrote out with no cross outs or revisions from start to finish, the majority of " The End(s) of Theory"—my response to his argument—and the final chapter of *Thinking Through Theory*.

To be friends with these folks and see them throughout the process and to see how their regular daily work and life fit into the single-authored book composing process was so crucial to me as a developing scholar and then tenured academic. Of course, through all of this time, Patricia Bizzell's work, collected in *Academic Discourse and Critical Consciousness* in 1992, was changing C/R. Only David Bartholomae has had a greater influence on C/R from 1980 to 2000. So I kept up with most of Bizzell's work as well. One cannot understand C/R then or now without Bizzell.

Finally, since tenure and the book, from about 1994 to the present, I have focused on two large areas of work. First, social class, first-generation college students, and composition. Of course, when Vygotsky argues that to understand language you have to theorize it in terms of social relations, sign, and sign image, the subject of social class as the prime social relation comes to the fore. So because the social relations part of this model was there in Vygotsky from the beginning—for Vygotsky higher psychological functions are internalized and transformed social relations—social class was also there from the beginning. One way to say all of this concisely and to reach an audience that might know Foucault but does not know Vygotsky or activity theory is to call the object of study "discourse" in the way Foucault uses that term in *The Archaeology of Knowledge*. (That book is one of the top three or four most important books in my life, right up there with the Bible.) When we begin to think of social class as discourse, as the intersection of language and power, as rhetoric, rather than something that the sociology or anthropology departments do, we have a chance of getting social class on the table in C/R. The discipline wants to talk about diversity, yet does not talk nearly enough about social class diversity, of our many and increasing numbers of first-generation college students. I was one of them. And they are the future of C/R. More of them are coming to four-year and research one universities, and the composition curriculum put in place in the last two decades is outdated and does not serve them. The recent work of Nancy Welch, Tony Scott, Doug Downs and Elizabeth Wardle, and Ann Penrose shows great promise, and I try to read everything they put out.

Foucault's notion of discourse (and later authorship) plays into future work I will do on the social formation of gay authorship and gay male literature. Tracking the changes in the gay community and the ways this has transacted with the formation of authorship and literature since Stonewall is a complete case study in multi-modal method from theory to history to empirical work, from start to finish. Obviously, this is of personal interest to me, but as one man who came out through literacy, that is by reading gay literature and identifying with it, it is also a literacy project. But this project is more than that; it is a way I hope to witness to a whole generation of gay men who are gone—who have died—largely due to public policy decisions of the Reagan administration. It is a witness and a testament to the creativity, the labor, that went into community building from Stonewall in 1969 and throughout the 1970s. As a younger member of that generation I saw some of the social formation first hand. Patrick Moore in *Beyond Shame* captures this utopian dimension of the work. As a survivor of what Larry Kramer early on called the gay holocaust, I feel I have an obligation to witness.

Taylor: Could you give an assessment of the major issues in composition and rhetoric today? To what extent are these related to or beholding to the issues that dominated early in C/R?

Zebroski: Three or four key issues come to mind. Obviously, given all I have said, the most important event of the next decade in C/R is going to be the radical shift in the student populations who come to university and into our classes and curriculum. We are on the verge of a period of change in C/R no less profound than occurred during open admissions in the late 1960s. Usually, this issue is set forth under the banner of diversity or, worse yet, multiculturalism. Of course, I am all for thinking about C/R in multicultural and "diverse" terms; we do so at University of Houston already where our students are already mostly not white, not traditional college age (18 years old). And they are mostly first-generation college students. The students at UH now look more like what the college students in the rest of the country will look like in ten or fifteen years if the trends the demographers are predicting are accurate. The most immediate effect of this tidal of wave of new student populations that the demographers are telling us is about to break is that the curriculum we have put in place in C/R over the last twenty years does not work for these students. Ann Penrose shows that given the usual curriculum both in and out of C/R, these first-generation college students simply leave. So we are going to have to change the standard college composition curriculum which has been built around academic discourse, argument, formulas for writing academic argument and writing in the disciplines that simply reproduce what the faculty in the disciplines say that they want. None of these standard C/R approaches seems to work with these new students.

These students—my students now: I taught freshman composition this year—are natural rhetoricians. They often speak fluently multiple languages, they frequently and easily code-switch, they live in several cultures, they cross borders like crazy. They constantly have to factor in, in a conscious way, culture and language and power in their thinking about their everyday lives. It would make sense to build a curriculum off of these strengths that I do not even have. These students are expert rhetoricians and are comfortable living ethnographically, expecting diversity, difference, multiculturalism.

They are also working like crazy—too much sometimes—so we need to put social class and working at the center of the curriculum. It is something first-generation students know a lot about as Tony Scott and Nancy Welch have shown. Add that up and C/R is going to have to put social class at the center of its reconceptualizing and rebuilding—from scratch if necessary—the college composition curriculum. I cannot say this too loudly: unchanged, our current approach will send the students of the future away from the university. We have to change the current college composition curriculum, in a principled way, knowing what we know about language, rhetoric, and writing development.

Second, I do not see current Writing Program Administration folks as grappling very much with this issue. What I see at best are debates about whether we should or should not use Graff and Birkenstein's textbook. I see more and more of the 4Cs program taken up with WPA identified speakers and peculiarly WPA issues of installing post-Fordist practices—contingent labor, outcomes assessment, outsourcing of C/R into the disciplines and corporate boardrooms. These practices are often defended by the use of what Nancy Mack has called the culture of fear—either we do these things, or they will be done to us. But if these practices increasingly keep students away from the university or flush them out of the university, can we simply accept them? Should we accept them without deliberation regardless? (Another argument I have heard: let's not talk about whether or not we are going to do these; rather let's talk about how we can do these practices.

Now I realize that all WPAs are well-intentioned, and I realize that they do bring an expertise to WPA work. No one does that work without good intentions and expertise. I have many WPA friends. Many WPAs even share my views about social transformation. But will we create a new curriculum for our new students if it is clear that current so-called "best practices"—a term borrowed from the "best practices" of the business world—are inadequate, in the sense of sending students away? Of discouraging students? Of making students feel like they have no stake in the university? Retention has been a major issue for some time, but it will become increasingly important when the next wave of first-generation college students hits the university. And retention is a problem according to the Penrose study because students do not feel welcomed into the university and its work because we are treating these folks as students rather than as fellow intellectuals, the way Antonio Gramsci thought of intellectuals. Will WPAs lead this curricular transformation?

I sometimes wonder if it might be better for all concerned including WPAs, if WPAs simply went off and formed their own discipline. WPA work would seem to have more similarities to what MBA programs do than what English or communication departments do. I would not have a problem hiring WPAs "outside" the discipline of C/R to do WPA work, though I also wonder how well a department would survive without WPAs. Would a post-Fordist English department, for instance, function without WPAs to manage contingent labor? How precisely? Can, in fact, one have contingent labor without WPAs or their equivalent?

But I also do not feel like the discipline of C/R has to keep the same form it has had for thirty years. It will not; it is changing as I speak. English and speech split at the start of the twentieth century. Both advantages and disadvantages resulted. Some writing departments have formed independently of English departments. No one argues that is beyond the pale. Some have argued that rhetoric should dump composition. Some have argued that rhet comp should abolish freshman composition. So maybe WPA and C/R should split? Why should we not think about that? Let me stress that this is a question I am posing, not an answer. My focus is always not with WPA, but with the success of the new wave of first-generation college students that are already beginning to show up on our doorsteps.

Third, to ask questions about WPA work is to raise the issue of sustainability. We need to theorize the current "boom" in the economy of C/R because if there is one sure thing we know about capitalism, it is that the "bust" is soon to follow. With the job market, for example, white hot in C/R, how are our strategic goals being distorted by this hot economy? Who loses out when newly minted graduates of doctoral programs in C/R have multiple offers and often engage in bidding wars—perfectly expected and accepted in capitalism and in a boom economy, of course. Is bigger always better? Is more (faculty, C/R courses fielded, majors in C/R, graduate programs in C/R, numbers served at the writing center, etc.) always better than less? In terms of the quality of the curriculum we offer? In terms of numbers of C/R positions advertised in the *Job Information List* of MLA? Can small be beautiful? Due to this boom (from which admittedly I too have benefited), we have gotten very good in C/R at getting bigger, at expansion almost for expansion sake, at taking over, at moving the C/R project from the classroom and into creative writing and into the dean's office and into the lecture rooms of faculty in other disciplines. Richard Miller, among others, has said he sees it as C/R's mission, a sort of disciplinary manifest destiny I suppose, to take over the role of being the teaching arm of the whole university. So what happens when that boom busts?

But sustainability is also about issues now beyond the discipline of C/R which is small potatoes in comparison. One reason I am in Houston and working at University of Houston is that this is the belly of the beast. Ground zero for the ecological catastrophe. Marx spent most of his days in London, the seat of capitalism of that day. Houston, the home to numerous multinational oil companies—at least at present—has over a hundred different language communities and has attracted the newest wave of immigrants. Houston is the contemporary example of what I imagine it was like for my father's mother and father to come to America from Poland before Poland even technically existed. Houston now has the feel of a world city, dynamic, large, ethnic, full of immigrants and the children of immigrants from Mexico, Latin America, the Caribbean, the former Soviet domains like Ukraine, but also India, Pakistan, Nigeria, Saudi Arabia and the Middle East. Houston is teeming with both unimaginable wealth and unimaginable third-world poverty, all within blocks of each other and often in the same blocks of the same neighborhood. The economy is booming here, yet Houston, at least, knows bust and has known it well recently. One only has to say Enron and Anderson Accounting. In this kind of economy in which the future is unclear, one goes to the university as one of the few remaining ways of insuring oneself and bettering oneself. In my father's generation, one did not need to go to college; one worked harder, did overtime, and fought through the union to consolidate those gains for your old age and for your children. Now, perhaps sadly, the only way of doing that, of buying social and economic insurance, is by extending one's education. Probably people should not have to go to college, but given the constant elimination and outsourcing of jobs, my students do not see any alternative.

The first-year student population at UH five years ago was already more than fifty per cent first-generation college students; every faculty person and administrator I have talked to since I arrived is sure that the figures are much bigger now. It is a place where most of my students spend more than an hour commuting on freeways and in terrible urban traffic just to get to campus and class. High gas prices are directly tied to my students and whether they can afford to get to campus.

So how is C/R's ideology about its own success and its assumption that success is infinitely elastic and inevitable into the near future related to the same ideology in American culture and in our public policy, to the ideology that my first-generation college students and often second-generation Americans bring to my classroom?

We are on the edge of an ecological global catastrophe. Huge SUVs are still being purchased. We still are acting like it is 1955 and the way we live will go on for another fifty or sixty years. How much are Americans really changing their lives with the ecological disaster in mind? How much is C/R talking about that, let alone dealing with it? I hate to put it in such scary terms, but will human life on the planet be sustainable over the next century?

Let me end optimistically. While a planetary shift in a way of life has not been demanded before now in history (it may have occurred in prehistoric times), cultures have had to change fast or die. Margaret Mead's title *New Lives for Old* points to that. But such transformation requires a composing of a new society including new concepts of self, of body, of economy, of the gods, of what passes as the good life or a high quality of life. The old gods are dying and new ones have not yet arrived, or if they have, they are being very quiet. The planet is not going to support 10 billion people or whatever it is currently at, each with their own SUV. I wonder if the planet can even feed that many people and for how long. Yet one of the most interesting cultural shifts occurring over two to three hundred years that I know of is the shift from the classical world, from the Roman Empire, from classical rhetoric, to the Byzantine world and the western medieval world. This period is called by classicists late antiquity. Peter Brown and many classicists currently working in this area have made fascinating discoveries. Brown, for example, shows in his book *The Body and Society: Men, Women, and Sexual Renunciation in Early Christianity* how a tightly integrated imperialist world culture, built on the idea of the centrality to the state of the patriarchal family, masculine supremacy, and its reproduction, was transformed within a couple of generations into world in which the solitary (*monochos,* i.e. monk) and communities of solitaries voluntarily renounced previous sexual and familial norms, practices, and desires. They constructed a much more ecological culture for a culture that after a thousand years was at its limits of expansion. In that process of transformation, at least at first, there was more equality between social classes and genders. But it involved a total reconceptualization of the worldview and a cutting back on what was thought of as material necessities for a complete and happy life. Simplicity and smallness and a new awareness of the individual were privileged. Now I am not arguing for the reproduction of that shift. I am simply saying that radical cultural change can happen and can be chosen. In part, that is what C/R is about—creating through language alternative worlds, countercultures, social formations. I believe we are on the brink of such a transformation. Whether the planetary catastrophe can be slowed down or averted may well lie with our response to one question: can we and our students imagine a world and our life where we live on less? Can we see small as beautiful? Of course, that is just the start, but I believe that we can and we shall and the C/R is already beginning its work in helping to enact new practices of what Foucault called the arts of living.

Taylor: As you see your career in the context of institutions, teaching colleges and major universities, what stands out? That is, how has each institution shaped you as a scholar, teacher, writer?

Zebroski: The effect of my institutional location has been enormous, second perhaps only to the theoretical stance I have taken. I see my experience at a wide range of universities over a long period of time to be an important resource that I bring to my current work at University of Houston where I hope to put together a Ph.D. in composition and rhetoric that prepares people for work at a variety of institutions including small liberal arts colleges, medium state universities, even local community colleges in the Houston area. The major binaries of our field—small school/large school; liberal arts college/tier I research university; private university/ public university; teaching/ research; to name just a few—construct our institutions and us; one almost needs to be an "organic deconstructionist" to unravel these binaries to the extent where one can clear a space to survive and live as a scholar, teacher, and writer in composition and rhetoric.

Let me start with some preliminary remarks about institutions. I find one of the most helpful (and hopeful) visions of institutions to be the one which Victor Turner constructed from his work in cultural anthropology and which can be found in his works like *The Ritual Process*. Turner argues that it is helpful to see institutions as a structure, but one that is in process and is a process or set of processes in change. We in composition rhetoric too often see institutions as monolithic and as unchanging. We regularly see award-winning articles calling for compositionists to be institution change agents. But Turner suggests this is a naïve view of institutions, that institutions are not static and monolithic, and we do not come to an institution as a change agent, so much as we come into a changing institution which we then with the collaboration of others may work to modulate. Even more important, Turner sees institutions as made up both of structures, that is hierarchies and statuses we are assigned to and inhabit, but also and more fundamentally anti-structures, liminal holes, gaps, and spaces—he also calls them interstices or inter-spaces—which largely define the structures. It is this constant dialectical process between structure and anti-structure that is the process that we call a university or a discipline or a society.

Resistance becomes possible on its own terms when one accepts Turner's idea of anti-structure. Turner's theory accounts for both the possibility of transformation and the near certainty of fossilization and reification of institutions or parts of them, in any society, large or small. So a scholar or teacher or writer interested in social transformation would benefit from an examination of Turner's theory.

Anyone who has worked or studied at both a large and a small university knows many aspects of this theory already through their everyday experience. The large university tends toward bureaucratization and fragmentation, rules for the sake of rules. The smaller college has its share of these too but often the forces that unite the campus are more obvious at a smaller school. Sometimes it is religious affiliation. I worked at a Roman Catholic university (Saint Edward's University in Austin, Texas) and a university affiliated with the Evangelical Lutheran Church (Capital University in Columbus, Ohio). Those faith communities had profound effects on those schools not so much in the dogma and religious practice—we used to joke at Capital that Lutherans were a minority in the student body and among the faculty; only one of the English faculty was Lutheran—but in a sense of commitment to something bigger, something more than the students, the job, and the pay. Larger schools may have such sub-communities but they tend to be dissipated when it comes to the university at large. Syracuse University where I worked for fifteen years, for instance, long ago broke its ties with the Methodist church and, despite the fact that Hendricks Chapel was at the head of the Quad, felt in many ways very much like a state university.

It is strange that the discipline of composition and rhetoric, as structured a collective as any, on the one hand pulls many doctoral students into its web by playing up the pleasures and joys of teaching which are many and seen as a strength, even an advantage, of studying in our field. But then once the student passes through the rite of passage of the doctoral program, and attains disciplinary status by getting a Ph.D., the student-become-professor is supposed to be off to a research I university to research. Or at least is supposed to be a writing program administrator. Teaching is supposed to be less an interest. Teaching jobs at teaching universities are too often looked down upon in doctoral programs. This sometimes feels like a kind of shell game; after undergoing the curriculum in most composition and rhetoric doctoral programs, one would think that the only jobs available, or the only good jobs available, were at research universities or, alternatively, were WPA positions.

But what impressed me in my career starting in 1982—and no one in my doctoral program ever mentioned this either—was that the teaching university is still very much alive and well. The small liberal arts university or the small state university rarely demands huge amounts of published scholarship though all of them want evidence of some sort of ongoing professional and scholarly commitment. Yet our graduate students in the major doctoral programs are not being made aware of such positions and certainly are not encouraged to apply for such positions or to desire to go to such schools, let alone to value the sort of work they do; in fact, one colleague who did eventually go on to a position at such a teaching university and really only wanted that from the start, was told by the former dissertation adviser how disappointing that decision was. All of the work of the adviser and the doctoral program put into this student, and then the person does not want to go to a tier I school, but rather just wants to teach—that was the sense of it. My experience at St. Ed's, Slippery Rock, and Capital calls this sort of conventional wisdom into question. The professionalism and the quality of teaching at these places were the highest of my professional career. I am still friends with folks at each of these institutions and see them regularly at 4Cs and in other forums, itself an interesting commentary on the stereotypes of professors at small and medium-sized universities; many are involved in the professional activity and ongoing research projects. I respect the work they do. And I would add that these folks also were quite up to date on new work in the field and kept their own research and scholarly projects alive.

Now I don't want to be accused of romanticizing the small university. Obviously, the teaching loads have a tremendous effect on one's ability to do anything else including scholarship. Each of the smaller liberal arts and state universities I taught at had 4/4 loads, all in composition and most of that in freshman composition. Over the years 2002-2007, for instance, I taught at least three freshman composition courses each term, over thirty sections of freshman composition total, in addition to about one section each term of critical writing or creative nonfiction, or advanced composition. As everyone knows, writing courses with from three to six papers each term to be graded, are labor intensive That is a heavy load no matter how many students per class. Capital had the best class rates at about 20 or so, fewer for upper division major courses, which was a treat. For those who do want to write and publish in the discipline, that is very difficult to do at the small school. But I also think we need to take stock of our graduate students at doctoral-producing institutions and note they mostly say that they want to teach, not do scholarship and certainly not do writing program administration. I do not have a problem with that. We need all sorts of people.

I was clear pretty much from the start that I did want to write and publish; my career has mostly traced a path across institutions that increasingly allowed me to do that. My five-year stay at Capital was, however, also shaped by a need to be closer to help take care of my mother. And my return to a large state university, the University of Houston, has occurred because I have the opportunity here of putting together a new innovative composition and rhetoric Ph.D. Still, despite its size, UH in some ways feels more like the smaller schools in its teacherly focus and in its interest in pedagogy, I think because our students are different from what many professors had experienced elsewhere. So they have to rethink what they learned about teaching. The majority of our students are the first generation of their family to go to college. They are often the children of immigrants. They are the most diverse student body I have ever worked with. This student population which looks more like what the college students at other universities will look like in a decade or two, will be the foundation of our Ph.D., which will be one of the few to focus explicitly and fully from the start on pedagogy and curriculum. Other Ph.D programs, of course, have that as a spinoff, as a byproduct, in their programs, but they also attend mostly to the politics of writing or to ethnicity and rhetoric, or to writing program administration or archival scholarship, or other specific areas, all legitimate areas to focus on, of course.

But our signature is that our RCP concentration—rhetoric, composition and pedagogy—will theorize the local, will produce teachers who are ready with strategies for reconceptualizing the college writing curriculum by generating innovative practices in individual courses, in majors and minors, in Masters programs and in community programs. So the interest and enthusiasm of UH for pedagogy have the feel of what one often encounters in a good department at a small or mid-size university.

Still, if I have any doubts where I am at, all I have to do is recall how quickly we were able to make major curricular changes at Capital and how long and involved even relatively simple changes here at UH seem to take. The term I came into Capital, I was asked to work up a syllabus and proposal for a creative nonfiction workshop course; I did that, submitted it, it was approved, and I was teaching the first section of that course the following fall term. A streamlined process. We could change the professional writer major almost instantly at Capital. The curriculum was less fossilized because of this; it could be changed nearly overnight. I think it is interesting that while many large universities do not have writing majors, the small and midsize universities I worked at had such majors years ago.

On the other hand, at UH, we do this work through several committees, and before we even start that process, we need to decide whether our students would benefit from a concentration within the literature department and its doctoral requirements, or whether we should take the longer route and set up an independent composition rhetoric degree under the aegis of English. When it came to the majors, there was never a comparable debate at the smaller universities I have worked at, in part because the literature faculty were well aware of the value of having a writing major and having the composition faculty very involved in it and in teaching freshman composition. About half my professional career has been spent at small and mid-sized universities teaching a good deal of freshman composition. I do not regret that; in fact, I believe it has enriched my work and my scholarship. I think all rhetoric and composition people should teach freshman composition at least once every two or three years. I think we in the discipline of composition and rhetoric tend to forget that the twentieth-century history of freshman composition entailed first that any English faculty person teach the course at least occasionally. John Crowe Ransom was an established and tenured faculty at Vanderbilt in the 1930s, a member of the famous Fugitive Group and a poet. Yet he still regularly taught freshman composition and had some interesting things to say about that. After a few more years, first-year writing was shunted off to the new literature faculty who taught it and the sophomore literature survey till tenure. By the 1950s and into the 1960s, TAs were increasing in numbers and the burden for teaching the freshman English course fell on them, especially after English fought speech communication for the course as John Heyda's historical work shows. Now established tenured faculty in composition and rhetoric rarely teach the course.

First-year writing is the most difficult but most important course we teach. So because I have spent about half of my professional life at smaller schools where the older way of doing things still holds on, I have taught first-year writing a lot. As I noted earlier, one of things that has taught me is that our student populations are changing and that our conventional wisdom about the first-year course and the undergraduate composition curriculum does not fit our changing students and that we are going to have to reconceptualize college composition over the next few years. It would seem that the old academic discourse curriculum worked fairly well for students in the 1980s but the students of the twenty-first century need something different.

Elizabeth Wardle is Associate Professor and Director of Writing Programs at the University of Central Florida in Orlando. She has published in journals such as *CCC, TCQ, Enculturation, WPA Journal*, and *Across the Disciplines*, among others. She recently completed a four-year longitudinal study of transfer from composition. With Doug Downs she is working on a textbook for Bedford/St Martin's to facilitate a writing-about-writing pedagogy in first-year composition. Her research interests center around the nature of composition as a course and a discipline.

The Conversation

Victor Taylor: Describe the dominant intellectual and academic context within which you decided to study composition and rhetoric?

Elizabeth Wardle: I began an MA program in English literature at the University of Louisville in 1997, after beginning (but not completing) an MA in Humanities, and completing a BA in philosophy. I had no knowledge of composition, and certainly no intention of studying it. I did, however, receive a TAship, and was required to take a Composition Theory and Pedagogy class before beginning. This class was extremely difficult for me, primarily because it privileged the theoretical when I wanted practical. Later, I came to appreciate that I needed to understand why and how writing worked before I could consider the daily teaching to-do list, but at the time the class did not win me over to the study of composition. Fortunately, teaching composition *did* win me over. As a teacher, I found myself constantly facing questions that seemed to require a researched answer if I wanted to help students become better writers. I wondered what benefits peer review had for the reader as well as the writer; I wondered how group work impacted writing; I wondered about the social and cultural influences on writing. My questions about my students and their writing led me to take another composition course, one on composition research, with Debra Journet and visiting professor Carol Berkenkotter. In this class, I found that extensive research and theory existed on topics of interest to me, particularly on the sociocognitive influences on the activities of composing. Here I found some, though not all, of the answers to the questions about writing I faced when I went into my composition classrooms. I determined to conduct a thesis study that looked at how students learned new genres through workshopping, and I applied to a PhD program in Rhetoric and Professional Communication at Iowa State University.

At Iowa State, I began a research project that linked writing in school to writing in the workplace. I had access to a new computer support specialist and was able to watch and talk with him as he struggled with the conventions of writing in a new and unfamiliar community. As I studied "Alan," I thought repeatedly about my composition students, who were also struggling with new and unfamiliar discourse conventions. In both cases, I found motivation (or lack thereof) to be a primary factor in how well (or poorly) the novice was able to learn new written genres and their conventions.

I was also fortunate to be named Assistant (and then later Associate) Director of English Learning Communities. In this capacity, I was able to see (and study) firsthand the struggles that teachers of all kinds faced as they tried to make composition courses relevant to their students. I watched intriguing partnerships between composition teachers and teachers of other disciplines, and I also watched completely failed partnerships. At the end of the day, though, regardless of the level of coordination and partnership, I found that nearly all composition teachers were frustrated by the goals of composition (which they understood as "teach students to write" generally, or specifically in the academy) and often subverted those goals to ones they felt better able to achieve (such as "teach about culture and power").

My understanding of the study of "Alan" and of the composition teachers was facilitated by sociocultural and cultural-historical theories that took into account not only the individual but also the context and the interaction between the individual, the community, the context, and other activity systems.

Taylor: What were the visible intellectual and/or disciplinary "contests" at the time and, in hindsight, what were the "invisible" but influential ones?

Wardle: When I began my doctoral program, my knowledge of the field centered around social and sociocognitive and activity approaches to composition—Berkenkotter and Huckin, Haas, Bazerman, Russell, McCarthy and Fishman, Bartholomae, Dias, Freedman, Medway, Pare. This was not necessarily the dominant intellectual context at the time. These approaches seemed to be competing with cultural theory (or, as Fulkerson calls it, "critical cultural studies" or CCS). Most of the composition journals at the time seemed to privilege critical cultural studies over sociocognitive research. Looking back, I see this as a battle arising from a false division between theory, research, and teaching. Obviously there were exceptions, but theory was the dominating lens and influenced what composition scholars looked for when they went into the classroom and when they wrote about classroom activities.

Much of the CCS work theorized and used narrative to explore and comment on issues of power, authority, sexism, racism, classism, in generalized ways—by which I mean it focused on empowerment generally, not necessarily empowerment of *writers* specifically. Here there was a clear departure from the earlier cognitive process research and the later sociocognitive research, both of which focused more directly on the teaching of writing and the activities of writing. The cultural studies work was often not tied directly to the activities of writing and writing instruction, nor did it use what Haswell calls RAD (replicable, aggregable, data-driven) methods to study those activities. CCS theorists were focused on how students might respond to an article on, say, class or race, whereas sociocognitive researchers might focus on how class background might affect students' writing processes, products, and attitudes about writing. CCS theorists might focus on citizenship in general, while sociocognitive researchers were more focused on citizen *writers* specifically. As a writing teacher and researcher, I found "empowerment" in general to be too large a goal for one classroom whose designated focus was writing; I was drawn more to the sociocognitive discussions of how students could be empowered as writers and users of language more specifically. At times, the critical cultural studies approaches of the 1990s often appeared to me to approach writing as literature did, as an activity used in the service of learning the content of cultural studies, and not as the primary object of attention itself. I believe that this contest was probably a predictable result of the fact that many compositionists were also literature specialists, or had begun their careers as literature specialists, and thus worked from many of the same assumptions. And that contest has continued to play out in interesting ways as scholars from my own generation, many of whom were never trained literary scholars, began to publish in the field.

Taylor: As you were making your way through graduate studies, who were some of the other key figures that shaped your understanding of the field and how do you view them today?

Wardle: As I mentioned above, some of the key figures who influenced me in graduate school included Berkenkotter and Huckin, Haas, Bazerman, Russell, McCarthy and Fishman, Bartholomae, Dias, Freedman, Medway, Pare. Others from outside the field also influenced me, particularly Vygotsky and Yrgo Engestrom, as well as Bakhtin. Later, as I became most interested in the role of first-year composition in the university, others became more influential: Petraglia, Crowley, Russell, in particular. I was persuaded by their claims that there is no such thing as "general writing skills" and that FYC is burdened with teaching this very non-existent thing in psuedotransactional ways. Though writing outside composition and outside the university is to accomplish some goal for some audience in a particular, transactional context, writing in FYC tends to be imitations of transactions for pretend audiences in genres I have elsewhere called "mutt genres." Given the scathing nature of the criticisms of FYC and the disheartening results of my own research on the learning community sections of composition, I was strongly persuaded by the abolitionist arguments for doing away with FYC. But I was also persuaded when Russell and others argued for making FYC a "writing-about-writing" class. I found that by replacing the goal of FYC with "teach students *about* writing," we were better able to teach transferable information, we posed an achievable goal that included content as well as process, and we solved our content problem and, thus, our transactionality problem. We were also enabled to empower students in very practical and specific ways linked directly to writing—we were enabled to help them understand themselves as writers, to understand how writing worked in the world, to understand how writing is used to make things work and to both subjugate and empower people. The rationale for such a course was more than convincing to me, but I did not see any of the scholars who argued it putting their ideas into practice within composition programs. It was only when I left graduate school and met Doug Downs that I realized such a curriculum could be implemented and had been in some classrooms. We found that my research made a strong case for the pedagogy, while his assessed the pedagogy, and that together we were able to take the next steps—making public arguments not only for the pedagogy but also for particular instantiations of it (see *CCC* June 2007 and September 2008), and also working at the programmatic level and textbook level to change pedagogies in more than one classroom.

All of this led me to think of our field as generational, with one generation struggling with the history of literature and composition, working sometimes from literary frames that emphasized consumption over production, and often making arguments for theories and pedagogies they did not have the disciplinary authority and autonomy to implement. My generation of rhet/comp scholars generally did not begin in literature. We enrolled in PhD programs to intentionally study composition. Many of us did not encounter adversarial relationships between literature and composition until we began our first jobs. When faced with negative attitudes about composition in our new departments, our reactions have included a willingness to leave English rather than make arguments for acceptance and recognition by literature faculty. For me, the divisions between literature and composition hold little interest, and I have very little desire to try to bridge a gap that has proven to be largely unbridgeable by the preceding generations. The fact that the gap should theoretically be bridgeable is irrelevant; if it is not getting bridged in practice, we are wasting valuable time. Every moment wasted justifying my discipline's knowledge to literature faculty is a moment that is not spent acting out of that knowledge to revise writing programs and pedagogies to better help writing students. My generation, trained by the David Russells and Andrea Lunsfords and Charles Bazermans of the field, came to voice and professional status believing we have the right to be a discipline and to have autonomy over our pedagogies and goals. And we are impatient when we are unable to act autonomously out of our disciplinary knowledge. Sometimes to our own professional detriment, we are unwilling to "keep our heads down" or "lay low" or "go with the flow" until we get tenure.

The practical work of instituting research-based, theoretically sound goals and practices in classes and programs staffed primarily by adjuncts

who often are not aware of the macro-level of Composition Studies seems
to me an important next step in our field's development. I don't think
this was a step that the scholars whom I admired and learned from were
generally free to take. It is a step that has everything to do with power
and authority; what power and authority do we have as a discipline to
change the way we teach (not just individually but programmatically)
and, thus, impact the lives of our students? Answering this question
requires putting aside distinctions and divisions between pedagogy
and theory, research and practice, cultural studies and writing studies,
teaching and administration. If we want to change the lives of our
student writers for the better, we must change the ways they are taught
to write, and we must change their conceptions of writing. For this to
happen, we must bridge the divide between macro-level composition
research and micro-level composition classroom practices; the meso-
level of the writing program must bridge the divide so writing courses
are structured vertically and comprehensively, and so that the teachers
of those various writing courses are empowered to understand and put
research and theory into practice in their classrooms, and thus change
the lives of their students. Writing program administration is where this
happens, or doesn't happen. Where we think creatively and strategically
about changing labor practices and curricular structures. Many of us
fell into writing program administration as untenured faculty in English
departments, and found that we needed every rhetorical strategy at our
disposal to navigate the treacherous terrain. Many of us left English
departments to administer independent writing programs, and many of
us left jobs where we wasted enormous amounts of energy appeasing
literature faculty. But we are finding new ways to structure and staff
writing programs and courses. We can only do this because we came to
professional status in a climate very different than the one encountered
by our mentors.

I would argue that earlier generations of rhet/comp scholars were
often powerless to act out of their research- and theory-based knowledge
because of the field's lack of status and power. As more independent
writing departments emerge, and as writing programs gain more power
and disciplinary authority even within some English departments and

universities, my generation is more able to act out of the knowledge we have as a field. We are grateful to those who came before who had to do this and paved the way for us, because their work has enabled us to assume we are entitled to act as a discipline and work to empower our students to understand themselves as writers and to better use writing as citizens in a democracy.

Taylor: You argue that "composition and rhetoric" is not a discipline, and you see problems with its present status. Would you elaborate?

Wardle: Our lack of disciplinarity results in our inability to seriously exert influence on writing-related matters. We disagree on our name, as well as our central project, making it difficult to even be recognized by the National Research Council. We have no broadly agreed upon set of methods, no internal means of determining appropriateness of methods, and few cooperative research agendas that would enable big questions to be answered piece by piece. We have a tendency to endlessly reinvent the wheel, resulting in few, if any, closed questions. Our ability to assert expertise and influence change has also been hampered by our historical lack of autonomy and place. Established disciplines have academic departments to house, budget, and support research and teaching. In contrast, Writing Studies has rarely had departments, and its home, English, has been largely inhospitable, using composition courses taught by non-specialists to fund literature majors and graduate programs. Partially because we have been hidden away in English Departments, fighting for any autonomy and voice, we have failed to gain much external credibility related to our expertise. Task forces on writing and writing assessment have rarely called on composition experts the way that task forces on other topics call on disciplinary experts on those topics.

I trace a lot of the current situation to the way the field of composition emerged. Unlike other academic areas, we did not begin with an area of study and then create coursework to teach it. Instead, we emerged from a single course prior to research. The course, English A, was originally created to solve an essentially non-disciplinary, non-research-based problem: students can't write. As a result of the creation of this grammar-and-usage Composition course, practitioners began to conduct research based on that original non-academic problem rather than any internal, scholarly one. As that research shaped a field of specialized study, the original mandate for the course, and the course itself, remained despite research over decades that suggested the "problem" ("students can't write") is a red herring and the "solution" (first-year composition) is an ineffective response to the (wrong) problem. As the original course was and remains remedial in the public imagination, knowledge about writing and the teaching of writing are similarly viewed as common sense about basic skills rather than specialized knowledge.

Our common teaching practices endlessly instantiate these assumptions. While graduate programs teach the field's research and theory, most undergraduate writing courses are neither informed by the same nor taught by Writing Studies experts. While much of the field now seems to agree that a truly contentless writing course is impossible, few directly teach the field's specialized knowledge in their writing courses.

So we are caught in a history that continually impedes us as we try to move forward. We do have a body of knowledge and some methods to grow that body of knowledge; we have journals and doctoral programs and conferences. We should be able to teach the knowledge of our field to students, and we should be able to effect change in writing instruction and assessment from kindergarten through graduate school. Why is it so difficult for us to do this? Because we are trapped in a system in which we are identified with one course; that course is seen as remedial; and that course is taught by non-specialists with little training who are often not even paid a living wage. Those instructors are generally not members of the field and the instruction in most writing programs thus continues to instantiate the misconceptions about writing that lead stakeholders to believe that one course can "inoculate" unprepared students so that they can write appropriately in every situation later. We must end this system. If we do not, I fear we will never be able to claim our disciplinarity, change misconceptions about writing, and empower students to be effective writers in their worlds. I believe change must occur at the level of writing program administration. WPAs must work with their administrators and stakeholders to educate for change; we must completely re-imagine the structures through which writing is taught. We must behave as though English A had never come into being, and instead imagine how writing can be taught—systematically and comprehensively—given our shared body of knowledge about it. If this means dismantling composition programs for a while, so be it. The system is broken and must be changed if we are to have any hope of fulfilling our promises of helping all students gain the rhetorical skills they need.

Taylor: I think that you have a very interesting historical point. While I was in grad school, late eighties/early nineties, there were two crises of "disciplinarity" around composition at Syracuse. The first was a tenure case in which a candidate submitted a collection of essays, which included course syllabi, as a "book." For weeks the rumor mill turned out tales of his rejection. First, the story went, a "book" isn't a "collection of essays"; and, second, the story continued, a "book" does not contain syllabi. The second crisis was more personal for me. The "dangling" faculty member was responsible for writing my composition and rhetoric exam, an exam that first had been rejected on the grounds that C/R was not a discipline. So, when the professor received tenure, my exam was approved—after being halted a second time for "format related issues." Once I received a "properly" disciplinary and "properly" formatted exam, I was allowed to take it.

I think this speaks to the problem of disciplines in general. Disciplines have an object(s) of study and methods of study. Composition struggles to make these institutionally visible. Chemistry has the periodic table of the elements and Bunsen burners, which makes it easier. To overcome the obstacles that we've discussed, doesn't composition have to "settle" either in the humanities or social sciences? The alternative is to develop a new category, which IDS attempts. I understand your final point, but with institutional credibility the ultimate test of survival, aren't the rules for the game pretty much established?

Wardle: I suppose that the rules are established. But those rules are also always changing. Disciplines are not static, nor are disciplinary structures, as interdisciplinarity attests. I believe it is possible for Composition to be a discipline according to our own values and practices, some of which are uncommon in other disciplines—inclusivity, attention to local context, etc. I think it is possible to be a discipline with agreed upon objects of study and a range of acceptable methods while still being true to the values that have identified us. To say there are a range of acceptable methods is to suggest that within those we choose what is appropriate given our local context and the expertise and interests of those involved. I believe that we can pursue disciplinarity while simultaneously working to change the institutional structures that make that difficult. We do have expertise and cultural capital to draw upon in making change, yet we so rarely call upon it publicly (this is changing with initiatives like the WPA's Network for Media Action). It is clear to me when I meet with administrators that "selling" good writing instruction and support and the vision of a comprehensive vertical writing curriculum is easy; bringing those visions into reality is not so easy, but the administrators I have worked with are open to hearing new ideas. I ask them to imagine the ends they would like and then together to imagine what structures exist, need to be changed, or need to be created to allow us to bring their desired ends into being. Can Composition and the Writing Program truly serve all faculty and students through consultations, classes, support, publication, celebration, and research from within a department that has other projects (like the analysis of literature) as its goal and which is identified within the Humanities and thus seems not to speak to the other, very different, colleges and schools? If not, then where do we need to be positioned in order to accomplish these ends? Being a provost-funded center is too unstable. Being a department requires, as you suggest, some affiliation with either the Humanities or the Social Sciences.

It seems to be an unresolvable dilemma, but I am not convinced that it is. I think we just have not hit upon the solution yet. Maybe we are, as you suggest, an interdiscipline. But to be truly effective in meeting our goals, we need some of the institutional stability and credibility that comes with being a discipline. Maybe it is possible to be a department that is not identified with any one school but rather that stands between and among them, thus free to act out of our own values in the service of students, faculty, and our object of study, writing. Of course, it is not necessary for the structures to be the same everywhere. Interdisciplinarity usually takes place in individual, unconnected sites. Once a number of centers for writing studies and independent writing departments and provost-funded writing programs and small writing programs within other departments begin acting not just as institutional units but as a network of professional units across institutions, they can function and be recognized as disciplinary.

I do believe that we have a number of initiatives that are moving us toward this; our professional conferences, media initiatives, writing experts who serve on the AP exam board or on national assessment panels are all examples of writing studies initiatives that pull from units across institutions and help identify us as disciplinary experts. But we still are not broadly recognized by the public as existing and having identifiable expertise beyond "grammar." And we have apparently been ineffective in changing misconceptions; the public, and even members of the academy, still tend to equate writing with grammar, to see writing instruction as "basic" and "remedial."

What will change this? Institutional structures must be adapted so that we can use our capital to change classroom and assessment practices, public attitudes, and knowledge about writing. Again, I'm not entirely sure what this will look like, but I am not willing to accept that the rules of the game are established and there is no possibility for change. If I've learned anything from activity theory, it is that activity systems constantly change, and the very sorts of contradictions that I've been discussing here are the root of that change.

Taylor: Since our discussion is taking place over the holiday season, I am forced to use a cooking analogy. The academy is a "kitchen"—just let me go with this—right? A lot of chefs, sous-chefs, ingredients, utensils, pots, pans, equipment, and unreasonable expectations. Everyone has a recipe and a special way to chop celery. The difference collapses, however, when one considers the outcome. Kitchens produce meals and the academy produces knowledge, which has higher stakes. If this analogy works at all, I think it speaks to your recent discussion in *CCC*. Your response, as

I read it, said, "let's accept different techniques and focus on goals." The problem is that in composition people have a difficult time separating the two or seeing a variety in the former. Isn't this one of major changes necessary to bring about new writing curricula?

Wardle: Maybe it is more accurate to say that I am arguing that techniques matter, but if they are not in the service of a thoughtful and meaningful goal, they don't get very far. If you are doing all that chopping of celery but you don't know what you are making or why, you are wasting a lot of time. We have spent a lot of time and attention on techniques, and sometimes those techniques have become our goals. We can see how fruitless this is in the kitchen analogy. Should my goal be to have the best celery-chopping technique ever? Well, that goal is okay if it is in the service of a larger goal—like quickly and efficiently chopping the celery for the stuffing for our Christmas dinner. Seeing writing as a process and teaching it that way, with drafts and peer revision and portfolio grading, has been very important for changing how students write and feel about themselves as writers. So much of our TA training and discussion, though, seems to focus only on technique. How do you set up a workshop? How do you give good feedback that encourages revision? How do you grade a portfolio? And these are important questions. But I notice that they sometimes become so important that the larger goal of a writing class seems to be eclipsed. When I started my job here at UCF this summer, I held the composition teacher orientation. I asked the teachers to take a look at the goals of the comp class and put aside the assignments and daily to-do list. I asked them to consider what the goals of comp should be, first, and then discuss ways to achieve these goals. As I walked around the room, I realized that almost no one was doing this. They were all talking about the specific assignments they teach and giving each other advice about how to teach those assignments. I kept trying to steer them back to the larger goals—what are we doing in comp and why? But they wanted to talk about techniques. I see this as a serious impediment to making any meaningful change in the writing curricula. I want to come up with goals and then techniques for achieving those goals *with* my teachers. Many of them, however, just want me to tell them what assignments to teach and how to teach them. I want them to seriously question the efficacy of various assignments in achieving the goals of the class; many of them want a to-do list.

So, yes, I agree with you that we must find a way to separate goals and techniques, and to involve everyone teaching comp in a discussion about this. I think part of the difficulty of doing this is that it is a theoretical problem—what are we doing here and why? What should we be doing here and why? What does research and theory show about the nature of writing and learning to write, and how does that impact what we even can attempt to do here? Theoretical discussions like this seem to be very difficult for people to have, as anyone who has ever taught a theory class can attest. But I also know, from teaching a theory class every year, that everyone can learn to do this, with practice and guidance. So part of my job as a WPA is to keep steering my teachers toward discussions of goals, and to expose them to the research and theory about writing so that they have some knowledge base for making a judgment about appropriate goals. Without some knowledge of the research and theory about writing, people make judgments about appropriate goals out of their assumptions about writing, and as we have been discussing, most people have serious misconceptions about the nature of writing and how people learn to write. And, as we've also discussed, many of the people teaching writing have no more training in the field of rhet/comp than those students in their classes. So the teachers need to be invited into the discipline—okay, let me say it like this—the teachers need to be invited to explore the knowledge of the field so that all of us together are then more disciplinary. We may not end up agreeing on what the goals of comp should be, but I would be a lot more comfortable about where we are going if we were all informed about the research on writing and having active and thoughtful discussions about what the goals of composition classes should be. And I'll also add that I am comfortable with having varied goals because I think we should not be relying on one writing class. If we have a vertical, comprehensive writing curriculum and many writing classes, then the goals for the various classes can and should be varied. It's hard to agree on a goal for composition because that one class gets burdened with all of our hopes and dreams and research and theory—no one class can enact all that.

David E. Kirkland is Assistant Professor of English Education at New York University and also serves as the national advisor for the Teachers Network Leadership Institute. His research focuses broadly upon urban youth culture, African American language and literacies, and urban teacher education. He has published numerous journal articles and book chapters and has received several awards for his scholarship and service. Currently, he is writing two books: *A Search Past Silence: Exploring Literacy in the Life Young Black Men* and *Social Justice: From Theory to Policy* (with sj Miller). He is also co-author of the recently published *Narratives of Social Justice Teaching: How English Teachers Negotiate Theory and Practice between Preservice and Inservice Spaces.*

The Conversation

Keith Gilyard: Much of your work has to do with trying to figure out how different populations, including specifically our folks in the city, in the 'hood, are strategically using language. How do you approach the notion of rhetoric and focus on that idea in your research?

David Kirkland: First and foremost, my work looks at youth culture, specifically as it relates to African American language, literacy, and urban education. I examine the ways youth use language compellingly to speak back to structures of power as well as to carve out spaces where they can live more prosperously. I have studied language and literacy in Hip Hop and in digital communities like Facebook. In both contexts, you see youth remixing languages, styles, and arguments to make sense of the present and speak back to their past and to the powers that have prevented the possibilities of that past.

Gilyard: When you bring these ideas up, you have to anticipate a number of arguments about the value of Hip Hop as a discursive strategy. How do you respond to critics who don't see the value of Hip Hop the way you describe it, that is, as a progressive and critical rhetorical practice?

Kirkland: Well, I think we can no longer make an argument that Hip Hop isn't relevant in terms of studying rhetorical devices. A significant body of work and opinion builds a compelling case that Hip Hop has complex and sophisticated rhetorical features—from the work of H. Samy Alim to the work of people like Ernest Morell, Maisha Fisher, Elaine Richardson, Gwen Pough, and many others. There's my own work, which looks critically at a range of social theories as they intersect with Hip Hop. Even what Lil' Wayne is doing, you know—talking about "my girls can't wear dat/dat's where my stash is at"—comments on his current situation inside the Ninth Ward in New Orleans. There is an African proverb that goes like this: Until the lion has letters to write history, the story of the jungle will forever glorify the hunter. Hip Hop gives the lion letters. It doesn't matter what the hell the lion is saying, but what's important is that the lion is recording and reporting on his or her story.

Gilyard: In some ways, this is like the conversation about African American language from the 1960s and 1970s. Like a replay. So much work had to be done to prove the language was systematic and had structure and rhetorical strategies. Seems like we have to do the same thing all over again.

Kirkland: The work still has to be done. We need to be descriptive about this literacy and map it. A lot of that has happened. But there's an issue of power, too. A lot of previous research had been done for whites. Blacks already knew that their language had a system because they used it systematically to enormous effect. Now we need scholarship that explains the way that people are transacting, persuading one another, making compelling cases to one another—both bending and using a new African American Language. We are talking about a new art of rhetoric. It would be problematic if we didn't study it in the first place and in its own right because we see with Hip Hop a revitalization. Youth and people in the city are creating languages of connection and critique and sometimes a language of accommodation. I mean we can criticize Hip Hop, but we would be missing a vital point if we fail to acknowledge the ways in which Hip Hop practitioners are creating a language that (1) belongs to them and (2) gives them a space and a way to communicate, to participate, and to be.

Gilyard: Do you make a distinction, as Cornel West does, between what he terms Prophetic Hip Hop and what we can probably just call Commercial Hip Hop? Often, when people speak of Hip Hop, they are referring exclusively to what's being released by large record companies. They generally don't know the whole universe of Hip Hop, the stuff coming out in these other spaces, these underground spaces that are sometimes progressive. There's a whole prophetic wing that we're not going hear on the radio and on the CDs from Sony and places like that.

Kirkland: Whenever we talk about Hip Hop as a singular, I think we are talking about a specific cultural movement or at least an aspect of counter culture that was created inside of urban communities. I think it's important to talk about Hip Hop, like you are doing, in pluralistic ways also. In a sense, we have Hip Hops. You're right no matter how we want to tag that. You can put any adjective you want to describe the Hip Hops, such as Prophetic Hip Hop, Conscious Hip Hop, Gangsta Hip Hop, Radical Hip Hop, whatever. That can be productive for certain kinds of analyses. But I also think that a deep structure sits at the core of Hip Hop. If Hip Hop has a deep structure, that deep structure speaks to those conditions of powerlessness that Geneva Smitherman talks about. It also speaks to the possibility of agitation. It articulates these ideas through movement, through dance, through—with rap being its verbal language—a sort of visceral hunger to be heard. It's very much the "Spoken Soul" of Claude Brown. It's Shirley Brice Heath's *Ways with Words*. It's the sorrow songs of W. E. B. Du Bois. It's all of that wrapped up and woven into one. It's not only a prophetic voice. It's a political voice, a voice of propaganda, a voice of provocation. It's also a voice of humanity. Sometimes it's used to expose our dirty little secrets. Other times it's used to express, in its simplest form, our hearts.

Gilyard: Well, that's part of our affirming our full humanity.

Kirkland: It's part of affirming our full humanity, and all of that stuff needs to be considered. If you only consider the good aspects, if you are selective with Hip Hop, then you get a kind of Hip Hop that can be used to make arguments to all people. You know, I'm at a point where I'm willing to accept Hip Hop on its own terms, its messiness as well as its beauty.

Gilyard: That's the only way to take it, really. That's the way we take everything else.

Kirkland: That's the way we take everything else. Some people don't have to make these kinds of distinctions. When we talk about white rhetorics and white art and white culture—and I know they get the privilege not to have to use the adjective *white* when they talkin about theirs but I'll use the adjective anyhow—we're not talking about them in their distilled forms. We're talking about ways to appreciate and celebrate those cultural productions in all their variations. For instance, in Shakespeare, we'll celebrate Othello's hands around Desdemona's neck or incest in *Hamlet*. These things make the texts full or round. They bring *humanity* to them. In Hip Hop, however, when such content is present, it's considered derogatory, a deviation from our humanity. It's like Hip Hop should only be a message of getting through struggle, getting over, a kind of positive, prophetic rhetoric. Well, if Hip Hop is prophetic, it's prophetic in the sense that it's bold enough to tell the truth.

Gilyard: That makes a lot of sense. That's the way I look at it. I guess you figure that no matter how intrusive the corporate prerogatives, a contesting voice, a contesting pulse is beating at the center of Hip Hop.

Kirkland: Yeah, I think the only way it can be commodified and co-opted is because it serves as a relevant voice for people. I think business people have noticed that it does serve as a voice for people. They have—as they always have—used this appeal to the common voice for economic ends. It has been commercialized. Yet, at its base, even in its most commercialized forms, there's something about Hip Hop that lends itself to the humanity of the popular class. So if we think about rhetoric not just as compelling people with arguments or as this science of persuasion but as the ability to make meaning of human situations, even the commodified forms of Hip Hop serve a powerful, political purpose.

Gilyard: I got you. I know you are also doing a lot of work on body inscriptions. There's a rhetoric to those as well. I guess that falls under visual rhetoric. Or we can discuss it as literacy.

Kirkland: I got into studying the body because of Hip Hop. I was studying some black kids in Detroit, just listening to them and noticing how and where they wrote stuff down. I started looking at their bodies, one place where they were writing. The tale is that these young men were not literate, that they didn't read and write. To be honest with you, when I looked at their report cards, that single piece of "evidence" bore these points out. If you asked them to read a canonical novel, they wouldn't read it or would struggle through it. But then you look at their bodies and see that those bodies bear the bruises of stories. You see on their bodies ink and flesh. You ask them to talk about the stuff that's on their flesh. Every tattoo serves some larger story.

Gilyard: Part of a narrative.

Kirkland: Part of a narrative by which they are able to make sense of themselves if not on paper, then on flesh.

Gilyard: So their bodies were functioning like Valerio's wall. You've seen Ralph Cintron's work about the boy's wall in his room?

Kirkland: Yes, I have.

Gilyard: Valerio was using the wall in his room to tell his whole story the best way he knew how.

Kirkland: Exactly. So you got youth seizing back space to tell their stories. You see it with tagging in Hip Hop—the graffiti art. You also see it with the body. They're taking back space. The black body is a site of contestation. For black men, it's a place that's been often written upon with bruises.

Gilyard: Brands.

Kirkland: Brands, slashes. Right. Each of these things tells a story about the human condition.

Gilyard: Castration.

Kirkland: Castration, right. What you see the young men doing now is taking the tattoo needle and rewriting the story of themselves on their flesh. So that tells us something else about rhetoric, that rhetoric is not just visual and it's not just heard. It has those semiotic and symbiotic qualities, but it also has other distinctions. There are questions of where you choose to write and how you choose to write it. This is what I call a *politics of place of inscription.*

Gilyard: Right.

Kirkland: Where you choose to write offers as much to your argument as what you choose to write. So when these youths choose to write on their bodies to reclaim that space, they're making a political statement. Make no doubt about it.

Gilyard: The political geography of inscription. I think recent critical work would back you. But I'm wondering what the sense of the youths themselves is. Do they see themselves to be doing all the things that you see? Or is this just your critic's eye?

Kirkland: Yes and no. They certainly understand that they have a story. I have one young man in my study whose brother was killed. When his brother was killed, he got a tattoo with his brother's name—BOSS—inscribed on his chest. He understood that the tattoo was a memorial to his brother. It served the cultural purpose of keeping his brother's memory alive. But what he didn't understand—

Gilyard: Memory work.

Kirkland: Yeah, memory work and also coping work and other kinds of political work, too. But what I don't think he was able to get—but that I was able to get at as an outsider reading the text—was the connection between his story and his brother's story. There was a narrative that he was writing in his brother's silence. There are things that are written about black men and not written about black men. Black men die tragically every day. Yet, in him and on him, his brother indeed lived; the bloodline continued. It's the human work of survival. You have another conversation that dehumanizes these subjects, that argues that they don't appreciate life. However, the tattoo—the embodied memorial—suggests that life is not only appreciated but memorialized and extended.

Gilyard: No question. They appreciate life.

Kirkland: Very much appreciate life.

Gilyard: Better believe that. So what do you think you'll be doing further along those lines?

Kirkland: Right now I'm doing work in what I call the Digital Underground, playing on the name of the early nineties rap group. My work in the Digital Underground continues the political work of trying to unpack urban youths' literate lives. You know, I've maintained that many more urban youth are literate than we choose to realize. And we have to describe how they're literate and understand rhetoric in ways that associate better with how these youths are literate. So I'm looking at literacies of urban youth in online social communities—*MySpace, Facebook, Second Life, Live Journal*—places where youth are reading and writing with verve and excitement. They're throwin' their raps up online. There's a technological component to it too, another level of sophistication.

Gilyard: Some people would argue that these kids are growing up with digital imaginations. I got that phrase from Jabari Mahiri. They may not even envision text or telling a story in the same way that an older generation might have thought about it. They readily conceive of telling stories in multimedia ways. The old way—like I'm doing with this tape cassette—is funny to them. It's sort of like when Hip Hop started. Some observers focused on the lyrics and declared that rap music was essentially urban poetry. Deejays thought that strange because they saw words as only one element of the mix and not necessarily the most important element. They were also focused on the beat, the break, the technology. So I think a lot of youth today don't see a separation between deejaying and lyrics. It's all one presentation to them.

Kirkland: Exactly. You have these interesting intersections. And with Hip Hop, overall, it's not just the deejaying and the emceeing. It's the deejaying, the emceeing, the dancing, the movement, the posture, the mindset, the recognition, all of it. It's multi-sensual in this sense. It's multimodal too. It's multidimensional. There's also the serene quality of it. It's the feedback, the call and response from the audience. So you got this relationship between multiple modes, not just between oral and written. It's even more complex and dynamic than that. It's an oral, written, and object relationship.

Gilyard: But you know where this can lead. Folks will take it to the cognitive level in a rigid way and say, "Well, there's a cognition capability difference going on now." They'll start talking about a post-literate America as an outcome of these digital imaginations. I know you ain't going there with it. You're just looking at literacy in an expanded way. But some folks will think it's a small step from our conversation to the conclusion that there's no point in teaching these kids the whole read-and-write thing because their minds are not set up for that. To me, you can get into some murky and dangerous waters.

Kirkland: Yeah. I was talking to somebody from the *New York Times* today. She thought my arguments, you know, could go down those lines. But I'd like to take that idea to its logical conclusion and then get back to more practical lines of argumentation. If we move toward a culture that does not value print, there's a question about whether students could continue to produce the visual, multimodal quality that students are now producing. I think the students value print very much. In fact, they seek out print to manufacture language. They find it and they forge it to make new meanings. So language isn't the issue. Language will, you know, remain represented through print inside of the new literacy and the new literate.

Gilyard: You mean print will stay represented.

Kirkland: Right. Print language will remain represented in some way. The past and the present are bonded. It's just that we can't think about literacy in the same linear ways because they are seeing and receiving different aspects of language. You have an elaborated code, an elaborated text such as that you see in novels. But these students don't exist in an elaborated textual world. They exist in an abbreviated textual world that's complemented by visuals, or in a world where visuals are complemented by abbreviated texts. You can look at it either way. There's a different relationship between print and the reader today versus the relationship in the past between print and the reader. I suppose one could say the imagination is different—without the hard cognitive claims about difference—but that imagination certainly owes something to print.

Gilyard: No question. See, I would argue that there is a special relationship between the spoken language and the printed code—and between critical writing and previous critical texts—because, after all, the printed version is based on the spoken version and the critical written version is based on the read version. You cannot replicate the dynamics of these relationships outside of an engagement with printed texts. Some people might say, well, students don't need novels because they have television and movies. They can develop literacy and critical abilities that way. But where's the transfer when we ask them for well-written critiques of novels and short stories? It's not always there.

Kirkland: I agree with you to a certain extent. We need to offer students opportunities to interact with multiple kinds of text. Moreover, the deeper issue is not just the oral-written relationship. Most binaries are problematic. Let's say that we concede to an oral-written relationship. Well, there's a visual-textual relationship we can talk about, also a relationship between the physical object and the senses. We have these multi-sensual, durable, complex relationships relative to the idea of literacy. One thing we have to do is to begin to explore literacy not simply as a linguistic idea between forms and features of oral and written language but as a relationship where visual, voice, sound, and other qualities, you know, come into play.

Gilyard: So anything that constitutes discourse, really.

Kirkland: Yeah. Anything that constitutes discourse, or as Derrida said, anything that is articulable is text.

Gilyard: This reminds me of Jim Gee's idea of discourses. He argues that we all get one discourse for free, a primary discourse; we acquire it rather than learn it. All the subsequent ones we have to pay for. That's literacy as opposed to acquisition.

Kirkland: But that's problematic because Gee is limiting us to a singular discourse.

Gilyard: Nah, he ain't saying that.

Kirkland: Well, primary means one.

Gilyard: But that's only the first one, the native tongue.

Kirkland: So he's limiting us to acquiring only one.

Gilyard: Maybe not. He's just not focusing on multiple acquisitions.

Kirkland: But it's not even just a question of multiple acquisitions. We have to address the notion of hybridity. In complex space, you're going to get a kind of generative fluidity and mixing. And that mixing is going to become something else. It's neither going to be one language or the other. It's going to be a third thing...

Gilyard: Now he gon read this, you know. (laughing)

Kirkland: That's okay.

Gilyard: You don't care? (laughing)

Kirkland: It's okay to bring up problems, and you have problems when you're limited to thinking in terms of a primary discourse when most people have various discourses that they acquire and various discourses that they learn primarily. It's complex, pluralistic, as I observe when I see people in New York City on the subway going from one community to the next. Some of them are kids acquiring multiple codes to deploy in multiple situations.

Gilyard: No question.

Kirkland: And embodying those different codes in multiple ways—on walls, bodies, parchment.

Gilyard: And nobody's teaching those codes explicitly.

Kirkland: Exactly. Yet they understand how to deploy those codes. So you get a hybrid sense of reality, a hybrid sense of self. The same thing happens when you think about print reading. Print is one of the registers, along with the visual register and other ways of reading and understanding the word and world around you. You deploy all of those understandings that you have acquired as well as all of those understandings that you have learned. Plus, in pondering this, I think we too need to shake up that notion of acquisition versus learning to see what it really means. Can you acquire and learn at the same time, and is there a relationship between acquisition and learning that's not explained by Gee in his earlier work? Of course, I do think that his earlier work is helpful; it gives us these questions.

Gilyard: You're on to a number of questions: Hip Hop, body inscriptions, digital...

Kirkland: Those are the main three I'm examining right now. Also, I have to return to the issue of power. We're moving towards a complex understanding of language and rhetoric, the kind of understanding that is necessary. But we are not moving towards as complex an understanding of power. Foucault talks about power as being relative, and he employs terms like *relationships of power,* which is interesting at one level but diminishes the notion that some people are more powerful than others.

Gilyard: You have to read my section on Foucault.

Kirkland: All right, I have to check that out. We have to reconcile those relationships between subordination and domination. The reason we're having a conversation about Hip Hop being included inside the rhetorical conversation or tradition—having the argument that it should not be excluded—is because it's by black people who are disempowered and not valued. Multicultural education is good at a certain level. Jim Banks, a good friend of mine, does outstanding work. But it responds to a specific tradition, to the practice of excluding women and African Americans from the mainstream conversation. Because of his work, they are included now, but only in an asymmetrical, subordinate relationship to the dominant stuff. So there's that conversation about power that needs to be had, you know. Trying to explore this notion of power in an honest and more complicated way will be essential to my work.

Gilyard: How is this playing out with respect to your teaching? You teach graduate students exclusively, at least on campus, and I was wondering how they have been responding to your takes on these various issues.

Kirkland: I enjoy my students, but many of them come from backgrounds where certain hegemonic ideas haven't been challenged. Certain ideologies were never questioned or torn down. So at first I meet resistance because I challenge some of those ideas. For example, I push the notion that literacy is something dynamic and multiple. I define literacy as a possibility, a possibility to use language and other symbolic material as a tool to participate in culturally valued activities, to construct identity, culture, or to critique power.

Gilyard: That's rich enough.

Kirkland: In a sense, everybody becomes literate. But for my students, my idea of literacy seems nebulous. Since I say everybody is literate, and have a broader definition of literacy than what they have used, they take it to the conclusion that I'm not for teaching students to read. Well, that's bullshit. I'm very much for teaching students to read. But I'm also for valuing the ways that students come to class reading. In order to value the ways that students come to class reading, you first have to conclude that they read. And you have to conclude that the ways that you read may be different from the ways that they read and somehow accept the ways that they read as valid and that you are in some ways illiterate to the ways that they read. If everybody is literate, then everybody is at once also illiterate in certain ways. So the question is about building upon the literacies of individuals but also extending those literacies so that we can have less illiterate spaces and more literate spaces.

Gilyard: You're making me think about the stances that some professors take in class. They figure they are fully literate relative to the subject matter of the class. If they don't know it, by definition it's not worth knowing. Where you're coming from is a challenge to all of that, which is very good. So there's some resistance in the classroom, but I imagine you work it out over time.

Kirkland: By the third week, we done rattled so much stuff up; I done critiqued everything that they believe. Then they get frustrated because they feel like everything they believed was a lie and, you know—

Gilyard: Well, some of it was.

Kirkland: It's disheartening to them. So then comes the work of building them back up. I value their literacies in the classroom as a way of demonstrating what I'm talking about. Toward the end, we come to a consensus. I generally get fairly high evaluations from my students. So I can't be doing too much damage.

Gilyard: Right. Now I read your recent piece, enjoyed it a lot, you know, "The New English Education." I want you to say a little more about it. How do you see this New English Education playing out?

Kirkland: One reason I wrote the essay is because we're in English Education and we're still talking about things that were talked about decades ago, even a century ago. We're still talking about the ways of reading that Louise Rosenblatt wrote about in 1938.

Gilyard: *Literature as Exploration.*

Kirkland: We're back to *Literature as Exploration*; we're back to New Criticism; we're back to an exploration of the canons. Essentially, we are back to the basics. At some level I think that gives us a good foundation, a significant foundation, by which to build a New English Education. But a foundation alone does not make a house. And we need to begin to build on that foundation in order to build some kind of fortress, you know, that we can call our discipline. This is where the New English Education comes in. At its root, the New English Education simply means that the study of English needs to keep up with the times. What things like Hip Hop as seen through a postmodern black lens give us are cases to rethink English—how it has changed and how English Education may need to change also. In fact, the category English as a site of study inside of a multicultural, multilingual, pluralistic place like the United States may be unhelpful. Maybe we need something that's more pluralistic like the study of Englishes. As for the idea of canons, we do great damage to the study of our humanity and to the study of who we are when we don't incorporate new texts and all Englishes that capture our fullness.

Gilyard: Let's back up for a second because I noticed that you used that term *postmodern blackness* in the article and again here. It can be seen as an oxymoron, right? If you're talking about postmodern in the sense of fractured or indeterminate, then how can the word describe blackness, a definable, discrete notion? It's like saying blackness is something specific but it's not something specifically specific. How do you work that out?

Kirkland: I'm adopting the term postmodern blackness from bell hooks, who is looking at—and I think the word nuanced is more helpful here than fractured—nuanced identities for black people—

Gilyard: For postmodern times. So postmodernity is really the era? The idea of blackness in a postmodern era?

Kirkland: The nuanced identity speaks to the era. This is central to all of my work. Things are not static; things are changing. Not only do we have the rupture of old structures, we have extensions of meaning. We have an appropriation of old codes that are re-accented, if you will, with new forms of meaning and new kinds of meaning. Let's take *fat*, for instance. The word *fat* don't mean fat no more. One of my research participants told me I had on a phat watch. He spelled *phat,* in this way, with a "ph." I was like, "My watch not that big." He was like, "Naw, that mean your watch is the shit." I was like, "Okay, I got you."

Gilyard: (laughing) You knew better than that.

Kirkland: (laughing) I was just playing. But it's that kind of transit, that kind of change and shift that postmodern blackness, at least in the sense that bell hooks talks about it, accounts for. And that shift happens with black people in a unique way. So you don't just get postmodernism; you get postmodern blackness that speaks to the nuances of black culture, that reveals something about the conditions of not only black people but also white folk.

Gilyard: No doubt.

Kirkland: And other folk.

Gilyard: Here's a question about nuances of black culture. Is Barack Obama going to be the first Motown president or the last Motown president or the first Hip Hop president? He says he listens to Jay-Z, but he also says he mainly gets with Gladys Knight, the Temptations, you know.

Kirkland: I don't think I have been able to draw those lines clearly. I think he might be both the first Hip Hop president and the first Motown president. Maisha Fisher writes that African American literacies, diasporic literacies, are situated within traditions. She also argues that African American literacies extend those traditions. Barack is very much within these traditions, even beyond Motown to the sorrow songs. If you listen to him croon in his speeches, you'll hear the voice of Douglass as well as the voice of Ida B. Wells as well as the voices of Shirley Chisholm, Malcolm X, Martin Luther King. Jr., and Jesse Jackson. You hear it all, the music, Hip Hop and Rhythm and Blues. You hear the soul of Ray Charles.

Gilyard: And there's a facial resemblance to Malcolm, but I don't say that much because I don't want people to focus on that.

Kirkland: There's dignity, a stature—

Gilyard: Don't keep comparing him to Malcolm now! No don't do that! We'll talk about it after November.

Kirkland: Okay. So my basic argument now is that he's situated within all these verbal traditions at once. This is the hybridity that we have to talk about. This is why—

Gilyard: And he's aware of it and foregrounds it. At Penn State, he came to a point in his speech where he was talking about insurance or jobs. He said something like, "You know it ain't right." Then he backtracked and explained, while the people laughed, "I want you to understand that some things are not right but this just *ain't* right." He knows that he's operating in various traditions.

Kirkland: That's right. And he extends those traditions. That's the other part. Hip Hop borrows. It is situated in the traditions of its past and it extends those traditions. So the question could be this: What is Post Hip Hop? Post Hip Hop may be Barack Obama and whatever his political movement embodies. But the immediate question is to consider how people like Barack Obama are situated within our traditions and remain nuanced enough and open enough in our approach to see where these traditions are going. It's good to see where we come from, but it's also good to know where we're taking this. If Barack Obama is an example, I think we're taking it in powerful directions.

Gilyard: He has to make it past these pundits. There's another study in rhetoric, right? You follow the campaigns and look at television every night and are just amazed at what these educated experts pretend not to know. Toni Cade Bambara used to talk about how on some dubious occasions she would be trying to slip out of the house and her grandmother would check her and ask, "What are you pretending not to know today?" I feel like her grandmother when I watch some of these pundits, these highly intelligent folks. Legitimate arguments exist on both sides of certain cases—the Florida primary, for example—and all these brilliantly trained pundits pretend that the other side doesn't make any sense at all. They know the other side makes sense. The question is whether you can work out the paradox. Yet they don't declare the matter a paradox or that the other side has a reasonable point with which they just happen to disagree intellectually or because of political expediency. They just pretend that any opinion counter to theirs is nonsensical. And then they come with these bogus facts. Lanny Davis is good at this.

Night after night, he'll say, "I got facts. The facts show that McCain is running ahead of Obama." This is his best argument for why Democrats should choose Hillary Clinton.

But Davis' facts, the result of a poll, are a prediction about a future set of facts, an actual election outcome, which we won't know about until November. That a person can make a prediction is certainly a fact. But it's also a fact that a prediction could turn out to be incorrect. If you listen to Davis seriously, you'll go from poll straight to inauguration. Or maybe he knows that we know he can't be serious.

Kirkland: And he's only talking about one prediction or set of predictions.

Gilyard: Yeah.

Kirkland: There's another set of predictions that critiques his set of predictions.

Gilyard: Yeah. This present commentariat is just wearing me out.

Kirkland: I think another conversation that has come up during this election season is the contrast between the rhetoric of Reverend Jeremiah Wright, a rhetoric of indignation and critique that we in the black community agree with, and the rhetoric of Barack, a rhetoric of possibility and hope that some of us also agree with. At some point we have to reconcile what those two rhetorics might mean to our progress and to our future. Again, situating those two rhetorics inside of the larger maelstrom of power and thinking about what power means and how power plays—

Gilyard: King is paradigmatic for that because he spoke of the hope—that part of him gets canonized—but he also brought the critique.

Kirkland: Yeah. But these are two different figures, not just different from King but from each other. It reminds me of our comments about Hip Hop. The Hip Hop that gets promoted and glamorized, at least by academics, is the prophetic message Hip Hop, the Hip Hop of hope and a particular kind of critique. This is versus some of the Hip Hop that comes directly from the conditions of our people. If there wasn't no hoes in my community, you know, they wouldn't be talking about no hoes. And I know I'm gon get jumped on by feminists for being misogynistic, but the truth is that when you hear Weezy talking about, you know, people selling pussy in the 'hood, it's because people selling pussy in the 'hood.

Gilyard: No question. Fortunately, I ain't had to buy none. But they was definitely selling it.

Kirkland: It was there. The implication sometimes is that it's all commodification and that people are just making up stuff. Well, probably not. You know, some of it is hyperbole, exaggeration. But for the most part those exaggerations start from a place of truth.

Gilyard: Plus it functions as memoir. In textual studies we've often made a distinction between memoir and autobiography in terms of there being different writer-reader contracts in play. As readers, we put the strict truth test on autobiography and we get mad when we get deceived. But some of it is that we are deceiving ourselves because we ought to know that those books are not anybody's absolute story. At any rate, we are not as demanding of memoir. Memoir is as much about the times and the situation as it is about you. Memoir doesn't necessarily have to be your story, but it's the story of your generation.

Kirkland: Yeah.

Gilyard: We're two black men riding around New York City. You might be driving. I can later write a memoir in which I tell the episode something like, "I was driving David around New York when we were racially profiled and stopped by the police." Now that wouldn't be technically true because you were doing the driving, but it's plausible enough. My episode would still be true to the times and the situation. And the essential fact that we were profiled and pulled over would remain. So when I relate that I was stopped DWB, Driving While Black, it could still ring true. It's true to the spirit of the times. In fact, I *have* been stopped DWB, just not with you. So in that sense the actual lyrics or raps have to get more memoir treatment than autobiography treatment. Folks criticize, "They rappin about stuff they ain't even do." Yes, at times, but they also are always talking about important things that occur. Whether they actually did it or not is only partly the story. And something is wrong anyway if you go for all of it. Some of it is just for fun. I mean, if you listen to "I Got a Story to Tell," you have to know that big ass corpulent Biggie is not lowering himself nimbly down the side of a building with a rope fashioned from bed sheets.

Kirkland: That's right.

Gilyard: That song is coming out of our badman tradition or the tradition of the tall tale. Now I admit it gets a little more complicated. For example, the only serious trouble Jay-Z has been in for years involved him stabbing a guy in the arm with a penknife because he thought the guy was bootlegging his CDs. Something like that. In any event, it's a case of Uzi rap and penknife reality. That's something to ponder. Still, if in a song, the character, mood, and sense of the times or sense of traditions are right, then the song could be good art.

Kirkland: You know the old conversations about black people and black art. Black art needs to serve the purpose of propaganda, Du Bois would say. Or Langston Hughes would say let our stuff just be. It seems that we have people saying that if it doesn't serve the positive purpose of propaganda then Hip Hop is not relevant. But my question is why does it have to serve that purpose? How come our art can't just be art? Like Langston Hughes said, we still chasing the Negro up the racial mountain. You know, it's time for us to come down and take our rightful place at the table.

Made in the USA
Lexington, KY
06 January 2015